THE HR EASY BUTTON

THE HR EASY BUTTON

A Practical Guide to Building
a Strong HR Foundation

KERRI M. ROBERTS

ISBN: 979-8-89694-254-2 - eBook

ISBN: 979-8-89694-255-9 - Paperback

To William Burke, my first HR boss and mentor, who challenged me every step of the way, pushed me to tackle the unknown, and forced me to see HR as data led, yet an art.

To my husband, who has been by my side since the very beginning of my career, first as a colleague, then as a friend, and now as my partner.

And to my son, who has always understood and supported the demands of a "working" mom.

This book is for you.

Contents

INTRODUCTION

In my twenty years navigating the corporate world, I've come to realize that the true essence of any successful organization lies in its people. As a female entrepreneur who has spent two decades focused on human resources (HR) and people operations, I've witnessed firsthand the pivotal role HR plays in shaping not just the success of a company but the culture that defines it.

This book is born out of my passion for and belief in the foundational elements that drive HR excellence. Over the years, I've worked across industries—from healthcare to distribution, finance to higher education, insurance to M&A—each experience reaffirming the significance of a solid HR framework. Sometimes, HR can be ultrapractical, so there are areas of the book where I'm going to offer some step-by-step instructions that you can simply plug and play in your business today. In other areas, truly an art. People are complex, situations are nuanced, and it's in the gray area where you can impact your culture and become an employer of choice.

This book is number one of three in a series, so over the course of all three books, we'll cover a total of thirteen HR functional areas. In the pages that follow, we'll delve into some of the key HR functional areas that I consider the bedrock of any robust HR strategy. Whether it's hiring and recruitment, smooth onboarding, performance management, or the legal side of things, each chapter offers insights and practical tools to help you navigate these critical areas.

In future books, we'll explore the importance of leadership development and talent management, the intricacies of benefits administration and employee wellness, and the often overlooked yet crucial aspect of internal communications as it relates to culture. This book aims to be more than just a guide; it's a tool kit designed to equip you with the knowledge and strategies needed to foster a thriving workplace.

As you embark on this journey with me, I hope you'll find not just answers but also the inspiration to create an environment where your people can excel. Because in the end, that's what HR is all about—empowering others to achieve their fullest potential and, in turn, driving your organization to new heights.

Let's get into it.

CHAPTER 1

Hiring and Recruitment

When navigating tight talent markets, it's essential to enhance your employer brand and offer competitive benefits that resonate with today's workforce. But how do you stand out? In today's competitive business landscape, talent acquisition has evolved far beyond simply filling open positions. It's now a strategic function that can significantly impact an organization's long-term success. As we delve into this chapter, we'll explore the critical components that make up a robust talent acquisition strategy, from the initial stages of strategic workforce planning to the complexities of HR law.

We'll begin with an introduction to talent acquisition and how it differs from traditional recruitment, setting the stage for why this function is vital for any organization looking to thrive. Next, we'll dive into strategic workforce planning, a forward-thinking approach that ensures that you have the right talent in place, both now and in the future. This planning is intrinsically linked to employer branding—the reputation your organization builds as a desirable place to work, which is increasingly important in attracting top talent.

Communication channels for posting jobs have become more diverse and complex, so we'll explore the various platforms and methods available, making sure your job postings reach the right audience. But it's not just about attracting candidates; screening and selection processes are equally critical. We'll discuss the best practices for evaluating candidates efficiently and effectively so that you're bringing the best fit into your organization.

Technology has become a cornerstone of talent acquisition, with tools ranging from applicant tracking systems to AI-driven candidate assessments. We'll examine how these technologies can streamline your processes and enhance decision-making. Additionally, D&I (diversity and inclusion) is no longer just a buzzword; it's a crucial aspect of talent acquisition that can't be overlooked. We'll address how to integrate D&I principles into your hiring practices to build a more inclusive workplace.

HR law is another essential component, with various legal considerations that can impact your recruitment efforts. Understanding the legal landscape is crucial to avoid pitfalls and ensure compliance throughout the hiring process. Finally, we'll wrap up the chapter with a look at best practices in talent acquisition, offering actionable insights and strategies that you can implement to enhance your organization's hiring success.

By the end of this chapter, you'll have a comprehensive understanding of the multifaceted nature of talent acquisition and the tools needed to build a strategic and effective talent acquisition process that aligns with your organization's goals and values.

Why Is Talent Acquisition Crucial for Organizational Success?

Talent acquisition goes beyond simply filling open positions; it involves strategically attracting, selecting, and retaining individuals who will contribute to a company's long-term growth and competitiveness. A well-executed talent acquisition strategy ensures that organizations have the right people in place to thrive in an evolving business landscape, or "the right people in the right seats on the bus,"[1] as Jim Collins says in his book *Good to Great: Why Some Companies Make the Leap . . . And Others Don't*. Let's dive into the key reasons talent acquisition is so crucial to organizational success.

Attracting and retaining top talent provides a significant **competitive advantage**. Skilled employees are the driving force behind innovation, efficiency, and quality. When a company has the right people on its team, it can outpace competitors and stay ahead in its industry. High-caliber talent pushes the boundaries of what is possible, giving organizations the edge they need to succeed. Effective talent acquisition is also vital for supporting an organization's **growth and scalability**. As a company expands or enters new markets, it must ensure that it has the necessary human resources to sustain that growth. A solid talent acquisition strategy guarantees that the right people are in place to meet increasing demands and support the organization's strategic objectives.

In addition to driving growth, talent acquisition has a direct impact on **employee retention**. By focusing on hiring individuals who align with the company's culture and values, organizations can improve employee engagement from day one. This cultural fit reduces turnover rates and boosts job satisfaction, leading to a more stable and motivated workforce, not to mention positively impacting the bottom line.

Cost efficiency is another benefit of strategic talent acquisition. Poor hiring decisions and high turnover rates can be expensive, both in terms of lost productivity and the resources required to replace employees. By

---

1   Jim Collins, Good To Great: Why Some Companies Make the Leap . . . and Other's Don't (Harper Business, 2001).

getting the hiring process right from the start, companies can reduce these costs and minimize the impact of prolonged vacancies on the business. Adaptability is key to navigating market changes and seizing new opportunities, and having the right talent in place allows an organization to do just that. A strong talent acquisition strategy ensures that the workforce is flexible and capable of responding quickly to shifts in the industry, enabling the organization to stay agile and competitive.

Finally, **improved performance** is a direct result of effective talent acquisition. When the most capable individuals are placed in roles that match their skills and potential, they can make the greatest impact. This leads to enhanced overall performance across the organization, driving better results and long-term success. Business owners are often behind the desired timeline for hiring, and so they just want a role filled and filled quickly. But talent acquisition is not just about filling positions; it's about building a workforce that aligns with the company's vision and goals. A strategic approach to talent acquisition can significantly influence an organization's ability to achieve sustainable success, foster innovation, and maintain a competitive edge in the market. When done right, it's extremely fulfilling and creates a workforce that is truly a team.

Next, let's clarify how talent acquisition is broader and more strategic compared to recruitment. **Talent acquisition** and **recruitment** are often used interchangeably, but they encompass different scopes and approaches in the hiring process.

Recruitment: A Tactical Approach

Recruitment is a critical process that focuses on addressing immediate hiring needs by finding the right candidates to fill current job vacancies. Unlike long-term talent strategies, recruitment tends to be more reactive, targeting specific roles that need to be filled in the short term. The process involves several essential steps, each designed to help organizations find, evaluate, and onboard the best possible candidates in a timely manner. I know there are some of you who are thinking, "*Give me a list and I'll run with it,*" and others who want to read the why and the how. So, I'll start with the list and then we'll get into the nitty gritty.

Hiring Process Overview

1. **Define the Role**

   o   Create a clear job description with key responsibilities.

   o   Establish salary range and compensation structure.

   o   Identify necessary skills and qualifications.

2. **Post the Job**

   o   Utilize job boards (Indeed, LinkedIn, industry-specific sites).

   o   Share on company website and social media.

   o   Encourage employee referrals with incentives.

3. **Screen Candidates**

   o   Review resumes and applications.

   o   Conduct phone screenings (15–20 minutes) to assess basic qualifications.

   o   Use an applicant tracking system (ATS) to streamline filtering.

4. **Interview & Assess**

   o Conduct structured interviews with behavioral-based questions.

   o Administer skill assessments or work samples if applicable.

   o Involve key team members in the evaluation process.

5. **Select & Offer**

   o Check references and conduct background screening.

   o Extend a formal offer letter with salary, benefits, and start date.

   o Negotiate as needed and finalize the hiring agreement.

6. **Onboard the New Hire**

   o Send a welcome email with preboarding details.

   o Set up IT credentials and provide a company handbook.

   o Assign a mentor or onboarding buddy for the first 90 days.

Now, let's get into the details. The first step in recruitment is **job posting and advertising**. This involves creating clear and accurate job descriptions that outline the responsibilities, qualifications, and expectations for the position. It should also consider a pay band for the role and what constitutes pay on the low end versus high end. Do not post a role without having a job description nailed down. Not having that description spells disaster for the new hire and the organization. These job listings are then posted on various job boards, the company's website, social media, and other channels to attract potential candidates. Sending a quick email or text to your personal network outlining the opportunity is a great idea as well. The goal is to reach as wide an audience as possible to increase the chances of finding a strong match for the role.

Next comes **candidate sourcing**, in which recruiters (either internal to your organization or through a contracted outside firm) actively search for potential candidates through different channels. This can include browsing job boards, attending career fairs, and utilizing social media to identify individuals who might be a good fit for the open position. Candidate sourcing ensures that the company has a diverse pool of applicants to choose from. Additionally, many great candidates are not necessarily on the job hunt, so this proactive approach might mine some options that wouldn't otherwise apply. Once candidates have been identified, the **screening and interviewing process** begins. Resumes are reviewed, and initial phone screens are conducted to assess each applicant's qualifications. The phone screen should take fifteen to twenty minutes total, focused on a set number of brief questions as a secondary screening method. From there, candidates may be invited to participate in one or more **interviews** to further evaluate their skills, experience, and fit with the organization's culture. This step is crucial for narrowing down the selection to the best possible candidates. Many say to hire slow and fire fast. This doesn't mean to take your sweet time during the process—it means to be intentional in the process and to move away from the "warm body" philosophy to an actual fit for the role, which is better for the candidate and the company long term. A person actively seeking a new role is typically hired between ten and forty-four days (depending on the level of role), and so the hiring manager needs to keep the process moving and the communication flowing to maintain engagement.

Finally, the process concludes with **hiring and onboarding**. Once a candidate has been selected, a job offer is extended, and negotiations around salary and benefits take place. After the offer is accepted, the onboarding process begins, which helps new hires transition smoothly into the organization. Onboarding includes tasks such as training, orientation, and integration into the company culture, ensuring that the new employee feels supported and prepared for their role.

Aspect	Recruitment	Talent Acquisition
Approach	Reactive: fills immediate job openings	Proactive: builds long-term candidate pipeline
Focus	Short-term hiring needs	Strategic workforce planning
Timeframe	Immediate hiring needs	Future growth and leadership roles
Process	Job postings, resume screening, interviews	Employer branding, talent pools, networking
Employer Branding	Minimal, role-specific	Strong emphasis on long-term attraction
Candidate Relationship	Limited to active job seekers	Engages passive candidates over time
Technology Use	Basic ATS for processing applicants	AI-driven insights, predictive analytics

Talent Acquisition: A Strategic Approach

Talent acquisition is a comprehensive and strategic process that proactively builds a strong talent pipeline that addresses both current and future organizational needs. Unlike recruitment, which is typically reactive and centered around filling immediate job vacancies, talent acquisition takes a long-term approach. It involves doing workforce planning, executing employer branding, and aligning talent strategies with business goals to ensure that the organization has access to the best talent, not just for today but also for the future.

Workforce planning is a key element that differentiates talent acquisition from recruitment. While recruitment responds to immediate hiring needs by filling current job openings, talent acquisition involves long-term planning to anticipate future hiring needs. This strategic approach is based on an analysis of business goals, industry trends, and projected company growth. On top of digging into these items to access talent needs, it's a great focus for your leadership team to attain alignment and vision cast for the future. By planning ahead, talent acquisition ensures that the right talent is available when the organization needs it rather than scrambling to fill vacancies as they arise.

Employer branding plays a critical role in both recruitment and talent acquisition, but there are distinct differences in focus. In recruitment, the primary goal is to promote specific job openings to attract candidates for immediate roles. Talent acquisition, on the other hand, goes beyond promoting individual positions and focuses on building a strong, recognizable employer brand. This involves consistently highlighting the company's culture, values, career development opportunities, and benefits to create a positive image that continuously attracts top talent. A strong employer brand helps organizations remain competitive in the talent market and ensures a steady influx of high-quality candidates. This moves an organization from a reactive to a proactive state. Together, workforce planning and employer branding form the backbone of a successful talent acquisition strategy. By taking a proactive and holistic approach, organizations can not only meet their current hiring needs but also position themselves to thrive in the future by building a robust pipeline of skilled talent.

Strategic sourcing is approached differently in recruitment and talent acquisition. Recruitment typically relies on traditional channels, such as job boards, career fairs, and similar platforms, to find candidates for open positions. While these methods can be effective, they tend to focus on active job seekers and may limit the reach of potential talent. Talent acquisition, on the other hand, employs a more diverse range of sourcing strategies. These include leveraging social media platforms, attending networking events, encouraging employee referrals, and developing talent pools. This approach not only targets active candidates but also engages passive candidates, broadening the pool of qualified individuals who may not be actively searching for jobs but could be a great fit for the organization in the future.

Candidate relationship management also varies significantly between recruitment and talent acquisition. In recruitment, the interaction between the company and candidates is often a one-time occurrence aimed at filling a specific position. Once the role is filled, the relationship may end. In contrast, talent acquisition focuses on building and maintaining long-term relationships with potential candidates. Even when there are no immediate job openings, talent acquisition teams continue to engage with promising individuals, ensuring that they have a ready talent pool to draw from when future needs arise. This ongoing relationship-building helps companies stay connected with top talent and reduces the time it takes to hire when roles do become available. HR folks typically aren't viewed as a part of the sales team, but this paragraph proves otherwise, right? It's a great idea to partner with the sales team to outline good scripts and ideas to be the best talent acquisition strategists possible.

Data-driven decision-making is another area where recruitment and talent acquisition diverge. Recruitment typically relies on immediate hiring metrics, such as time to fill and cost per hire, to measure success. While these metrics are useful, they focus primarily on the short-term effectiveness of the hiring process. Talent acquisition, by contrast, takes a broader, long-term view. It utilizes data analytics to track metrics, like quality of hire, employee retention rates, and the effectiveness of different sourcing channels. This data-driven approach aligns hiring practices with the overall business strategy, helping organizations optimize their talent acquisition efforts to meet both current and future needs. If you aren't already tracking these metrics, now's a great time to set up a simple dashboard and make it happen. You'll be more respected from the overall leadership team if you can show some data that proves success (or identifies resource allocation needs).

Diversity and inclusion are handled differently in recruitment and talent acquisition. In recruitment, the focus may be on meeting diversity targets for specific roles to ensure that the hiring process reflects the company's immediate diversity objectives (more typical in larger organizations). This can involve targeting underrepresented groups to fill particular vacancies. However, in talent acquisition, diversity and inclusion are integrated into the entire hiring strategy. Rather than simply filling quotas, talent acquisition aims to build a diverse workforce that aligns with the company's long-term goals and values. This approach fosters an inclusive workplace culture that promotes equity, making sure that diversity is considered at every stage of the hiring process and throughout the employee life cycle.

Onboarding and development are also approached with different scopes in recruitment versus talent acquisition. Recruitment typically ends once a candidate is hired and given a basic onboarding process. The primary focus is on enabling the new hire to quickly assume their role and meet immediate job requirements. Talent acquisition, however, extends beyond hiring to include a comprehensive onboarding process that prioritizes long-term integration. In addition to making sure new hires feel welcomed, talent acquisition considers their career development from the start. This involves creating clear career paths and providing the necessary resources to help employees grow and succeed in the organization, resulting in higher retention rates and long-term employee satisfaction.

Recruitment is a critical component of the hiring process, addressing immediate needs and vacancies. However, **talent acquisition** takes a broader, more strategic view, focusing on building a continuous pipeline of qualified candidates, aligning hiring practices with long-term organizational goals, and creating a strong employer brand. This strategic approach ensures that the organization not only fills its current positions but is also well-prepared for future growth and challenges, fostering a sustainable competitive advantage.

Strategic Planning

Aligning talent acquisition with organizational goals and workforce planning is essential for several reasons. This strategic alignment ensures that the organization has the right talent to achieve its objectives, supports business growth, and enhances overall performance. Supporting business objectives through talent acquisition requires a strategic approach that aligns with the company's long-term vision and mission. Strategic workforce planning plays a crucial role in this process by making sure the organization has the talent necessary to meet its strategic goals. By looking ahead and forecasting future needs, talent acquisition helps prepare the company to achieve its objectives by identifying the skills and positions needed for success.

Goal fulfillment is also central to talent acquisition. By clearly identifying the skills and competencies required to meet specific business goals, the recruitment process can focus on attracting and retaining individuals who embody these qualities. This alignment ensures that the workforce is well-equipped to drive the organization forward and meet its objectives. Enhanced competitive advantage is another key outcome of aligning talent acquisition with organizational goals. A well-executed strategy attracts top talent, meaning individuals who bring innovation, productivity, and a competitive edge to the company. These high-performing employees can set the organization apart in a crowded marketplace.

Employer branding plays an important role in this competitive advantage. When talent acquisition is aligned with the organization's goals, it strengthens the company's employer brand, making it more attractive to high-caliber candidates who are the right fit. A strong employer brand reflects the company's values and culture, drawing in talent that is both skilled and aligned with the company's mission. Improved organizational performance is another direct result of aligning talent acquisition with business objectives. When the right people are placed in the right roles, job satisfaction and performance naturally improve. This optimal role fit not only enhances individual productivity but also contributes to the organization's overall success. Finally, skill alignment ensures that the company acquires the capabilities crucial for its success, both now and in the future. By focusing on the skills necessary to meet current and upcoming challenges, talent acquisition creates a workforce that is resilient, adaptable, and ready to support the organization's long-term growth. HR data shows a skills gap in many organizations, and while much of that is due to evolving technology changes, some can be attributed to hiring for the job of today but not considering the needs of tomorrow.

Facilitating growth and scalability is a key advantage of aligning talent acquisition with workforce planning. By taking a proactive approach to hiring, organizations can prepare for growth and scale effectively.

This forward-thinking strategy means the company is not caught off guard by rapid expansion and can fill crucial roles ahead of time, allowing it to grow smoothly without disruption. Resource allocation is another benefit of strategic talent acquisition. By hiring based on thoughtful workforce planning rather than reacting to immediate needs, organizations can minimize costs associated with high turnover and poor hiring decisions. With this approach, resources are used efficiently, reducing the financial and operational burdens of filling roles repeatedly.

Enhancing employee retention and satisfaction begins with ensuring a good cultural fit during the talent acquisition process. When employees align with the company's values and culture, they are more likely to engage fully with their work and stay longer in their roles. A strong cultural fit fosters a positive work environment and increases the likelihood that employees will contribute to the company's success over the long term. Career development also plays a critical role in retention. By aligning talent acquisition with organizational goals, companies can offer clear career paths and development opportunities to their employees. This focus on growth not only enhances employee satisfaction but also reduces turnover, as employees are more likely to stay with an organization that invests in their future. This of course assumes your organization has clearly developed organizational goals. If it doesn't, let this be your sign to start there, or you're likely setting yourself (and your future new hires) up for some heartache later.

Adaptability to market changes is another key outcome of a well-aligned talent acquisition strategy. When an organization aligns its hiring strategies with its broader business goals, it gains the agility needed to respond quickly to changes in the market. This adaptability enables the company to seize new opportunities and remain resilient in the face of challenges, ensuring long-term sustainability. Addressing skill gaps is also critical to maintaining competitiveness. Continuous workforce planning helps companies identify and close skill gaps, stay innovative, and respond effectively to industry trends. This focus on skill alignment keeps the organization prepared to meet current and future demands. Cost efficiency is a significant benefit of aligning talent acquisition with organizational goals. One way this is achieved is through reduced turnover costs. By focusing on hiring candidates who are not only qualified but also a strong long-term fit for the company's culture and strategic direction, organizations can lower turnover rates. This, in turn, reduces the frequent costs associated with lost productivity and the need to rehire and retrain when positions remain vacant or new hires don't work out.

Effective utilization of resources is another cost-saving aspect of strategic talent acquisition. By hiring with long-term objectives in mind, companies can ensure that their human resources are optimally deployed. This approach minimizes wasted efforts and unnecessary hiring, contributing to better financial performance and a reduction in operational costs. By taking a more thoughtful, planned approach to talent acquisition, businesses can stretch their budgets further and operate more efficiently overall. Aligning talent acquisition with organizational goals and workforce planning is crucial for building a resilient, capable, and engaged workforce that can drive the organization's success. This alignment supports business objectives, enhances competitive advantage, and enables the organization to prepare for future challenges and opportunities. By taking a strategic approach to talent acquisition, organizations can achieve sustainable growth, improve performance, and maintain a strong, positive culture.

Developing a talent acquisition strategy that supports an organization's objectives involves a comprehensive approach that integrates workforce planning, employer branding, sourcing strategies, and data-driven decision-making. Here's an outline to guide the process:

1. Understand Organizational Goals and Objectives

- **Identify Business Goals**: Meet with key stakeholders to understand the organization's short-term and long-term goals. Don't forget to include the mission, vision, and values in this conversation.
- **Align Talent Needs**: Determine the skills, roles, and competencies needed to achieve these goals. Let yourself dream during this initial phase. Don't hold yourself back by thinking of skills your team already has, or ones found in your professional network. Think bigger.

2. Conduct Workforce Planning

- **Current Workforce Analysis**: Assess the current workforce to identify skill gaps, strengths, and areas for improvement. Remove the person from this process and look at the roles and what they should bring to the table, then identify any gaps that exist (and they likely do).
- **Future Workforce Needs**: Forecast future talent needs based on business growth, market trends, and technological advancements. Also take into consideration any potential retirements or resignations.
- **Succession Planning**: Develop a plan for leadership and critical roles to ensure business continuity. Every key position (not just C-Suite roles) should have a successor identified, even if that successor is a need-to-hire person.

3. Build a Strong Employer Brand

- **Define Employer Value Proposition (EVP)**: Highlight what makes the organization a great place to work, including company culture, values, and career opportunities. How do you differentiate yourself in the market as an employer?
- **Promote EVP**: Use social media, company websites, and job postings to consistently communicate the EVP to potential candidates. This is a fun job to give your marketing team—but make sure they collaborate with HR to capture the essence of life at your company.
- **Nurture Employee Advocacy**: Encourage current employees to share their positive experiences and promote the company culture. Consider using quotes from your engagement or satisfaction survey or shoot some quick videos asking employees why they like working at your organization. And if you've never conducted an employee engagement or satisfaction survey, here's your reminder to do so. You can find sample questions by using AI and you'll get great data on what's working as well as where you can focus for the upcoming year.

4. Develop a Comprehensive Sourcing Strategy

- **Diverse Sourcing Channels**: Utilize job boards, social media, career fairs, university partnerships, and employee referrals to reach a wide talent pool. Consider creating an employee referral program to incentivize this behavior. And put some actual cash behind it to truly incentivize your people to participate.
- **Passive Candidate Engagement**: Build relationships with potential candidates who may not be actively looking for a job but could be a good fit for future openings. LinkedIn is a great place to start.

- **Talent Pools**: Create and maintain a database of potential candidates for critical roles to streamline future hiring processes. Consider adding a calendar invite reminding yourself to follow up with these candidates on a systematic basis to stay top of mind.

5. Implement Effective Recruitment Processes

- **Job Descriptions**: Create clear and compelling job descriptions that accurately reflect the role and its requirements. If your job descriptions haven't been audited lately, make sure each line is reviewed prior to posting a new role.
- **Selection Criteria**: Develop standardized selection criteria to ensure a fair and consistent evaluation of candidates. Map out your minimum qualifications and the qualities that are nice to have. And think of your top performers and what it is about them that makes you want to clone them in the role. (If you don't have company values, this little clone exercise is a great way to develop those.)
- **Interview Process**: Use structured interviews and assessments to objectively evaluate candidates' skills, experience, and cultural fit. Consistency is key in eliminating or reducing any potential bias. Create some interview guides and stay consistent with asking the same questions at the same point in the process. Remember, we are hiring the best fit for the role and not auditioning for our new best friend.

6. Leverage Technology and Data Analytics

- **Applicant Tracking System (ATS)**: Use an ATS to streamline the recruitment process, track and communicate with candidates (utilizing automation), and manage job postings. These are far more affordable than you may think and save so much time.

- **Data-Driven Decisions**: Analyze recruitment data to identify trends, measure the effectiveness of sourcing channels, and improve the hiring process.
- **Predictive Analytics**: Utilize predictive analytics to forecast hiring needs and identify potential skill gaps.

7. Focus on Candidate Experience

- **Transparent Communication**: Maintain clear and open communication with candidates throughout the recruitment process. Let them know you received their resume and communicate potential timelines. Always decline them if not moving them forward; don't forget, there is a real human on the other side that is dreaming of their future. Don't leave them hanging.
- **Timely Feedback**: Provide timely feedback to candidates to keep them engaged and informed.
- **Positive Onboarding**: Develop a comprehensive onboarding program to ensure new hires are well-integrated and productive from day one. This includes a training outline, culture integration, technology guides, and as much as you can provide to set the proper tone.

8. Promote Diversity and Inclusion

- **Inclusive Job Descriptions**: Ensure that job descriptions and postings are inclusive and free from biased language. Ask AI to double-check your language to make sure you will appeal to all genders and types of people.

- **Diverse Sourcing**: Actively source candidates from diverse backgrounds and underrepresented groups.
- **Bias Training**: Provide training to hiring managers so they can recognize and mitigate unconscious bias in the recruitment process.

9. Measure and Optimize

- **Key Performance Indicators (KPIs)**: Define KPIs, such as time to fill, cost per hire, quality of hire, and employee retention rates, to measure the success of the talent acquisition strategy.
- **Continuous Improvement**: Regularly review and analyze recruitment metrics to identify areas for improvement and optimize the talent acquisition process.

10. Foster a Collaborative Recruitment Culture

- **Stakeholder Involvement**: Engage hiring managers and other stakeholders in the recruitment process to align with organizational goals. Consider if you want an internal team member focusing on recruitment or if you want to hire an outside firm. Either way, there will still need to be an in-house point person to lead this charge.
- **Cross-Functional Teams**: Create cross-functional teams to collaborate on talent acquisition initiatives and share best practices.

Developing a talent acquisition strategy that supports organizational objectives requires a strategic and holistic approach. By aligning workforce planning, building a strong employer brand, leveraging technology, and focusing on candidate experience, organizations can attract and retain top talent that drives business success. Regular measurement and optimization ensure that the strategy remains effective and responsive to changing business needs.

Employer Branding

A strong employer brand is essential for attracting top talent and differentiating your organization in a competitive job market. Let's dive into the key elements of a strong employer brand. The employer value proposition (EVP) is a clear and compelling statement that outlines what employees can expect from the company and, in return, what the company expects from them. It serves as the foundation of the employer-employee relationship and is a key driver in attracting and retaining top talent. A strong EVP typically includes several important components, such as career growth opportunities, a supportive company culture, competitive compensation, comprehensive benefits, work-life balance, and alignment with the organization's core values. For an EVP to be effective, it must be consistently communicated across all channels and touchpoints, ensuring clarity and transparency throughout the employee experience.

As an example, here is the EVP for Salt & Light Advisors:

At Salt & Light Advisors, we are more than a consulting firm—we are a purpose-driven community dedicated to transforming HR practices while empowering our team to thrive personally and professionally. Based in Missouri, we specialize in creating impactful solutions for our clients, and we start by fostering a workplace where our employees feel valued, supported, and inspired.

What Makes Us Different?

1. Purpose-Driven Work with Real Impact

Every project we take on is an opportunity to make a meaningful difference. Whether we're helping a small business build its HR foundation or enhancing employee engagement for a growing team, our work is rooted in purpose and guided by integrity.

2. Work-Life Balance Tailored to You

Your time is yours to design. At Salt & Light Advisors, we trust our team to choose schedules that balance their professional ambitions and personal priorities. Whether it's attending a child's recital, pursuing a passion, or simply having time to recharge, your life comes first.

3. Freedom to Work Anywhere

Work from the comfort of your home or wherever life takes you. Our remote-first culture ensures that you have the flexibility and resources to do your best work, wherever you are.

4. A Candid, Loving, and Transparent Environment

We believe in open communication, kindness, and authenticity. Our team operates in a culture of trust where every voice is heard, and every heart is valued. Feedback is given with grace, challenges are faced with compassion, and growth is celebrated together.

5. Advocates for Women's Worth

As a woman-owned business, we are unapologetically committed to elevating women in the workplace. We pay above-market salaries because we know the value women bring to leadership and business. Here, your contributions are not just recognized, they're rewarded.

6. Rooted in Faith and Integrity

Our firm reflects the values of our founder—a woman of strong faith who leads with servant leadership and humility. We honor our commitments, act with integrity, and are guided by principles that align with our purpose.

A company's culture is vital to its identity and should be expressed through a well-defined culture (or EVP) statement. This statement encapsulates the company's values, mission, and vision, which collectively shape the organization's character and direction. Employee stories and testimonials are also essential in showcasing the real-life embodiment of the company culture. These stories provide potential candidates with a glimpse into the authentic work environment and highlight how employees live the company's values. Visuals and descriptions of the workplace environment also contribute to a tangible representation of the culture, offering candidates a sense of what it's like to work in the organization.

Career development opportunities are an important aspect of an EVP, reflecting the company's commitment to employee growth. Information on professional development programs, mentorship opportunities, and continuous learning initiatives demonstrates how the company invests in its workforce. Clear career pathways, with outlined opportunities for internal promotion and progression, help employees see a future in the company, fostering engagement and retention. Work-life balance (or integration) is another critical component of a strong EVP. Companies that prioritize employee well-being provide policies and benefits that support flexible working arrangements, remote work options, and wellness programs. Additionally, employee assistance programs, mental health resources, and family-friendly policies support employees both professionally and personally, creating a holistic work environment that values their overall well-being. You can be creative here—and don't forget to ask your team what they would enjoy or want. They undoubtedly will have ideas for you.

Recognition and rewards play a pivotal role in employee satisfaction and motivation. Competitive compensation packages that include salary, bonuses, health benefits, and retirement plans are the foundation of a robust rewards system. If you haven't conducted a compensation data study in the past year, you need to. I recommend you contract with someone who has access to updated data that ties to level of education, geographic location, and more to be sure you're getting the best information to inform your decisions on hiring, raises, and bonus pay. Beyond financial incentives, employee recognition programs that celebrate individual and team achievements contribute significantly to boosting morale. These programs not only acknowledge hard work and contributions but also foster a culture of appreciation where employees feel valued and supported.

Social responsibility is another key area that shapes an organization's reputation and attractiveness to employees. Corporate social responsibility (CSR) initiatives highlight a company's commitment to making a positive impact on the community and the environment. Whether through sustainability efforts, charitable activities, or ethical business practices, a strong CSR presence demonstrates that the company values more than just profit. Ethical business practices and governance further solidify trust in the organization, ensuring that employees and stakeholders are aligned with the company's mission and values.

Diversity and inclusion (D&I) are essential elements of a thriving workplace. D&I policies and initiatives make every employee feel welcomed and included, regardless of their background. Support for employee resource groups and diversity-focused events or programs promotes a sense of belonging and community in the organization. This commitment to diversity and inclusion not only fosters a positive work environment but also attracts a broader pool of diverse talent, enhancing innovation and problem-solving.

Employee engagement is driven by effective communication and feedback mechanisms. Open and transparent communication channels between leadership and employees are crucial for building trust and collaboration. Regular employee surveys and feedback loops allow for continuous dialogue, providing employees with the opportunity to voice their opinions, concerns, and suggestions. When employees feel heard and valued, it increases engagement and strengthens the overall organizational culture and values.

Also, the brand naturally draws candidates who are a cultural fit, increasing the likelihood they will thrive and contribute positively to the organization. This alignment not only improves the hiring process but also enhances long-term employee engagement. The candidate experience is greatly enhanced by a positive employer brand. From the first point of contact through the recruitment process, a strong brand ensures a consistent, engaging experience that leaves a lasting impression. Candidates are more likely to stay engaged and excited about the possibility of joining the company when the process reflects the company's positive values.

Beyond attracting new talent, a strong employer brand also plays a critical role in retaining current employees. When employees feel proud of their company and its values, they are more likely to stay over the long term, reducing turnover and increasing loyalty. This pride can lead to word-of-mouth referrals as well. Satisfied employees are likely to recommend the company to their personal and professional networks, helping expand the talent pool through organic referrals.

Lastly, a compelling employer brand attracts higher-quality applicants. These individuals are genuinely interested in the company's mission, culture, and goals, and they are more likely to be a strong fit for the organization. As a result, the overall quality of applicants improves, making the hiring process more efficient and successful.

Building a strong employer brand involves clearly defining and consistently communicating what makes your organization a great place to work. By focusing on EVP, company culture, career development opportunities, work-life balance, recognition, social responsibility, diversity and inclusion, and employee engagement, companies can attract top talent, differentiate themselves in the job market, and create a positive and appealing workplace environment.

Communicating an employer brand effectively to potential candidates is crucial for attracting top talent. Let's explore some **effective ways to communicate the employer brand.**

1. A career website is a crucial tool for showcasing your employer brand and attracting top talent. Create a dedicated careers page that highlights your company culture, values, employee testimonials, and available job openings. To make this section engaging, include videos, photos, and stories that give candidates a glimpse into your workplace environment and what it's like to work for your company.

2. Social media is another powerful channel for promoting your employer brand. Regularly share content on LinkedIn, Facebook, Twitter, and Instagram to highlight employee achievements, company culture, and corporate events. Consider implementing employee takeovers, where employees take control of the company's social media accounts for a day to offer a behind-the-scenes look into their experiences.

3. Job descriptions should not only outline the role and responsibilities but also emphasize the company's culture and values, showcasing what makes it an attractive place to work. Use compelling language that speaks to the candidates' aspirations. Plus, it's important to create descriptions that use inclusive language that appeals to a diverse range of applicants and reflects your company's commitment to diversity and inclusion.

4. Employee advocacy is a key driver of authenticity. Feature employee testimonials and stories on the company website and social media to provide genuine insights into the work environment. Establish a referral program that encourages employees to refer candidates from their networks and share job openings on their personal social media platforms. Recruitment marketing involves creating targeted campaigns on social media, job boards, and professional networks to reach specific talent pools. Additionally, sharing blog posts, articles, and videos that highlight the company's strengths, industry insights, and employee experiences helps position your company as an employer of choice.

5. Networking and attending events are excellent ways to engage potential candidates. Participate in career fairs, industry conferences, and other networking opportunities to meet talent and showcase your employer brand. You can also host open houses, webinars, or other company events where potential candidates can interact with current employees and learn more about your organization.

6. Providing an exceptional candidate experience is essential for a successful recruitment process. Ensure that all communication with candidates is personalized and reflects your company's culture and values from the first point of contact through to the hiring decision. Providing timely feedback and keeping candidates engaged throughout the process shows that you value and respect their time. Employer review sites like Glassdoor and Indeed can significantly impact your brand's perception. Actively engage with reviews by responding to both positive and negative feedback, showcasing transparency. Encourage satisfied employees to share their experiences by leaving positive reviews on these platforms.

7. Video content is a compelling way to promote your employer brand. Create culture videos that highlight your company's work environment, team activities, and employee experiences. Day-in-the-life videos are particularly effective, providing potential candidates with a realistic view of what it's like to work in different roles in the organization.

8. Lastly, partnerships and community involvement can enhance your employer brand. Establish educational partnerships with universities, colleges, and professional organizations to engage emerging talent and promote your company as an employer of choice. Highlight your involvement in community service, volunteer activities, and corporate social responsibility initiatives to demonstrate your company's commitment to making a positive social impact.

Sourcing Candidates

Sourcing refers to the proactive process of identifying, attracting, and engaging potential candidates for open positions in an organization. It focuses on finding talented individuals, often before they formally apply for a job, and is an essential part of building a robust talent pipeline.

Sourcing candidates from inside the organization, known as internal sourcing, offers several advantages and some challenges when compared to recruiting external candidates. One of the most significant benefits of internal sourcing is that internal candidates are already familiar with the company's culture, values, and processes. This understanding leads to a smoother transition into new roles, which reduces the time and cost associated with onboarding and training. Additionally, promoting from within has a positive impact on employee morale and job satisfaction, as it provides a clear path for career progression and can lead to improved retention rates. Internal sourcing also offers cost savings and efficiency. The hiring process for internal candidates tends to be faster and less expensive than external recruitment, allowing organizations to fill key roles quickly. Furthermore, hiring internally reduces the risk associated with new hires because managers can make decisions based on the candidate's proven performance in the company. This provides more confidence in the candidate's ability to succeed in their new position. Internal sourcing also encourages employees to develop their skills and seek growth opportunities, fostering a more versatile and skilled workforce.

However, internal sourcing comes with challenges. A primary one is the limited pool of candidates, which may restrict diversity of thought and experience. This limitation can hinder innovation and creativity. Additionally, promoting one internal candidate over others can create resentment or competition among employees, potentially affecting team dynamics and morale. Another challenge is the risk of stagnation and complacency, as overreliance on internal hiring can limit the influx of fresh ideas and perspectives from outside the organization. Internal candidates may also lack the specific skills or experience required for certain roles. This can create gaps in expertise that need to be addressed through additional training and development. While internal sourcing can be beneficial in many ways, it is important to balance it with external recruitment to ensure a diverse, dynamic, and innovative workforce.

I have seen organizations post roles internally to check the box and show current employees they would consider an internal hire, with no intention of hiring anyone internally. I urge you to stay away from business practices like these. Even if you have a good intention in that decision, it comes across dishonest, and employees see straight through it. Candor and intentionality are always the best policy.

Sourcing external candidates offers several benefits that can enhance an organization's capabilities. One of the most significant advantages is the introduction of fresh perspectives and innovation. External candidates bring diverse experiences, ideas, and approaches that can spark creativity and drive innovation in the organization. This diversity in thinking helps companies stay competitive and adaptable in ever-changing markets. Additionally, sourcing externally opens up a larger talent pool, giving the organization access to a broader range of candidates, which increases the likelihood of finding the best fit for specific roles. Another key benefit is that external candidates often bring specialized skills and expertise that may not be available in the organization. This can be particularly valuable in filling critical skill gaps or meeting specific organizational needs. Furthermore, external hires can introduce knowledge of industry benchmarks and best practices, helping the company improve its processes and performance by learning from other sectors or industries. Nearly every job change I had in my career was being an external hire without industry experience. I joined a distribution company in the HR department from healthcare in the IT department. I then went into the mortgage industry, followed by higher education, followed by insurance (where I made my move from strictly HR to Operations). The most similar move I ever made was from insurance to an M&A (mergers and acquisitions) firm that purchased insurance agencies. Each time there was a hill to climb with some internal staff members because I was new to each industry. But overall, I brought external business experience that helped elevate each company to the next level, which was the ultimate hiring goal. Sometimes you must disrupt a bit to level up. An organization has to evaluate that prior to the hire.

However, sourcing external candidates also comes with challenges. One of the main difficulties is that external recruitment tends to be more expensive and time-consuming compared to internal hiring. Costs may include advertising, working with recruitment agencies, conducting multiple rounds of interviews, and potentially covering relocation expenses. Additionally, external candidates may take longer to adapt to the company's culture and values, affecting their initial performance and integration into the team. I have experienced this personally, and it takes a strong person to continue to bring their A-game when others may not be overly welcoming. Another challenge is the uncertainty and risk that come with hiring someone from outside the organization. When a new hire doesn't have a proven track record in the company, there is a higher risk of misalignment in terms of work ethic or cultural fit. This can lead to higher turnover and additional hiring costs. Moreover, frequent external hiring can have a negative impact on internal morale. Employees who feel overlooked for promotions or opportunities may become demotivated, which could result in increased turnover among existing staff.

Back in my corporate HR days, I had a senior leader who sent over a family member as a referral. I assumed (because it was the co-CEO who sent the resume, and it was his family member) that hiring her was not an option. We essentially created a role to fit her skillset, even though it wasn't a direct hiring need at the time. I had the person report to me. Then the person moved roles and reported to someone else. Over time, she moved to yet another department. The sad reality to this story is, while she was a great person, we should have handled the situation differently. I realized too late that **hiring through referrals doesn't replace a structured hiring process.** Even when hiring someone through a trusted recommendation, **always assess skills and cultural**

fit thoroughly. It's vital for the company, and years down the road when that employee quit on her own accord, it ended up being better for her to find something that was truly a fit for her skills and experience.

Balancing external and internal sourcing is essential to maintain a dynamic workforce while ensuring that current employees feel valued. Both internal and external sourcing have their own sets of benefits and challenges. A balanced approach that leverages the strengths of both can be most effective. Internal sourcing boosts morale, reduces costs, and leverages existing knowledge, while external sourcing brings fresh perspectives, specialized skills, and industry best practices. Organizations should consider their specific needs, culture, and strategic goals when deciding on the best approach for sourcing candidates.

Let's dive into the **job posting** aspect of recruitment. While I don't love the post-and-hope mentality, there is some success that can be gained. Job boards serve as online platforms where employers can advertise open positions and job seekers can explore opportunities. These platforms, such as Indeed, LinkedIn, Monster, and niche sites like Dice (for tech roles) and MedReps (for medical sales), provide companies with a broad reach to attract candidates actively searching for jobs. Job boards have extensive access to a large pool of potential hires, ranging from general job boards to specialized platforms for specific industries. So employers can find candidates with varying backgrounds.

To maximize the effectiveness of **job boards**, companies should employ specific techniques. First, job postings need to be optimized with clear, detailed, and engaging descriptions to attract relevant talent. Including essential responsibilities, qualifications, and perks of the role gives job seekers a comprehensive understanding of the position. Don't forget to add your mission, vision, and values, as well as your EVP. Additionally, utilizing relevant keywords increases the chances of job postings appearing in search results, improving visibility. Finally, regularly updating and refreshing job postings keeps them at the forefront of search results, maintaining their visibility to job seekers.

Social media platforms have evolved into valuable recruitment tools, providing businesses with opportunities to tap into extensive networks while leveraging engagement features. Social media's strength lies in its ability to facilitate targeted advertising. LinkedIn, Facebook, and X (formerly known as Twitter) allow businesses to reach specific demographic groups, professionals in particular industries, and individuals with specific skill sets, all while engaging directly with potential candidates. Employers can implement various techniques to harness social media's recruitment power. For example, on LinkedIn (which is my favorite for professional recruiting), recruiters can utilize LinkedIn Recruiter to actively search for and connect with potential candidates while also sharing job openings and content about the company's culture. Facebook offers companies the opportunity to post job openings on their pages and relevant groups, as well as run Facebook Ads to target specific recruitment audiences. Lastly, X allows businesses to share job openings with the use of industry-specific hashtags while interacting with niche communities, amplifying the reach of their job postings to relevant talent.

Employee referral programs are a valuable recruiting tool that encourages current employees to refer candidates from their personal and professional networks. This method often results in high-quality candidates, as employees typically recommend individuals who align well with the company's culture and job requirements. Referred candidates tend to perform better and have a higher retention rate, making this an efficient method for recruitment.

Additionally, employee referrals are cost-effective compared to traditional hiring methods, reducing the need for extensive advertising or recruitment agency fees. To optimize employee referral programs, businesses should implement incentive programs that reward employees for successful referrals, such as offering bonuses or other perks. Some organizations used a tiered system (entry level roles get a $ bonus while leadership level roles earn you a $$$ bonus). I recommend making the reward one that motivates an employee to participate. Typically, $50 is not enough to make an employee care to participate in your recruiting efforts, but $500+ does the trick. If you're struggling to justify the expense, think about the cost of utilizing an external recruiter, paid ads, or the cost of turnover for hiring the wrong person. A simple and user-friendly referral process is also essential, ensuring that employees can easily submit referrals with clear guidelines. Regularly promoting the referral program in the company keeps it top of mind, motivating employees to continuously contribute to the recruitment process.

Recruitment agencies are specialists in sourcing and placing candidates, offering businesses a way to leverage their expertise, particularly for hard-to-fill roles or specific industries. These agencies have vast networks and industry knowledge, allowing them to identify suitable candidates more efficiently. Recruitment agencies can save companies a significant amount of time by handling various stages of the hiring process and freeing up internal resources for other essential tasks. To get the most out of a recruitment agency, it's crucial to select one with a strong track record in your specific industry or for the types of roles you need to fill. Clear communication is key. So, providing the agency with detailed job descriptions and expectations ensures that they understand what you're looking for. Additionally, staying in regular contact with the agency allows you to monitor progress, adjust strategies if needed, and keep the recruitment process on track. I have partnered with many recruitment firms over the past two decades. Some focus on executive recruitment, others on sales roles, and still others on more entry-level positions. Some are industry specific, while others assist with your recruitment strategy and provide tracking tools. If you're looking to outsource this task, shop around or ask a trusted professional in this area what they recommend. Recruiters aren't a one-size-fits-all operation.

Career fairs provide an excellent opportunity for employers and job seekers to meet in person and make meaningful connections. These events allow employers to showcase their company, its culture, and current job openings, creating a space for networking and direct interactions. The benefits of attending career fairs include the chance for face-to-face engagement with potential candidates, which can leave lasting impressions and foster immediate connections. Moreover, career fairs help increase brand awareness, as companies have the opportunity to boost their visibility among job seekers in the local market or specific industry. Thorough preparation is essential to make the most of career fairs. Employers should bring informative materials, such as brochures, business cards, and engaging displays that present the company's values and open positions. During the event, it's important to actively engage with attendees, answer questions, and collect resumes to identify potential fits. Afterward, prompt follow-up with promising candidates can set the stage for deeper discussions and move the hiring process forward. If you have any personality hires at your company (meaning the folks who represent your culture extremely well and can't seem to meet a stranger in this life), bring them to these events. And don't forget the cool swag.

Your company's **career page** is a crucial tool for attracting candidates who are already familiar with or interested in your organization. A well-structured career page allows candidates to apply directly, creating a smooth and efficient application process. Additionally, the company has complete control over how its employer brand is presented, allowing you to highlight your company's culture and values, along with the benefits of working there. To optimize your careers page, ensure that the design is user-friendly and easy to navigate on both desktop and mobile devices. Providing detailed information about job openings, the company's mission, available career paths, and benefits is key to attracting the right candidates. Engaging content, such as employee testimonials, videos, and blog posts, can further showcase the company culture and inspire potential candidates to apply.

Networking is also a key strategy in recruiting because it utilizes personal and professional relationships to identify potential candidates. This method can offer a more personalized approach to recruitment, as it builds on established connections and referrals. Networking allows employers to reach targeted individuals with specific skills or experience, enhancing the likelihood of finding well-suited candidates. A significant benefit is the direct connection, where referrals can come from trusted sources who understand both the candidate's capabilities and the company's needs. Effective networking techniques include attending industry events, such as conferences, seminars, and meetups. These gatherings provide opportunities to meet potential candidates face-to-face and establish meaningful connections. Employers can also leverage professional associations related to their industry, participating in their events and activities to expand their network. Another valuable technique is engaging with alumni networks, which can connect you with individuals who have graduated from programs relevant to your field. By building these connections, employers can create a pool of qualified candidates for current and future job openings.

Internship programs offer companies a powerful tool to both develop talent pipelines and evaluate potential future employees. These programs serve as a trial period for both the intern and the company, allowing both parties to assess fit. From the company's perspective, internships help identify high-potential candidates and train them according to the company's specific needs and culture. These programs provide interns with valuable experience, giving them insight into the work environment and expectations.

To maximize the benefits of an internship program, companies should develop structured programs that outline clear goals and provide mentorship. This allows interns to gain meaningful experience while contributing to the organization's goals. Partnering with universities and colleges is an effective way to attract top talent, as these institutions provide a steady flow of motivated students eager for hands-on experience. For interns who perform well, offering conversion opportunities into full-time roles can solidify their commitment and contribute to the company's long-term growth. And while (in most cases) an unpaid internship is legal, I don't recommend it. These folks are performing work for you; let's pay them at least minimum wage for their time and efforts.

A great way to create a solid flow of interns is to develop a relationship with a local university and offer to come in and guest speak. Oftentimes, programs like to have business professionals come in and speak on a variety of topics. I've done seminars on employee benefits, LinkedIn utilization, self-trust, and several other subjects. Students enjoy the real-world experience coming into academia; it gives professors a break from their lesson plans, and it gets you in front of students, with the ability to highlight an excellent organization (yours) where they could become an intern.

Candidate Screening and Selection

Efficiently screening resumes and applications is a key aspect of the recruitment process, helping employers quickly identify the most suitable candidates. Let's look at some best practices for streamlining the process.

Develop Clear Criteria

Define Job Requirements: Start by clearly identifying the essential skills, qualifications, and experience needed for the role. This includes both hard and soft skills, as well as the minimum years of experience or specific qualifications, like certifications. Additionally, outline any preferred attributes, such as industry knowledge or advanced technical skills, which are not mandatory but can help further distinguish candidates. If you already have people in this role, have them review the current job description if you haven't done so already. They can provide great insights into where updates may need to be made. If it's a newly created position, they can also share the job description with internal collaborators to make sure all needs for the role have been articulated.

Standardize Evaluation Criteria: To ensure consistency and objectivity, create a checklist or scorecard to evaluate each application against the job requirements. Assign weights to different criteria based on their importance. For instance, technical skills might hold more weight than customer service experience for a software development position. Many applicant tracking systems (which we'll discuss next) can help you do this utilizing automation.

Use Technology and Tools

Applicant Tracking System (ATS): An ATS is one of the most effective ways to screen applications. These systems automatically filter resumes based on predefined criteria, allowing recruiters to focus on the most relevant candidates. Use keyword searches to identify resumes that include essential skills, qualifications, and experiences relevant to the role. If you don't have an ATS, I'd recommend you chat with your current HR and payroll technology provider to see if they have an add-on module available to you. There are also recruitment strategy firms that provide an ATS as part of their services.

AI and Machine Learning: Many companies now implement AI tools that intelligently screen resumes, ranking candidates based on their fit for the position. These tools can even use predictive analytics to help identify candidates who are more likely to succeed based on past performance data from similar roles. Many people are afraid to utilize these tools, but if you have a report that can help you make a better-informed decision, wouldn't you want to read it? Utilizing AI in your recruitment process, I believe, is the same thing.

A structured screening process helps recruiters efficiently manage and evaluate a high volume of applications while maintaining consistency in the hiring process. Here are some steps to create a more structured and effective screening process:

Conduct an Initial Screening

Automated Responses: Implementing an automated response system allows you to immediately acknowledge receipt of applications. This helps to set expectations for the candidates and informs them about the next steps in the process. Plus, we've all applied for jobs. It can be an emotional, stressful time. Let's treat people with kindness and communicate throughout the process.

Basic Qualifications Check: During the initial screening, quickly eliminate candidates who do not meet the basic qualifications, such as minimum education requirements or years of experience. This can be done manually or through an ATS to filter out those who do not meet the job's essential criteria. Be gracious and respond to every candidate, even the declinations. If you have an ATS, this will be a quick and simple process, allowing you to treat people with the respect they deserve.

Conduct a Detailed Screening

In-Depth Review: For candidates who meet the basic qualifications, conduct a more detailed review of their resumes and cover letters. Focus on specific job-relevant experiences, achievements, and soft skills that align with the role.

Consistency and Red Flags: Look for inconsistencies in employment history, unexplained gaps in the resume, or frequent job changes. While some red flags are not automatic disqualifiers, they can indicate potential issues worth investigating in interviews. Don't forget that the average tenure (at the time I published this book) is three years and four months. So, I wouldn't recommend penalizing the average. You'll miss out on amazing candidates if you do.

Utilize Prescreening Questions

Application Form Questions: Including custom questions in the application form is a useful method for gauging the candidate's suitability early in the process. These questions help filter candidates based on their experience or knowledge of the industry. And while it's an extra step, this will also help you hear back only from the most engaged candidates, which is what you want.

Knockout Questions: Use these questions to immediately disqualify candidates who don't meet non-negotiable criteria. For example, asking about specific certifications or willingness to relocate.

Behavioral and Situational Questions: Including questions on how candidates have handled relevant scenarios in the past helps assess their behavior in real-world situations. Similarly, include skill-based questions to measure critical abilities related to the role. You can also introduce behavioral assessments in this step as well, which I highly recommend. There are a million out there, but remember, you want to use one that is the most legally defensible if someone claims they weren't hired because of the assessment results. They are not all created equal.

Prioritize Key Qualifications

Focus on Core Competencies: As you move through the screening process, prioritize candidates whose skills and qualifications most closely align with the job description. Highlight their relevant experience and achievements, along with how well they match the core competencies needed for the position.

Look for Growth Potential: Beyond matching current job requirements, assess candidates' growth potential by reviewing their career progression and openness to learning new skills. Look for signs of adaptability and initiative in their previous roles.

Involving multiple reviewers in the resume-screening process ensures a more balanced and comprehensive evaluation of candidates. Let's look at how it can be done effectively.

Use Collaborative Screening

Multiple Perspectives: By involving several team members in the screening process, a company benefits from diverse perspectives. Each reviewer might notice different strengths or weaknesses in a candidate's application, leading to a more thorough evaluation. This would be after the initial qualifications are met.

Consistency: It's essential that all reviewers follow the same evaluation criteria to ensure fairness and consistency. This also helps prevent bias by having standardized assessments.

Hold Calibration Meetings

Alignment: To create uniformity in the evaluation process, calibration meetings are useful for aligning on standards. These discussions help reviewers sync on how they're interpreting the job requirements and evaluation criteria. This should occur prior to posting the role and then again after each interview.

Consensus: After individual reviews, the team can reach a consensus on which candidates should progress to the next stage of the hiring process. These discussions can also clarify discrepancies in initial assessments.

Maintaining a positive candidate experience is critical to preserving a company's reputation and encouraging top talent to stay engaged. How can this be done? First, let's focus on clear communication. This includes two primary elements, the first being timely updates. Keeping candidates informed of their application status is a simple yet impactful way to show respect for their time and effort. Timely communication, whether positive or negative, helps keep candidates engaged in the process. The second is feedback. While not always possible, providing constructive feedback to those who don't move forward can leave a positive impression and help them in future applications. That said, if you have a loose cannon for a hiring manager, I don't recommend you provide any feedback other than the legal jargon (we have chosen to go with other candidates at this time). Offer feedback only if it is compliant and helpful.

The second way to preserve a company's reputation and encourage top talent to stay engaged is through respect and professionalism.

Don't forget what it feels like to apply for a job and dream of what would come along with this amazing career switch. It's important to respect candidates' time. Review applications promptly to keep the process moving efficiently. If candidates experience delays without updates, they may lose interest or have a negative impression of the company. You are likely not the only place they are applying at if they are actively job searching, so don't lose out on the right person because you weren't prioritizing the time for candidate reviews. Also, ensure that your correspondence is professional. It is important to maintain professionalism in all candidate communications, from email responses to interview arrangements. It reflects the company's values and sets a positive tone for the candidate's experience.

Continuous improvement in the screening process enables the company to remain efficient and effective in hiring. How do you do this? First, let's analyze some metrics. I recommend you start by tracking KPIs. Keeping an eye on key performance indicators—like time to fill, cost per hire, and quality of hire—helps measure the efficiency and success of the screening process. This data allows for informed adjustments where necessary. Next, identify bottlenecks. Analyze the process to identify any delays or inefficiencies, such as unnecessary steps or overly lengthy reviews, and streamline those areas. The second thing you can do is gather feedback. There are two types of feedback that would be helpful during this process:

Candidate Feedback: Asking candidates for feedback about their experience can provide valuable insights into how they perceive the screening process and highlight areas for improvement.

Internal Feedback: Similarly, collecting input from hiring managers and recruiters can help identify any pain points or areas where the screening process could be refined to be more effective.

Efficiently screening resumes and applications involves a combination of clear criteria, advanced technology, structured processes, and continuous improvement. By defining job requirements, leveraging tools like ATS and AI, using prescreening questions, prioritizing key qualifications, involving multiple reviewers, maintaining a positive candidate experience, and continuously analyzing and improving the process, organizations can streamline their screening process and identify the best candidates more effectively.

Now, let's talk assessment methods. Effectively assessing candidates involves using a range of methods to evaluate their skills, personality, and fit for the role. Different approaches can help a company gain a comprehensive understanding of the applicant's potential. Interviews are one of the most common ways to assess candidates. They provide a direct method for evaluating a candidate's suitability for a role. There are different types of interviews that can be used depending on the company's specific needs.

- **Structured interviews** follow a set of predetermined questions presented to all candidates in the same order, allowing for a more standardized comparison. I would use a structured interview for the phone interview portion as well as the initial on-site interview.
- **Unstructured interviews** are more informal, with questions varying based on the conversation's flow, offering more flexibility but less consistency. I would recommend that an interview be unstructured only after the candidate has passed minimum qualifications, a phone interview, and a round of structured interviews.
- **Behavioral interviews** focus on how candidates handled past situations, providing insight into their problem-solving and decision-making abilities. I recommend baking this into your structured interview process and then considering a behavioral or cognitive assessment (through an outside vendor), depending on the role.

- **Panel interviews** involve multiple interviewers assessing the candidate at the same time.
- **Video interviews** are conducted remotely using video conferencing tools and offer convenience for remote candidates. That said, even at my fully remote company, I did in-person meetings with each person prior to hiring, as I believe that personal connection is very important, especially if you don't know the person outside the work interaction.

Aspect	Structured Interviews	Unstructured Interviews
Format	Pre-determined questions, standardized process	Conversational, varies by interviewer
Consistency	High: every candidate assessed the same	Low: may differ per candidate
Bias Risk	Low: reduces interviewer bias	High: influenced by interviewer preference
Best Used For	Ensuring fairness in hiring, legal compliance	Exploring personality, cultural fit

The benefits of interviews include the opportunity for personal interaction, where a candidate's communication skills, personality, and cultural fit can be directly observed. Many organizations don't prioritize making time for phone interviews, but on-site interviews can often be avoided after a quick phone interview, which can reveal a candidate's communication skills (or lack of) or professionalism (or lack of). However, interviews can also be time-consuming and may be subject to interviewer bias, making it important to use them alongside other assessment methods. Let's run through a barrage of items you can add to your interview process.

Psychometric tests are another valuable tool in the assessment process, as they measure a candidate's cognitive abilities, personality traits, and emotional intelligence. Different types of psychometric tests can be used depending on what is being evaluated. **Aptitude tests** assess a candidate's logical reasoning, numerical ability, and verbal skills, providing insight into their cognitive capabilities. Not all positions warrant a cognitive assessment, but if it's a more highly skilled or executive level that may be on the technical side, they are a great option. **Personality tests** evaluate behavioral tendencies, helping employers understand how the candidate might fit in the team or company culture. **Emotional intelligence tests** assess a candidate's ability to understand and manage their own emotions as well as others'. The key benefits of psychometric tests are their standardization, which allows for objective comparisons between candidates, and their predictive validity, which can indicate a candidate's likely job performance and cultural fit. However, some candidates may prepare specifically for these tests, which can distort results, and there is a potential cultural bias, as the tests may not fully account for cultural differences between candidates.

Skills assessments are an essential tool for evaluating a candidate's technical and practical abilities that are directly relevant to the job. These assessments take on various forms depending on the specific skills being measured. For example, **technical tests** focus on specific technical proficiencies, such as coding for software developers, providing a clear indication of a candidate's level of expertise. **Task-based assessments** require candidates to complete projects or tasks that mirror the responsibilities they would take on in the role, offering a practical demonstration of their abilities. Another method is the use of **case studies**, in which candidates are tasked with analyzing and solving a business scenario, showcasing their problem-solving and analytical skills. The benefits of skills assessments include a job-relevant evaluation of the candidate's abilities and objective evidence of their competencies. However, there are some challenges, such as the resource-intensive nature of designing and evaluating these assessments and the possibility of candidate anxiety affecting performance.

Work samples, in which candidates complete tasks or projects they would perform on the job, are another effective way to evaluate capabilities. This method includes **portfolio reviews**, through which candidates present previous work, allowing employers to evaluate their prior experience. **Job simulations** are another approach, providing candidates with real-world tasks so the organization can assess their performance under realistic conditions. Additionally, some companies may use **trial periods**, in which candidates work on a project over a short time frame to demonstrate their abilities. The main advantage of using samples is the **realistic evaluation** they provide, offering insight into how well the candidate can perform the actual tasks of the job. Furthermore, this approach is **performance-based**, focusing on tangible results rather than theoretical knowledge. However, it can be **time-consuming** for both the employer and the candidate, and ensuring **fairness** across candidates can be challenging, especially when evaluating diverse portfolios or projects. And while I know companies do some of the above without compensating a person for their time, I don't recommend that. If you hire the person, it's not a great start to the relationship.

Assessment centers provide a comprehensive evaluation of candidates by using a combination of assessment methods over one or more days. These centers typically involve **group exercises**, in which candidates participate in discussions or problem-solving activities, simulating real-world collaboration. **In-tray exercises** are also common, mimicking the role's organizational demands and asking candidates to prioritize emails or manage tasks. Additionally, **role-playing** scenarios are used to assess how candidates would handle specific job-related situations, giving insight into their decision-making and interpersonal skills. The primary benefit of assessment centers is their **comprehensive evaluation**, as they offer a holistic view of a candidate's abilities, personality, and potential. The use of **multiple assessors** also helps reduce bias, leading to a more objective and balanced evaluation. However, these centers can be **costly**

to organize and require significant logistical planning, making them resource-intensive for companies to implement.

The hiring process can be overwhelming, but it doesn't have to be. My consulting firm has a free **Hiring Process Steps** guide that walks you through the key stages to attract, assess, and onboard top talent effectively. This helps you avoid making hiring mistakes, saves time with a structured process, and improve the candidate experience. If you'd like the free guide, go to saltandlightadvisors.com/transformyourhiringprocess and snag it.

Let's go deeper into the five different types of interviews.

Structured interviews are a highly effective approach to evaluating candidates by ensuring consistency and fairness throughout the process. In a structured interview, each candidate is asked the same predetermined set of questions, allowing for a uniform assessment of skills, experiences, and qualifications. Preparing in advance is crucial, starting with a list of standardized questions that align with the job description and the core competencies required for the role. To guarantee fairness, it's essential to also create a scoring system to evaluate candidate responses consistently. The interview should be conducted in a consistent environment for all candidates, where they are provided with the same information about the interview process and format to minimize any potential bias. During the interview, it is important to focus on job-relevant questions that assess the specific skills, knowledge, and abilities needed for the position. Avoid any questions that are unrelated to the job, as they can introduce unnecessary bias.

Open-ended questions are particularly useful in structured interviews, as they encourage candidates to share more detailed information about their past experiences. For instance, asking, "Can you describe a time when you successfully managed a challenging project?" allows candidates to elaborate on their problem-solving abilities and approach to challenges. Throughout the interview, taking notes is essential to document responses accurately and provide a fair comparison between candidates. With a standardized form, the answers and scores are recorded systematically. As a reminder, any of these documents or notes used in the process are to be kept in a candidate's file, whether hired or not, for a specific period (as determined by the state you operate in).

Finally, to ensure objectivity, evaluating candidates objectively based on the scoring system helps minimize subjective bias. This allows interviewers to compare candidates' performances based on their responses and overall scores, creating a fair and consistent selection process. Structured interviews, when conducted properly, can greatly enhance the reliability of hiring decisions and promote equal opportunity for all candidates.

Behavioral interviews assess a candidate's past behavior as a predictor of their future performance. These interviews focus on how candidates have handled real-life situations, providing insights into their competencies, decision-making processes, and interpersonal skills. To start, it's essential to identify core competencies relevant to the role, such as teamwork, leadership, or problem-solving. Once these competencies are identified, interviewers can craft questions that target them. For instance, asking about conflict resolution in a team allows candidates to demonstrate their ability to navigate interpersonal challenges.

A helpful structure for these interviews is the STAR method (Situation, Task, Action, Result), which encourages candidates to provide detailed responses that outline the context, their responsibilities, the actions they took, and the outcomes of their efforts. A question like "Can you tell me about a time when you had to resolve a conflict in your team?" is an example of using the STAR method to gain a clear and structured response. To gain deeper insights, interviewers should probe for details by asking follow-up questions that encourage a candidate to elaborate on their thought processes and actions. This might involve questions like "What specific steps did you take to improve communication in the team?" Throughout the interview, it's important to look for patterns in the candidate's behavior across different scenarios. By doing so, interviewers can assess consistency in how the candidate handles various challenges and responsibilities. Finally, evaluation based on evidence is key. Interviewers should focus on concrete examples provided by the candidate and avoid making assumptions based on generalizations or incomplete information. Because most companies struggle to determine what questions to ask to get to the above outcomes, we've developed hiring guides for that very reason. We built them segmented by the level of the role in an organization.

Here's a sample question on the topic of accountability for an entry-level person to get you started:

Question: Tell me about a time when you weren't able to finish a task before the deadline. What did you do?

Potential Follow-Up: Why were you unable to finish the task? Were there consequences for the task not being complete?

Here's a management-level question on the same topic (accountability):

Question: Tell me about a time when you delegated a project or task to a direct report and it didn't go well. What happened, and how did you handle it?

Potential Follow-Up: Did you approach the employee? What was the result of the situation?

Situational interviews, on the other hand, present candidates with hypothetical scenarios that reflect challenges they might face in the role.

This type of interview is particularly useful for assessing how candidates approach problem-solving and decision-making in real time. To conduct an effective situational interview, it's important to develop relevant scenarios that are closely aligned with the responsibilities of the position. For example, asking, "If you were leading a project and discovered it was behind schedule, how would you handle the situation?" provides insight into how the candidate manages time-sensitive and high-pressure situations.

In situational interviews, it's crucial to assess problem-solving skills by asking the candidate to walk through their thought process and the steps they would take to address the scenario. Additionally, focusing on the candidate's decision-making abilities, particularly under pressure, helps interviewers evaluate how they weigh risks, make trade-offs, and mitigate potential consequences. Interviewers should also consider the practicality of the candidate's proposed solutions, looking for evidence of both innovation and feasibility. For fairness and consistency, it's helpful to compare responses across candidates using a standardized evaluation framework. This allows for a more objective comparison of how each candidate approaches the same scenario, helping interviewers identify the best fit for the company's values and problem-solving needs.

When conducting interviews, it's essential to follow general best practices to ensure a smooth and effective process. Setting the tone at the start of the interview is crucial for building rapport and establishing a welcoming environment. Begin with a brief introduction about the company and the position to give the candidate context and clarity. Making the candidate feel comfortable encourages them to communicate openly and honestly, which can result in a more productive conversation. During the interview, active listening is key. Pay close attention not only to the candidate's verbal responses but also to their nonverbal cues, such as body language and facial expressions. Give them the space to fully express their thoughts without interruptions, which shows respect for their responses and allows you to gather all the necessary information.

Remaining objective is another critical component of effective interviewing. To avoid biases or preconceived notions about the candidate, focus solely on their qualifications and the content of their responses. Using a standardized evaluation form helps maintain consistency across all interviews so that each candidate is assessed fairly based on the same criteria. I've had colleagues who have "gone with their gut" in an interview process instead of using structured interview questions. On multiple occasions I've seen this turn into a case of an unqualified hire or a cultural mismatch. Following a structured interview process not only avoids potential bias, it also helps you avoid hiring based on the first impression alone. We may "click" personally with someone, but that doesn't make them qualified for the job.

It's also important to provide opportunities for the candidate to ask questions about the role and the company. This not only clarifies any uncertainties for the candidate but can also reveal their level of interest and understanding of the position. Their questions can offer insights into what matters most to them in a job, helping you gauge cultural fit.

Finally, make sure to follow up promptly with all candidates after the interview. Inform them about the next steps and provide an estimated timeline for when they can expect to hear back. If possible, offer constructive feedback to candidates who were not selected, as this can leave a positive impression of your company and help them in their future job searches (if appropriate).

While we are talking interviews, if a candidate is coming on-site, you need to recognize that you are either getting them excited about joining the team or turning them off during their on-site experience. Creating a positive on-site encounter is vital to leaving a lasting impression on candidates during the recruitment process.

Upon arriving at the office, candidates should be greeted warmly and made to feel welcome, as this sets a positive tone for their visit. Ensure that the interview environment is comfortable and professional to help candidates feel at ease and confident throughout the process, allowing them to perform at their best. Offering a tour of the office and introducing them to potential team members can make them feel valued and give them a sense of the company's culture. I wouldn't spend time doing this if it's not a top-rated candidate, but I also hope you're learning that you aren't bringing non-top-rated candidates into your organizations for formal interviews.

Let's go deeper into the topic of tech as it relates to recruitment and talent acquisition. An applicant tracking system (ATS) is a critical tool for efficiently managing the recruitment process. It serves as a comprehensive software application that simplifies various stages of hiring, from posting jobs to onboarding candidates. One of its key functions is job posting and distribution. With an ATS, recruiters can create and distribute job postings to multiple platforms, including job boards, social media channels, and the company's career page, all from a single interface. This not only ensures that job descriptions are consistent across different platforms but also automates the posting process, saving recruiters valuable time. Furthermore, the ATS's ability to broadcast job openings to a wider audience increases the likelihood of attracting a diverse and qualified talent pool.

The ATS also excels in application management by organizing candidate data in a centralized database. This repository collects all applications, making it easy to manage and access relevant information. Additionally, the system's resume-parsing feature extracts details from resumes and cover letters, which reduces the need for manual data entry.

Each candidate is represented through a comprehensive profile that includes not only their application materials but also interview notes and communication history. These profiles are searchable, allowing recruiters to filter candidates based on criteria such as experience, skills, and qualifications, which makes the process more efficient. Profiles can be shared with hiring managers for real-time collaboration. And automated responses are a must-use in the system.

When it comes to screening and filtering candidates, the ATS offers powerful tools to automate this often-time-consuming process. It uses keyword-matching algorithms to identify resumes that align with the job description, filtering out candidates who do not meet the basic qualifications. Recruiters can also customize prescreening questions to automatically disqualify those who fail to meet essential criteria. Additionally, candidates are scored and ranked objectively based on their qualifications, which allows recruiters to prioritize top talent efficiently from a large applicant pool.

The ATS also simplifies interview scheduling and management by automating various logistical tasks. Through calendar integration, recruiters can schedule interviews without worrying about conflicts, and candidates receive automated invitations and reminders.

In the case of panel interviews, the system can seamlessly coordinate multiple interviewers and consolidate their feedback in a centralized location. This organized approach reduces the administrative burden on recruiters, and the interview process runs smoothly for both candidates and hiring teams. Communication and collaboration are streamlined through an ATS by offering centralized communication and effective team collaboration tools. With unified messaging, recruiters can manage all interactions with candidates from one platform, whether via emails, texts, or in-app messages, ensuring consistent communication. The system also provides customizable email templates that help maintain a professional tone across all candidate correspondence.

Beyond communication, the ATS enhances teamwork by allowing recruitment teams to share notes, comments, and feedback on candidates. This promotes a more collaborative hiring process. Additionally, approval workflows in the system facilitate the smooth advancement of candidates through different stages so that the decision-making process is organized and clear.

While I would love to make a helpful recommendation here on what system works best, the reality is that it depends. If you want a recruitment strategy alongside an ATS, I have a referral partner I love in this space. Otherwise, I rarely recommend you add a new tool that isn't connected to what you already have. Unless you find a system with an API that already has examples of the connection working smoothly, look at the HR and payroll tool you already utilize and see what they can add on for you.

In terms of analytics and reporting, an ATS provides valuable insights into the recruitment process. Recruiters can track important metrics, such as time to fill, cost per hire, and source effectiveness, allowing them to assess the efficiency of their hiring strategies. Oftentimes, organizations aren't tracking these metrics at all, which begs the question, How do you determine the success or failure of your recruitment or HR team? The system also allows for the creation of custom reports, enabling a deeper analysis of recruitment data to identify trends and improve performance. Furthermore, the ATS guarantees compliance with employment laws by maintaining detailed records of all recruitment activities, including audit trails. This is particularly useful for maintaining a clear history of decisions made during the hiring process. Additionally, diversity-reporting capabilities support inclusive hiring by providing data on diversity metrics, which helps in promoting equitable recruitment practices.

The onboarding process is also simplified through ATS integration, which is a huge win and a time-saver for the HR or payroll teams. By integrating with onboarding systems, the ATS creates a smooth transition from candidate to employee. It handles the collection and storage of necessary documents, making the onboarding process more organized. New hires benefit from automated welcome messages that set the tone for their new role, along with a structured onboarding schedule. The system also assigns onboarding tasks to new hires and tracks their completion, ensuring that nothing is overlooked as they become familiar with their new responsibilities. With this seamless transition, new employees are supported right from the start.

An applicant tracking system (ATS) is a vital tool in modern recruitment, offering a range of functionalities that enhance efficiency, consistency, and collaboration throughout the hiring process. By automating routine tasks, centralizing data, and providing powerful analytics, an ATS allows recruiters to focus on strategic aspects of talent acquisition, ultimately leading to better hiring decisions and a more streamlined recruitment process.

AI and automation are playing a transformative role in talent acquisition by streamlining processes, improving candidate experience, and enabling more informed decision-making. Key innovations in this space include AI-powered chatbots, predictive analytics, and automated screening tools, each contributing to a more efficient and responsive recruitment process.

AI-powered chatbots have become integral to initial candidate engagement, offering real-time interaction throughout the application process. These chatbots are available twenty-four seven, meaning candidates can receive immediate responses to inquiries regardless of time zone or business hours. This constant availability enhances efficiency, as chatbots handle repetitive tasks, like answering frequently asked questions, scheduling interviews, and guiding candidates through the application process. This automation leads to an improved candidate experience, as they are guaranteed timely and consistent communication. For example, chatbots can guide candidates through application procedures, help schedule interviews by syncing calendars, and even prescreen candidates by asking qualifying questions to ensure that they meet basic job requirements. Some HR and payroll systems have this feature, or it's a fairly simple add-on to others.

Predictive analytics in recruitment leverages historical data and machine learning algorithms to improve hiring decisions and anticipate future talent needs. By analyzing data from past hires, predictive analytics identifies patterns and traits associated with successful employees, helping hiring managers make better decisions. This proactive approach aids in talent management by forecasting future hiring needs based on business growth trends and market dynamics, allowing companies to prepare accordingly. Predictive models also contribute to reducing employee turnover by identifying candidates who are more likely to remain with the organization over the long term.

Examples of the use of predictive analytics include predicting candidate success based on previous hiring data, managing talent pools by identifying passive candidates who could be suitable for future roles, and improving diversity by analyzing hiring patterns that favor diverse candidates if that's your organization's goal.

AI and automation in talent acquisition not only enhance operational efficiency but also improve the overall hiring experience for both recruiters and candidates, paving the way for more strategic and data-driven approaches to recruitment.

Automated screening tools use AI to streamline the early stages of candidate evaluation by filtering and ranking applicants according to predefined criteria. These tools greatly enhance efficiency by reducing the time recruiters spend manually reviewing resumes and applications, allowing them to focus on top candidates more quickly. Automated screening creates consistency by applying the same evaluation standards to all candidates, which helps reduce bias in the selection process.

Furthermore, these tools are scalable, enabling recruiters to handle large volumes of applications, especially during peak hiring periods. For example, resume-parsing technology extracts key information from resumes and compares it against job requirements. Keyword-matching algorithms further enhance this process by identifying resumes that best match the job description, while some screening tools can even conduct initial skills assessments, such as coding tests for software developers.

AI and automation extend beyond screening, with applications in intelligent sourcing and candidate engagement. Intelligent sourcing uses AI algorithms to scan databases, job boards, and social media platforms to find candidates who meet specific job criteria. This proactive approach enables recruiters to identify potential talent early on, and automated tools can send personalized outreach messages to passive candidates, encouraging them to apply. In terms of candidate engagement, automation supports nurture campaigns that keep candidates informed and engaged through regular updates and relevant content. Additionally, AI can be used to collect and analyze candidate feedback, allowing organizations to continuously improve their recruitment processes.

AI and automation also play a role in onboarding, where they streamline workflows by automating document collection, training schedules, and new-hire orientation. This automation leads to a smoother, more efficient onboarding experience. Furthermore, AI can tailor the onboarding process to fit the new hire's specific role, location, and preferences, offering a more personalized approach that can improve the transition from candidate to employee.

AI and automation are significantly transforming talent acquisition by enhancing efficiency, consistency, and effectiveness. Chatbots provide real-time engagement and streamline communication, predictive analytics enable data-driven hiring decisions, and automated screening tools expedite the initial stages of candidate evaluation. Together, these technologies improve the candidate experience, reduce time to hire, and help organizations build stronger, more diverse teams. By leveraging AI and automation, companies can stay competitive (and more efficient) in the evolving landscape of talent acquisition.

At the time of publishing, there have been several shifts in the professional world when it comes to **diversity and inclusion**. Many organizations are doing away with their formal programs and the leadership running them. And while the purpose of this book doesn't align with me weighing in on that topic, I do want to include some insights as to why D&I is important to consider when it comes to talent acquisition and recruitment.

A diverse workforce represents a broad spectrum of differences among employees, such as race, gender, age, ethnicity, cultural background, sexual orientation, and physical abilities. Embracing diversity in an organization leads to a range of benefits that significantly contribute to business success. One key advantage is enhanced creativity and innovation. Teams composed of individuals from diverse backgrounds bring varied perspectives and experiences, which can lead to a wider variety of ideas and more creative solutions. Employees with different worldviews can approach problems from multiple angles, often uncovering solutions that more homogeneous teams might overlook. For example, in product development, diverse teams are better equipped to design products and services that cater to a wider audience, while in problem-solving, they can help identify potential challenges and opportunities that others may miss.

Another major benefit of diversity is improved decision-making. With a broader range of insights, a diverse team can conduct more a comprehensive analysis, considering various perspectives that enhance the depth and quality of decisions. Diversity also reduces the risk of groupthink, fostering critical evaluation and encouraging open debate. This is especially valuable in strategic planning, where input from diverse teams ensures that market segments and cultural nuances are well accounted for, leading to more robust business strategies. Additionally, in risk management, diverse viewpoints are instrumental in identifying and mitigating risks that might otherwise go unnoticed.

A key advantage of diversity in organizations is the attraction and retention of top talent. An inclusive culture promotes employee satisfaction, as individuals feel more valued and respected in a diverse workplace. Such environments tend to boost employee morale, making the company more attractive to high-caliber professionals from various backgrounds. In fact, organizations known for valuing diversity are often seen as forward-thinking, drawing interest from a broader talent pool. For example, companies with a reputation for inclusivity tend to experience lower turnover rates, as employees are more likely to stay in a place where they feel appreciated and understood. This leads to more consistent retention of top performers and contributes to overall workplace stability.

Diversity also drives broader market reach. Employees from diverse backgrounds contribute invaluable insights into different customer segments, making it easier for companies to tailor products, services, and marketing strategies to specific cultural preferences and demographics. This global competence allows businesses to operate effectively across various markets. For instance, diverse marketing teams are more capable of developing campaigns that resonate with a wide array of audiences. Similarly, customer service teams that reflect diversity are better equipped to address the unique needs and concerns of a broader customer base, fostering stronger customer loyalty and satisfaction.

Moreover, diversity enhances a company's reputation. Organizations recognized for their diversity and inclusion initiatives often enjoy a more positive public perception, which strengthens their employer brand. This reputation not only attracts potential employees but also appeals to partners and customers who prioritize inclusivity. Companies that integrate diversity into their corporate social responsibility (CSR) strategies are often viewed as more socially responsible, and positive media coverage further boosts their brand image. For instance, businesses that actively promote diversity may receive accolades or recognition, which enhances their appeal to consumers and employees alike.

Financial performance is another area where diversity makes a significant impact. Studies have consistently shown a correlation between diverse workforces and improved profitability. This is largely due to the innovation and creativity fostered by diverse teams, which lead to market growth and expanded revenue streams. Diverse companies often see better performance metrics, as they are able to innovate more quickly and effectively. For example, research indicates that companies with high diversity scores tend to outperform their less diverse competitors, showing higher revenue from innovation and increased market share.

From a compliance standpoint, diversity also offers legal protection. Companies that embrace diversity are more likely to adhere to equal employment opportunity laws, reducing the risk of discrimination lawsuits and related legal challenges. Implementing robust diversity policies not only helps businesses stay within legal frameworks but also fosters workplace harmony by creating an inclusive environment where conflicts and grievances are less likely to arise. Organizations with strong diversity practices are more likely to avoid costly legal issues and maintain a positive, respectful workplace culture.

A diverse workforce is a strategic asset that drives creativity, innovation, and improved decision-making. It enhances a company's ability to attract and retain top talent, broadens its market reach, and strengthens its reputation. Additionally, diversity positively impacts financial performance and ensures compliance with legal standards. By fostering an inclusive culture, organizations can leverage the full potential of their diverse employees, leading to sustained success and competitive advantage in the marketplace.

Fostering diversity and inclusion in an organization requires intentional actions, such as creating inclusive job descriptions, reducing bias in the selection process, and creating diverse candidate pools. These strategies are key to cultivating a more diverse and equitable workforce. Creating inclusive job descriptions begins with the use of gender-neutral language. Avoid gendered terms, like *he* or *she*, and opt for neutral alternatives, such as *they*. Similarly, revise job titles to avoid excluding candidates based on gender, like replacing *salesman* with *salesperson*. It's also important to balance wording so the description appeals to all genders, avoiding overly aggressive or nurturing language.

Additionally, focus on essential skills and qualifications by listing only the core competencies and avoiding excessive requirements that could discourage diverse applicants. Including a statement about the company's commitment to diversity and highlighting inclusive benefits, such as parental leave and flexible work arrangements, can also attract a broader range of candidates. Finally, be mindful of accessibility by making sure that the job description is written in clear, simple language and is accessible to individuals with disabilities, using readable fonts and alternative text where necessary.

Reducing bias in the selection process is another crucial strategy. Implementing blind recruitment practices, such as removing identifying information (like name, gender, and age) from applications, can significantly reduce unconscious bias. Similarly, using standardized evaluation forms means that all candidates are assessed consistently. Structured interviews, in which predefined questions and scoring rubrics are used, help further reduce bias by objectively assessing candidates based on set criteria. Including diverse interview panels, which bring varied perspectives, and providing bias training to interviewers can also minimize individual biases. Furthermore, using AI and automation to screen resumes based on objective criteria can further mitigate human bias, while predictive analytics helps make data-driven hiring decisions.

To ensure diverse candidate pools, organizations must expand their sourcing channels. Posting job openings on diverse job boards and websites, such as those catering to specific communities (e.g., diversityjobs.com or Women in Tech), can help reach a broader range of talent. Partnering with professional associations, like the National Society of Black Engineers or the Society of Women Engineers, can also enhance recruitment efforts. Additionally, employee referral programs should be inclusive, encouraging employees to refer candidates from diverse backgrounds and offering incentives for successful referrals.

Partnerships with universities and community organizations are effective in recruiting diverse talent, particularly through campus recruitment at institutions with diverse student populations and community outreach at diversity-focused career fairs. Internships and apprenticeships targeting underrepresented groups, coupled with mentorship and development opportunities, further support diversity initiatives. Finally, tracking diversity metrics throughout the recruitment process and continuously gathering feedback allows organizations to refine their practices and address any barriers to achieving diversity goals.

Legal and Ethical Considerations

Ensuring compliance with legal requirements during the hiring process is critical in helping organizations avoid legal risks and promote fair and equitable employment practices. Employers must be aware of several key legal aspects and adhere to the law throughout the hiring process.

Equal employment opportunity (EEO) laws play a fundamental role in protecting individuals from discrimination during hiring and employment. These laws protect individuals from being treated unfairly based on personal characteristics, such as race, color, religion, sex (including pregnancy, gender identity, and sexual orientation), national origin, age, disability, and genetic information. Employers are required to provide equal opportunities in all aspects of employment, including hiring, promotion, and compensation. Key laws governing EEO include **Title VII** of the Civil Rights Act of 1964 (which prohibits employment discrimination based on race, color, religion, sex, and national origin) and the **Equal Pay Act** of 1963 (which mandates equal pay for equal work regardless of gender). Additionally, the **Age Discrimination in Employment Act** (ADEA) of 1967 protects individuals over the age of forty, and the **Americans with Disabilities Act** (ADA) of 1990 prohibits discrimination against individuals with disabilities, ensuring that they receive reasonable accommodations.

Data privacy regulations are also critical in today's hiring processes, as employers must protect candidates' personal data. Employers are required to obtain consent before collecting, processing, and storing candidates' data, guaranteeing transparency about how that data will be used. Data security measures must be in place to protect sensitive information, and candidates must have the right to access their data and be informed about its use. Laws like the **General Data Protection Regulation** (GDPR), which applies to organizations operating in the European Union (EU) or those dealing with EU citizens' data, and the

California Consumer Privacy Act (CCPA), which governs businesses in California, provide strict guidelines on data protection and grant individuals significant rights over their personal information. The **Fair Credit Reporting Act** (FCRA) also regulates the use of consumer data, particularly in the context of background checks, and requires that candidates be informed and give their consent before such checks are conducted. By adhering to these legal requirements, employers can ensure a fair, inclusive, and legally compliant hiring process, protecting both their organization and their employees from potential legal challenges.

Let's dig a little deeper into **background checks** regarding legal considerations. These are standard practices for employers aiming to verify a candidate's qualifications and assess their suitability for a position. However, these checks must adhere to legal requirements to guarantee fairness and transparency throughout the hiring process. A crucial aspect of conducting background checks is the need for disclosure and consent. Employers are required to inform candidates that a background check will be conducted and must obtain their explicit consent before proceeding. This makes sure that candidates are aware of the process and can provide informed approval. Furthermore, the information gathered during background checks must be accurate and relevant to the job in question. Employers must ensure that the data they rely on reflects the candidate's qualifications without extraneous or outdated information that could unjustly influence hiring decisions. In cases where an adverse action is taken based on the results of a background check, employers are obligated to notify the candidate and provide them with an opportunity to dispute any inaccuracies in the information provided. This process is essential for maintaining fairness and transparency in hiring. Additionally, **ban the box laws** in certain jurisdictions prevent employers from inquiring about a candidate's criminal history on job applications, meaning qualifications are considered before criminal history is reviewed. This approach promotes fair hiring practices by allowing candidates to be evaluated based on their skills and experiences before any background information is considered.

Immigration and employment eligibility are critical components of the hiring process, as employers must verify that all employees are legally permitted to work in the country. This verification is typically conducted using Form I-9, which employers must complete for each employee to confirm their identity and employment authorization. The form serves as a crucial step in ensuring compliance with immigration laws. In addition to the I-9 form, many employers choose to use E-Verify, an optional online system that allows them to confirm an employee's eligibility to work in the United States. E-Verify provides an additional layer of assurance regarding an employee's legal status, helping mitigate potential legal issues related to hiring practices. The primary legal framework for immigration and employment eligibility is the **Immigration Reform and Control Act** (IRCA) of 1986, which mandates that employers verify the employment eligibility of all employees. Complementary regulations from the Department of Homeland Security govern the use of E-Verify and other employment verification processes.

Understanding and adhering to legal requirements related to hiring is essential in avoiding legal issues and creating a fair and inclusive hiring process. Key areas include offering equal employment opportunities, preventing discrimination, protecting candidate data, conducting fair background checks, and verifying employment eligibility. By following these guidelines, organizations can foster a compliant and equitable hiring environment.

Ethical considerations in recruitment are pivotal in establishing a foundation of trust and maintaining a reputable organizational culture. By adhering to key ethical principles, such as honesty, transparency, and fairness, companies can foster an environment of integrity while creating a positive experience for both candidates and employees.

These ethical practices help create an equitable recruitment process that is not only compliant with legal standards but also supports long-term organizational success. Honesty in recruitment involves being forthright about every aspect of the job and the organization. Providing accurate and truthful information about the job role, company culture, compensation, and potential career growth opportunities is essential. Honesty builds trust between the employer and potential employees, laying the groundwork for a strong and lasting working relationship. It also sets realistic expectations, reducing the chances of future misunderstandings or job dissatisfaction. Moreover, an honest recruitment process enhances the company's reputation, making it more attractive to top talent. This principle can be upheld through offering precise job descriptions, transparent salary information, and candid communication about both the role's opportunities and challenges.

Transparency in recruitment means being open and clear about the selection process, criteria, and timelines. Transparency contributes to a positive candidate experience, as applicants feel informed and valued throughout the recruitment process. It also promotes fairness by ensuring that all candidates are evaluated based on the same clear and consistent criteria. Transparency fosters trust and engagement among employees as well, which can lead to higher loyalty and satisfaction. Organizations can practice transparency by outlining the recruitment process in detail, providing candidates with timely updates, and offering feedback to those who were not selected to help them improve for future opportunities. Fairness is a fundamental principle of ethical recruitment, making sure that all candidates are treated equitably and assessed based on their qualifications, skills, and potential without bias. Fair recruitment practices encourage diversity and inclusion by offering equal opportunities to candidates from various backgrounds. Fairness also helps organizations comply with anti-discrimination laws and fosters a respectful organizational culture, which can improve employee satisfaction and retention. Fairness can be achieved through bias training for recruiters, standardized evaluation criteria, and diverse interview panels to provide varied perspectives and mitigate potential biases in the decision-making process.

Let's dive into talent acquisition and recruitment metrics, shall we? Key performance indicators (KPIs) serve as essential tools for evaluating the effectiveness of talent acquisition efforts. By tracking metrics, such as time to fill, cost per hire, and quality of hire, organizations can gain valuable insights into their recruitment processes, optimize their strategies, and make informed decisions. These KPIs not only help assess efficiency and cost-effectiveness but also contribute to improving the overall candidate experience and long-term success.

One critical KPI is **time to fill**, which measures the number of days between when a job opening is posted and when a candidate accepts an offer. This metric reflects the speed at which an organization can fill open positions, impacting business operations and team productivity. Generally, organizations aim for a shorter time to fill, though this can vary depending on market conditions and the role's complexity.

Another essential KPI is **cost per hire**, which calculates the total recruitment expenses—including advertising costs, recruiter fees, and technology investments—divided by the number of hires. This KPI helps assess the efficiency of the recruitment budget and allows organizations to evaluate the cost-effectiveness of different sourcing methods. A lower cost per hire is desirable, but it is also crucial to maintain a balance between cost, quality, and speed of hiring.

Quality of hire is a more complex KPI, focusing on the long-term impact of new employees on the organization. This metric is often measured through performance evaluations, retention rates, and the new hire's contribution to team productivity. A high quality of hire indicates that the recruitment process is effectively selecting candidates who fit both the role and the organizational culture, leading to long-term success.

In addition to these core KPIs, organizations often monitor the **offer acceptance rate**, which reflects the percentage of job offers accepted by candidates. A high offer acceptance rate signals that the organization is appealing to top talent and that job offers align with candidates' expectations. Similarly, **source effectiveness** measures the performance of different recruitment channels, helping organizations prioritize the most productive sources for high-quality candidates.

Finally, **retention rate** evaluates the percentage of new hires who stay with the organization over a specified period. A high retention rate suggests that the recruitment and onboarding processes are successful in identifying candidates who are a strong fit for the company.

Collaboration between HR teams and decision-makers is enhanced through data visualization. By presenting key recruitment metrics and insights in the form of easy-to-understand dashboards and reports, stakeholders can make informed decisions more quickly and effectively. Empowering recruitment teams with these insights fosters data-driven decision-making, leading to improved hiring outcomes, better resource allocation, and overall process enhancements. Not to mention, many HR pros I run across often talk about their desire to have a "seat at the table." An executive leadership team will beg you to join the meeting if you're regularly supplying them with data that clearly helps guide and direct them in decision-making. And if you're at an organization that doesn't value that input, well, that's for another book.

To implement data analytics in recruitment successfully, companies need to invest in training their HR teams in data analysis and interpretation. This ensures that recruitment professionals can effectively utilize analytics tools and techniques to extract meaningful insights from the data. Just like having your sales team come in and work with recruiters, it's a great idea to have your quality or business intelligence team work with HR staff on how to curate, interpret, and utilize data. In addition, organizations should focus on technology integration, making sure that their applicant tracking systems (ATS) or human resource information systems (HRIS) have built-in analytics capabilities or are integrated with external analytics platforms. This streamlines the collection, analysis, and application of recruitment data, driving better recruitment strategies and outcomes.

Future Trends in Talent Acquisition

As workplaces continue to evolve, three significant trends are reshaping how organizations structure their workforce and engage with employees: remote work, the gig economy, and flexible work arrangements. Each of these trends reflects the changing priorities of both workers and organizations, driven by advances in technology, shifting economic conditions, and new expectations for work-life balance.

Remote work has become a prominent feature of modern workplaces, allowing employees to perform their duties from locations outside the traditional office. This shift is enabled by advances in technology, such as cloud-based tools, video conferencing, and collaboration software, which ensure productivity and communication even from a distance. Remote work provides employees with greater flexibility, helping them manage personal and professional commitments more effectively. It also broadens the talent pool for organizations, allowing them to hire skilled workers globally, which can lead to increased diversity. While remote work often results in higher job satisfaction due to reduced commuting stress and more autonomy, productivity outcomes vary. Some employees thrive in a remote environment, while others may struggle with focus or feel disconnected from their teams. From a financial perspective, remote work can save organizations substantial overhead costs related to office space and other resources.

The **gig economy** refers to a labor market characterized by short-term, flexible jobs often facilitated through digital platforms. They are oftentimes classified as 1099 contractors; therefore, workers in the gig economy enjoy flexibility and independence, choosing when, where, and how much they work. They often bring specialized skills to short-term projects, providing valuable on-demand services to various industries. However, the gig economy also presents challenges, particularly regarding job security and benefits, which are less common in gig work compared to full-time employment. On a broader scale, the gig economy creates new economic opportunities for freelancers and independent contractors while helping organizations manage fluctuating workloads without the commitment of permanent hires. As the gig economy grows, there are ongoing regulatory discussions about labor rights and protections for gig workers across different regions. You'll want to make sure a contractor is actually a contractor (based on IRS standards). Misclassifying workers can lead to penalties and compliance issues. My consulting firm has a free **Contractor vs. Employee Guide** which will help you determine the right classification based on IRS guidelines. The guide assists with understanding legal implications, avoiding fines and misclassification errors, and making confident hiring decisions. If you'd like to grab it, go to saltandlightadvisors.com/contractororemployee.

Lastly, **flexible work arrangements** offer employees the ability to tailor their work schedules to meet personal commitments. These arrangements can include flextime, compressed workweeks, part-time schedules, or job-sharing opportunities. Flexible work arrangements are increasingly popular with younger generations and have become an important factor in attracting and retaining top talent. They also enhance employee engagement by providing greater autonomy over work-life integration, contributing to higher job satisfaction. For organizations, flexibility enables operational agility, allowing businesses to adapt to changing market conditions and resource demands. However, managing remote and flexible teams can pose challenges for managers, requiring strong communication strategies, trust, and clear performance metrics to ensure team success. I've talked several times on my podcast about managing remote teams and workers, and I love to point out that it's simply managing employees who are humans. So, whether you sit together or not, there are going to be difficulties. Seek to understand, provide clarity, and communicate often.

These emerging trends reflect a shift toward more adaptable and responsive work environments driven by technological advancements, changing workforce demographics, and evolving employee expectations. As organizations navigate these trends, they must balance flexibility with effective management practices and address regulatory considerations to maximize the benefits for both employees and the business. Embracing these trends strategically can foster innovation, improve employee satisfaction, and strengthen organizational resilience in a competitive global landscape.

Talent acquisition is undergoing significant transformation due to advancements in technology and innovative practices that enhance both efficiency and candidate experience. These innovations are reshaping how organizations attract and hire talent, making recruitment more data-driven, automated, and personalized.

While we addressed it previously in this chapter, I anticipate that AI, chatbots, automation, and data will be continuing trends moving forward. Let's be honest—we still have a bit to go in the HR field in that arena, but we are making progress. Emerging technologies, like **virtual reality (VR) and augmented reality (AR)**, are beginning to influence recruitment in innovative ways. Virtual interviews using VR and AR technologies simulate real-world job environments, allowing candidates to demonstrate their skills and suitability for the role in a more dynamic and immersive way, even when remote. These technologies are also revolutionizing training and onboarding by offering engaging, hands-on experiences that enhance learning retention and employee engagement.

Lastly, **employer branding and candidate experience** are critical elements shaped by new technologies. Organizations are increasingly leveraging digital content marketing—through videos, blogs, and social media platforms—to showcase their culture, values, and employee testimonials, all of which help attract top talent. AI-driven personalization tools enhance candidate communication by providing tailored interactions throughout the recruitment journey, creating a more engaging and positive candidate experience. These innovations are making talent acquisition more agile, personalized, and data-driven, helping organizations attract and retain top talent in a competitive labor market.

Remote work and global talent acquisition have transformed the way organizations approach hiring in the digital age. Virtual hiring events, online assessments, and collaborative tools have made it easier to recruit talent globally, breaking down geographical barriers and expanding the reach of talent acquisition. This shift has allowed companies to tap into diverse global talent pools that might have been inaccessible in traditional, office-based recruitment models.

Furthermore, technology has enhanced the ability to account for cultural differences in recruitment practices. Companies are increasingly adopting recruitment processes and engagement strategies that prioritize cultural sensitivity, fostering an inclusive and respectful environment for candidates from different backgrounds.

Continuous learning and development is another area where technology is driving change in talent acquisition. AI-driven skill assessments are now used to evaluate candidates' technical abilities and soft skills, providing employers with valuable insights into their potential for growth in the organization. These assessments help recruiters identify candidates who not only are qualified for the current role but also have the capacity for long-term development. Additionally, organizations are utilizing technology to create personalized learning and development plans for employees. These tailored pathways align individual career goals with organizational objectives, ensuring that employees can grow and thrive while contributing to the company's success.

Innovative practices and technologies in talent acquisition are revolutionizing how organizations attract, assess, and retain talent in a competitive global landscape. By leveraging AI, data analytics, automation, VR and AR, and a focus on candidate experience and diversity, organizations can optimize recruitment processes, enhance employer branding, and build a skilled, engaged workforce prepared for future challenges and opportunities. Embracing these innovations strategically enables HR professionals to stay ahead in talent acquisition and drive organizational success in the evolving digital age.

CHAPTER 2

Onboarding

A great hiring process doesn't end when an offer is accepted, it's just the beginning. Effective onboarding ensures that new hires integrate smoothly, understand expectations, and contribute to the business quickly. This chapter covers every aspect of onboarding, from preboarding to role-specific training, with a focus on small business efficiency. By the end, you'll have a structured framework to set up new employees for long-term success.

Employee onboarding refers to the comprehensive process of integrating a new employee into an organization, preparing them for their specific role, their team, and the broader company culture. This process begins once the job offer is accepted and typically continues through the new hire's initial employment period, which can last from a few weeks to several months. (That time frame is identified by your organization based on the needs.) Effective onboarding is crucial as it sets the foundation for an employee's journey in the organization, ultimately influencing their performance, engagement, and retention.

The **importance of effective onboarding** cannot be overstated. It facilitates a smooth transition and enhances productivity by helping new employees assimilate quickly into their roles and teams. By establishing clear expectations regarding job responsibilities, performance standards, and organizational goals, onboarding aligns new hires with the company's mission and vision, making it clear how they can contribute to the organization's success. Additionally, onboarding plays a vital role in employee engagement and retention. It fosters cultural assimilation by helping new hires understand the company's values and norms, thereby creating a sense of belonging and commitment. Engaging onboarding experiences can significantly increase job satisfaction, leading to lower turnover rates as employees feel valued and supported from day one.

Moreover, onboarding includes essential training initiatives that equip new hires with the skills and knowledge they need to perform their jobs effectively. It introduces employees to growth opportunities in the organization, encouraging a culture of continuous learning and career advancement. A well-structured onboarding process also contributes to organizational efficiency by ensuring that administrative tasks, such as paperwork, equipment setup, and IT access, are handled promptly, thus minimizing disruptions to workflow.

In terms of employer branding, a positive onboarding experience significantly enhances an organization's image, making it more attractive to top talent. First impressions matter, and a well-executed onboarding process reflects positively on the employer brand, leading to favorable word-of-mouth recommendations from satisfied employees. Furthermore, onboarding is crucial for ensuring compliance and safety in the workplace. It provides new hires with necessary training on workplace safety, legal compliance, and company policies, effectively reducing risks and liabilities associated with noncompliance.

When talking onboarding with clients, regardless of whether it's in a white-collar or blue-collar environment, I remind them that how you onboard indicates to the employee how professional, serious, dedicated, organized, and prepared the company is, which means you set an example for what you expect. If the office manager, team leader, or HR person conducting onboarding is ill-equipped, tech isn't ready, or plans run late or don't seem prioritized, how can you hold the new hire to any different standard down the line? Overall, effective onboarding is a strategic investment that not only enhances employee performance and satisfaction but also reinforces the organization's commitment to its workforce and long-term success.

Employee onboarding serves several critical objectives designed to help new hires adjust smoothly to their roles, integrate into the team, and align with the organization's overall mission. The following two primary goals focus on enabling social integration and making sure that new hires are performance-ready early in their employment.

Social integration helps new employees build relationships with colleagues, supervisors, and other key stakeholders. This relationship-building is crucial for creating a sense of belonging and fostering collaboration, which contributes to a more cohesive work environment. Onboarding also helps new hires understand the company culture— its values, norms, and unwritten rules—allowing them to align their behaviors with organizational expectations. Additionally, social integration helps new employees quickly become part of their team's dynamics. By understanding group norms and the team's specific goals, they can contribute more effectively to projects and collective objectives. As a result, their early involvement is both meaningful and productive.

The second primary objective is to ensure **performance readiness**. During onboarding, new hires are given a clear understanding of their job roles, responsibilities, and performance expectations, helping them see how their individual work contributes to the broader organizational goals. This clarity minimizes confusion and sets the stage for success by aligning expectations from the outset. Moreover, onboarding programs typically provide the necessary training and resources to develop the skills and knowledge new hires need to perform their roles effectively. By supporting new employees in developing these capabilities, companies set them up for success so that they can quickly adapt to job tasks and responsibilities. Ultimately, this approach accelerates the transition to full productivity, minimizing any downtime typically associated with the learning curve for new employees.

Onboarding also plays a vital role in increasing **employee retention and engagement**. When new hires are engaged from the beginning of their employment, they are more likely to feel satisfied in their roles and develop a sense of loyalty to the organization. Demonstrating a commitment to their success from the outset reduces turnover, as employees feel valued and supported.

Another critical objective is ensuring **compliance and safety**. Effective onboarding provides new employees with essential training on company policies, procedures, safety protocols, and legal compliance, protecting both the organization and its workforce from potential risks. Additionally, the onboarding process should provide opportunities for feedback and adjustment. By regularly soliciting feedback from new employees and making necessary adjustments, companies can address any concerns early, allowing for a more personalized and effective onboarding experience.

Achieving these onboarding objectives aligns new employees with the organization's mission, values, and strategic priorities, contributing to a cohesive and high-performing workforce. A well-structured onboarding process enhances the overall employee experience, leading to higher job satisfaction, increased engagement, and improved retention rates.

Moreover, effective onboarding accelerates the time it takes for new hires to become fully productive contributors, which has a positive impact on organizational efficiency and overall performance. By investing in comprehensive onboarding, organizations not only create a smoother transition for new employees but also reap long-term benefits in terms of productivity, engagement, and retention.

Let's walk through some practical steps in the process.

Onboarding Activities

Time Frame	Key Activities
Preboarding	☑ Send welcome email with first-day details ☑ Prepare necessary paperwork (W-4, I-9, direct deposit, etc.) ☑ Set up email, system logins, and equipment ☑ Assign a mentor or onboarding buddy ☑ Schedule key meetings (HR, manager, team introductions)
First Day	☑ Give office tour (or virtual walkthrough) ☑ Provide onboarding packet (handbook, policies, org chart) ☑ Introduce team and leadership ☑ Review job expectations and key responsibilities ☑ Ensure payroll and benefits enrollment is completed
First Week	☑ Schedule initial training sessions (systems, processes, compliance) ☑ Set short-term goals with manager ☑ Encourage participation in team meetings ☑ Answer questions and check for concerns

First 30-90 Days	☑ Schedule regular check-ins with manager and HR
	☑ Monitor progress on goals and provide feedback
	☑ Gather feedback on the onboarding experience
	☑ Begin professional development conversations
	☑ Confirm cultural integration and engagement

First 90 Days of Onboarding

- **Preboarding (Before Day 1)**

  - Send welcome email and required paperwork.

  - Assign IT credentials, email, and set up workspace.

  - Provide company handbook and policies for review.

- **First Week**

  - Introduce to team and assign onboarding buddy.

  - Conduct company culture and HR policy training.

  - Provide technology training (email, software, communication tools).

- **First Month**

  - Schedule regular check-ins with manager.

  - Assign small projects for hands-on learning.

  - Discuss performance expectations and career development.

- **First 90 Days**

  - Conduct a formal 60-day review (manager and employee feedback).

  - Assess integration with team and workload.

  - Adjust development plan and set long-term goals.

Now for the details - Offer Acceptance to First Day

The period between a candidate accepting a job offer and their official start date, commonly known as the preboarding phase, is essential for setting the tone for a positive and productive onboarding experience. This phase includes several strategic steps that ensure that the new hire feels welcomed, supported, and prepared for their new role.

The first step in preboarding is to confirm the candidate has officially accepted the offer and agreed upon a start date. Once this is established, a personalized welcome email or letter should be sent, expressing excitement for their upcoming arrival and outlining the next steps in the process. This can be sent by HR, a department head, or that person's direct leader. Additionally, introducing the new hire to their future team members via either email or a virtual meeting can help start building relationships early. This early communication sets a positive tone and fosters a sense of belonging before the new employee even walks through the door (or logs on remotely).

Completing necessary documentation and administrative tasks during preboarding makes for a smooth transition once the new hire begins. This includes providing the candidate with employment agreements, confidentiality contracts, and noncompete clauses, as applicable. Benefits enrollment should also be handled during this period, so that the new hire understands their health insurance, retirement plan options, and other perks available to them. Finally, payroll setup is crucial. The new hire's information needs to be filed correctly and ready, guaranteeing that payment processes, such as direct deposit and tax forms, are in place from day one.

If any of the above steps for your organization are manual (meaning a piece of physical paper is being used), there are efficiencies to be had. If you have an HR and payroll system, everything can be done electronically. If you don't, you will be pleasantly surprised by the affordable options available to businesses of all sizes. My small but mighty team is four people at the time of writing this book, and we utilize a system that's under $100 a month and allows me to electronically onboard. It also tracks time and provides simple-to-process payroll.

A seamless first day often hinges on the efficient setup of technology and access to necessary systems. Preboarding includes coordinating with the IT department to prepare any required equipment, such as laptops, phones, and hardware, that the employee will need to perform their job effectively. Additionally, new hires should be granted access to essential software, tools, and networks in advance. If necessary, offering initial training or tutorials on the organization's systems and platforms can help the new hire feel comfortable with the technology they will be using. Add this to your training checklist. (And if you don't have a training checklist, this is your reminder to make one.)

I had a client who rushed the hiring process and took the approach that they would figure it out when the employee got onsite. The individual had no logins ready; the new hire paperwork was disjointed (and therefore ended up incomplete), and the first day felt like chaos. As you can imagine that employee didn't show up for day two. At that point, other candidates had been declined and had to be re-contacted, and several had already accepted other positions. A first impression sets the tone for an employee's engagement and retention. I've always liked the old saying, "Do it right, do it light. Do it wrong, do it long." It definitely rang true in my client's situation. The extra preparation is always worth it.

Providing new employees with the right information and resources ahead of time can reduce first-day anxieties and set clear expectations. Sharing the employee handbook, for instance, gives the new hire a chance to familiarize themselves with company policies, procedures, and organizational culture. Offering background information on the company's history, mission, values, and structure further deepens the new employee's understanding of how their role fits into the broader organizational context. Including a list of frequently asked questions (FAQs) and providing contact details for HR, IT support, and other relevant departments ensures that any uncertainties can be addressed quickly and efficiently.

Sending a welcome package or swag is a creative way to build excitement and demonstrate the company's appreciation. This can include company-branded merchandise, a personalized welcome letter from leadership, or any items that reflect the company's culture and values. These thoughtful gestures not only foster a sense of belonging but also help new employees feel like part of the team even before their first day. Sending a package to the new employee's home includes their family or loved ones in the excitement. Plus, they may even share it on their social media, which positively impacts your brand awareness and positions your company as an employer of choice.

Providing a clear agenda for the first day and beyond is crucial for setting expectations and giving the new hire a road map for their onboarding journey. Sharing a detailed schedule that includes meetings, orientation sessions, and key tasks for the first day helps the new employee know what to expect. Additionally, prescheduling introductory meetings with key team members, stakeholders, and mentors allows the new hire to start forming important connections and gaining a better understanding of their role and the people they will be working with. Seeing this training or onboarding agenda shows a new hire that you are prepared for them and that they work in a professional environment. Not only does that positively contribute to their experience, but it also sets the tone for your expectations of them moving forward. By thoroughly addressing these aspects of preboarding, organizations help new hires have a smooth and engaging transition, which sets them up for success from day one.

Maintaining engagement with the new hire between the time they accept the offer and their official start date is key to ensuring that they feel welcomed and prepared. Regular check-in calls or emails serve as an effective way to provide updates, answer any questions the new employee may have, and reassure them that their transition is being thoughtfully managed. These communications not only foster a sense of connection but also help alleviate any anxieties the new hire might have about their upcoming role, especially if the start date is weeks away. This continued dialogue builds excitement and reinforces the employee's decision to join the organization. Additionally, organizations can invite the new hire to virtual social activities or informal gatherings with their future colleagues. These events provide a relaxed setting for relationship-building and help integrate the new hire into the team culture before their first day. Such activities enhance camaraderie and create an inclusive environment, easing the new employee's entry into the workplace.

Efficiently managing logistical details before the new hire's start date is critical, particularly for those relocating or attending in-person orientations. For employees who need to travel, assisting with travel arrangements, such as securing accommodations or providing information on the best routes, can ease the stress of relocation or commuting. If applicable, organizations should also provide detailed information on parking facilities, public transportation options, and office access procedures. This practical support ensures that new employees are well-prepared for their arrival, whether they are joining the organization in person or remotely.

Onboarding Program Design

Structured onboarding programs and ad hoc approaches represent two distinct methods for bringing new hires into an organization, each offering its own set of advantages.

Structured onboarding programs are characterized by their consistency and standardization, providing a reliable framework for integrating employees. Because these programs follow a well-defined sequence of activities, all new hires receive the same information, resources, and training. This structured approach creates a uniform experience, which promotes cohesion across different departments or locations and aligns new employees with the organization's values and goals. In this way, structured onboarding ensures that employees share a common understanding of the company culture and expectations, regardless of where or with whom they work.

In terms of efficiency and clarity, structured onboarding programs streamline the process for both the employee and the organization. Clear expectations about roles, responsibilities, and performance are communicated early on, helping new hires quickly understand their duties and how they contribute to the organization's success. Predefined timelines and milestones mean essential administrative tasks, such as paperwork and training, are handled efficiently, which minimizes downtime and helps accelerate the employee's path to full productivity. This organization and structure are particularly beneficial for managing time and resources effectively, contributing to a smoother transition for the employee.

A key advantage of structured onboarding programs is their ability to enhance employee engagement and retention. By incorporating engagement activities, such as team introductions, social events, or mentoring opportunities, these programs foster early relationships and create a sense of belonging for the new hire. This can lead to increased job satisfaction and a greater likelihood of long-term retention, as employees who feel supported and connected to their teams are more likely to stay with the company.

The combination of clear communication, social integration, and mentorship helps new hires build confidence and feel valued from the very beginning. From a compliance and risk management perspective, structured onboarding programs are crucial for ensuring that all employees complete mandatory training on workplace policies, safety procedures, and legal requirements. Every new hire is informed about the company's compliance obligations and safety protocols, which reduces the organization's risk and liability. Additionally, structured programs often incorporate centralized tracking systems so that all documentation, such as employment contracts and benefits forms, is completed accurately and on time, helping the organization maintain thorough and up-to-date records.

In contrast, **ad hoc approaches to onboarding** are more flexible and informal, allowing for a personalized experience that may better suit the specific needs of the employee or the department. However, without the consistency and defined processes of a structured program, ad hoc onboarding may lead to inconsistencies in the information provided or gaps in training and compliance that could leave the new hire feeling unsupported or unclear about their role.

Therefore, while structured onboarding programs offer significant advantages in terms of consistency, engagement, and compliance, an organization must carefully weigh the benefits of both approaches depending on its goals and the needs of its employees. One of the primary benefits of this approach is its flexibility and customization. Unlike structured programs, ad hoc methods allow managers to tailor the onboarding process to meet the specific needs and preferences of each individual hire or team. This adaptability ensures that the process is relevant to the new hire's background, skills, and career goals, which can increase engagement and create a more meaningful onboarding experience. This personalized approach also benefits managers, who can shape the onboarding to highlight aspects of the role or team dynamics that are most important for the new hire's success.

Another significant advantage of ad hoc onboarding is its **speed and responsiveness.** When organizations face urgent needs or require specialized roles to be filled quickly, ad hoc methods provide the flexibility to onboard employees without adhering to rigid timelines or formal procedures. This approach allows organizations to react swiftly to immediate challenges or changes, providing the agility necessary to meet time-sensitive demands. For example, if a new hire is needed to address an urgent project, the ad hoc approach can expedite training and focus on immediate role-specific tasks, helping the employee get up to speed more quickly.

Ad hoc onboarding also encourages creativity and innovation in the onboarding process. Since it is not constrained by a strict framework, this method allows organizations to explore new and creative ways to engage employees. Whether it's experimenting with gamification, leveraging new technologies, or creating interactive learning experiences, ad hoc approaches can help make the onboarding process more dynamic and engaging.

Additionally, the flexibility of this approach supports continuous improvement—managers can gather feedback on what works well and what doesn't, allowing for ongoing adjustments to improve the experience for future hires and stay current with industry trends.

However, there are several considerations to bear in mind when using an ad hoc approach. One potential drawback is scalability. As the number of new hires increases or organizational needs become more complex, maintaining an ad hoc approach may require significant resources and become difficult to manage effectively. Additionally, the consistency of the onboarding experience may be compromised in an ad hoc process. Since the method lacks standardization, there's a risk that key elements may be overlooked, resulting in gaps in training or preparation that could hinder long-term employee success.

Finally, balancing employee experience is essential with ad hoc onboarding. While flexibility and personalization are critical for engagement, the process must still include structured elements that provide clarity, role alignment, and necessary compliance training. Striking this balance ensures that new hires feel both supported and empowered to contribute to their teams from the outset, leading to higher satisfaction and retention in the long run.

Let's address the final 10 percent here. I've laid out the necessary considerations, but I want to offer some real talk. If you are choosing an ad hoc approach because you haven't taken the time to prepare effectively, that is not the goal. With AI and other tools, you can create a great plan when appropriate. Choosing between structured onboarding programs and ad hoc approaches depends on organizational priorities, culture, and resources. While structured programs offer consistency, efficiency, and compliance benefits, ad hoc approaches provide flexibility, customization, and innovation opportunities. Ultimately, organizations may benefit from combining elements of both approaches to create a balanced onboarding experience that meets the unique needs of new hires while aligning with strategic business objectives.

Let's move into **orientation**. The first day for a new hire is a critical moment in shaping their experience and setting the tone for their future with the organization. A well-thought-out first-day agenda helps ease any initial anxiety, fosters a sense of belonging, and ensures that the new hire feels valued and supported. As an HR leader, I've seen firsthand how a welcoming and structured start can impact retention and engagement over the long term.

One of the first things on the agenda is a **welcome and introduction**. This typically begins with an HR or office representative greeting the new hire, offering an overview of the day's activities, and addressing any immediate questions they may have. This step not only makes the new hire feel comfortable but also sets a professional tone for their integration.

From there, **introductions** to immediate team members and department colleagues are essential. These early introductions help the new employee establish initial connections and put faces to the names they may already be familiar with.

Offering a **welcome kit**—often including company swag or branded items—can also be a small yet meaningful gesture, making the new hire feel like a valued part of the team right from day one. If you've already sent these items to their home, consider placing on their desk or mailing to their home a handwritten welcome note from another member of the team or a senior leader.

Another vital element of the first day is the **office tour and facilities orientation**. This walkthrough provides the new hire with an understanding of the physical layout of the workspace, introducing them to key areas, like their workstation, break rooms, restrooms, and common spaces. During this time, it's also important to assist with **IT and equipment setup**, helping the new hire get logged into necessary systems and familiarizing them with tools and software they'll need for their role. This can greatly minimize first-day frustrations and set up a new hire for productivity from the start.

The next step is introducing the new hire to the company's core frameworks through **company policies and documentation**. Providing the **employee handbook** and reviewing critical policies, such as attendance, code of conduct, and leave policies, gives the new hire a clear understanding of expectations. Making sure that any outstanding **paperwork**—like tax forms, benefits enrollment, or confidentiality agreements—is completed helps streamline the administrative side of onboarding. **Company culture and values** play a significant role in helping the new hire understand the *why* behind organizational behaviors and decision-making. Discussing the company's mission, vision, and values highlights how these aspects shape everyday work. Additionally, helping the new hire understand **team dynamics**, including team goals and how their role fits into the broader organization, reinforces their importance to the team's success.

Providing **training and onboarding sessions** on the first day, tailored to the new hire's specific role, ensures that they are adequately prepared to meet the demands of their job. This training typically includes both a general **orientation session**, covering the organizational structure and strategic priorities, as well as **role-specific training** that dives into their responsibilities, tasks, and immediate goals. A thoughtful gesture that further fosters camaraderie is arranging a **team lunch or welcome meal**. This casual setting allows the new hire to get to know their colleagues in a more relaxed environment, promoting team bonding and helping break the ice.

As the day progresses, it's important to set aside time to **set goals and align expectations**. This conversation outlines both short-term and long-term performance expectations, as well as how success will be measured. It also provides an opportunity to clarify the support systems in place, including access to mentors, coaches, and professional development opportunities. Don't forget to cover the job description and any outstanding questions on that topic. If you and the new hire can both answer the question "What does success look like for this role?" then you are doing great.

When new employees gain a **contextual understanding** of the company's history, they get a sense of how the organization has evolved over time, its founding principles, and the key milestones that have shaped its trajectory. This context builds a connection between the employee and the company, making them part of a larger narrative. Moreover, understanding the company's mission allows new hires to grasp its purpose and core values, offering insight into why the company exists and what it aims to achieve. These elements are not just abstract concepts but serve as the foundation for how business decisions are made and why the company operates in a certain way. This is a great portion to have an executive or senior leader cover with the new hire. It is time on their calendar well spent.

Alignment with organizational goals is equally crucial. Sharing the company's vision helps new hires see the long-term direction the organization is moving toward. They learn about the desired future state and how their individual role contributes to that vision. It shifts their perspective from viewing their tasks in isolation to seeing how their work fits into the bigger picture. Additionally, when new hires understand the company's strategic goals, they can align their daily efforts with those goals, ensuring that their contributions are in sync with broader organizational priorities. This sense of purpose enhances focus, motivation, and accountability.

Beyond understanding the company's direction, **cultural integration** plays a major role in onboarding success. Introducing new hires to the company's values helps them navigate the behavioral expectations, organizational norms, and decision-making processes that define the workplace culture. These values are the backbone of what is celebrated and prioritized in the organization, whether it's collaboration, innovation, or customer-centricity.

Equally important is familiarizing them with the **organizational structure**. Understanding how different departments function, reporting lines, and key stakeholders not only clarifies workflows but also helps employees know whom to approach for guidance and collaboration, ensuring that they are integrated into both their team and the wider organization effectively. Another important benefit of this information is how it influences **engagement and commitment**. When a company takes the time to share its history, mission, and vision with new hires, it demonstrates a commitment to transparency. This builds trust and sets a positive tone, making new employees feel valued. When employees are engaged with the company's story and strategic direction from the outset, they are more likely to feel a sense of belonging and loyalty. This investment in the company's future motivates them to contribute actively to its success.

Understanding the company's history, goals, and strategic priorities can directly impact an employee's ability to make informed decisions. New hires who understand the broader organizational context are better equipped to align their actions with the company's objectives. This **empowerment** fosters innovation, as employees feel confident proposing new ideas and improvements that support the organization's goals. In this way, the company benefits not only from the skills the new hire brings but also from their fresh perspective on how to improve and evolve existing processes.

Finally, ending the day with a **follow-up and check-in** reinforces that the new hire's experience matters. This end-of-day conversation allows HR or the hiring manager to address any lingering questions or concerns and set the stage for what comes next. Gathering **feedback** from the new hire about their first day is helpful for continuous improvement and shows the organization's commitment to an exceptional employee experience.

Role-Specific Training

Tailoring training to a new hire's specific roles and responsibilities is an essential component of effective onboarding and long-term employee success. When organizations provide targeted, role-specific training, they enable new hires to build job proficiency and ensure alignment with broader organizational objectives. This not only equips employees with the skills necessary to perform their job duties but also accelerates their integration into the workplace culture.

First and foremost, job proficiency and performance are significantly enhanced through role-specific training. This type of training focuses on developing the skills, knowledge, and competencies a new hire needs to perform their specific tasks effectively. By focusing on relevant workflows, processes, and best practices, employees become familiar with the tasks they will encounter daily. Additionally, new hires are trained to develop technical proficiency, mastering the specific tools, software, and equipment essential to their roles. This early emphasis on skill-building equips employees to handle the demands of their position from day one, boosting their confidence and enabling them to contribute meaningfully to team goals.

Moreover, role-specific training helps new employees align with organizational objectives. By understanding how their work contributes to broader company goals, new hires gain clarity about the purpose behind their tasks and the performance standards expected of them. This alignment fosters a sense of accountability, as employees are empowered to meet specific metrics and deadlines that directly impact the company's success. Because clear performance expectations are laid out during training, employees understand what success looks like in their role, which not only improves individual outcomes but also enhances team and organizational performance.

Equally important is the role that training plays in adapting employees to the company's culture. While general onboarding introduces company values, role-specific training goes a step further by incorporating cultural norms and behaviors that are crucial for success in a given role. This training emphasizes appropriate communication styles, professional conduct, and teamwork expectations, ensuring that new hires align with the company's ethos and values in their day-to-day interactions. By integrating these cultural elements into role-specific training, organizations create an environment where new hires not only perform well but also thrive in the company culture.

From a retention perspective, role-specific training has a profound impact on employee engagement and satisfaction. Employees who feel competent and well-prepared in their roles tend to be more satisfied with their jobs. This satisfaction stems from the confidence gained during training, as employees are better equipped to handle their responsibilities. Additionally, by investing in targeted training, organizations signal a commitment to career development, demonstrating that they are invested in their employees' long-term growth. This approach encourages loyalty and reduces turnover, as employees feel valued and supported from the outset.

One of the most practical advantages of role-specific training is the reduction in ramp-up time. New hires become productive more quickly when they receive focused training that equips them with the tools and knowledge necessary for their specific role. By minimizing downtime and smoothing the new hire's integration into the team, role-specific training enhances overall workplace efficiency and reduces disruptions, allowing teams to maintain high levels of productivity even as new members join.

Finally, role-specific training plays a critical role in risk management and compliance. Every industry and role has its own set of compliance requirements, from safety protocols to legal obligations. By providing targeted training that addresses these specific requirements, organizations can ensure that employees are well-versed in regulatory standards, reducing the likelihood of errors or noncompliance. This not only protects the organization from potential legal issues but also safeguards its reputation and operational stability.

Assigning **mentors** or "buddies" to new employees can significantly enhance their onboarding experience and contribute to their long-term success in the organization. This practice fosters a supportive environment where new hires can thrive, allowing them to acclimate more swiftly to their roles and the company culture. It's a simple process, but I don't see organizations executing it regularly. Considering it's almost zero cost and provides so much value, let's make it happen!

There are several key benefits associated with having mentors or buddies that organizations should consider. Before we jump in, here's just a quick note that a mentor can be at a peer level. (And in the case of new hires, that's the perfect idea.) So don't let the idea that this is just another leadership task turn you off with this programming. One of the most immediate advantages of mentoring is the accelerated learning and integration it facilitates. Mentors or buddies offer personalized guidance, answering questions and clarifying expectations while sharing insights about the company culture, norms, and organizational dynamics. This direct support helps new hires navigate the learning curve more efficiently, as mentors can provide tips, tricks, and practical advice based on their own experiences. Such guidance is invaluable, especially during the critical early days of employment when new hires may feel overwhelmed.

Furthermore, having a mentor or buddy greatly enhances engagement and confidence among new employees. These experienced colleagues help facilitate early connections with other team members, promoting a sense of belonging and inclusion in the organization. This early relationship-building is crucial for employee morale. Mentors also boost new hires' confidence by offering encouragement, constructive feedback, and reassurance, which helps them feel more assured in their abilities and contributions from the outset.

I worked at a very large organization for a couple of years during my HR corporate career. The employer had over twenty thousand employees, and as you can imagine, it was easy to get lost in the shuffle. We implemented a new hire "buddy program" that was simple, and it worked wonders. We wrote templated emails about the program for the manager to send and even took the lead for scheduling buddy sessions to eliminate the burden from the department. We outlined topics for them to discuss at their meetings if they struggled to find connection points. Around six months into the program, in one of our bi-annual surveys, we asked a new hire about their experience. The individual shared that without the buddy program, they would have quit within their first month. They found themselves overwhelmed and their buddy helped them to stay engaged and even helped to remove some obstacles for them. It doesn't have to be anything elaborate, but I highly recommend you consider implementing a program like this for your organization. You may take for granted how much it's needed.

In addition to emotional support, mentors play a vital role in knowledge transfer and skill development. They share job-specific insights and information about daily tasks that formal training sessions may not cover. By providing hands-on learning opportunities and coaching on technical skills, mentors ensure that new hires develop the competencies necessary for their roles. This targeted skill enhancement can lead to a more effective workforce, as employees are equipped with the tools and knowledge they need to succeed. Mentorship also aids in providing cultural and organizational insight. Mentors help new hires understand the company's values, traditions, and unwritten rules, facilitating smoother cultural integration. They can guide new employees through the complexities of organizational politics, helping them avoid common pitfalls while fostering effective working relationships. This support is essential in creating a cohesive work environment where new hires feel comfortable and empowered to engage fully.

Moreover, mentors contribute significantly to career development and networking. They provide advice on career advancement opportunities, professional development resources, and pathways for growth in the organization. Additionally, mentors introduce new hires to key stakeholders, decision-makers, and potential mentors, which helps expand their professional network and visibility in the company. This networking can prove invaluable for career progression and personal growth.

The presence of a mentor or buddy also positively impacts retention and satisfaction. Having this support system can alleviate isolation and uncertainty, leading to increased new-hire satisfaction and reduced turnover rates. When organizations demonstrate an investment in the success and development of new employees, it fosters a sense of loyalty and commitment. By nurturing this relationship, mentors play a crucial role in retaining talent and enhancing overall employee engagement.

To implement an effective mentoring program, organizations should establish clear expectations for both mentors and buddies. Outlining their responsibilities and time commitments helps ensure that the relationship is productive and beneficial for both parties. Additionally, providing training and resources for mentors equips them with the necessary skills, such as effective communication techniques and conflict resolution strategies. Finally, establishing a feedback mechanism to evaluate the effectiveness of the mentoring relationship allows organizations to adjust as needed. And that leads to the continuous improvement of the onboarding process.

Let's talk about **MVV (mission, vision, values).** Effectively communicating an organization's values, expected behaviors, and unwritten rules is crucial for aligning employees with the company culture and fostering a cohesive work environment. Clear communication means that all employees understand not only what is expected of them but also how they can contribute to the organization's success.

Several key strategies can be implemented to achieve this. One of the most effective methods is through formal communication channels. An employee handbook serves as a comprehensive reference guide that includes the organization's values, expected behaviors, and policies. New hires can refer to this document throughout their employment, reinforcing their understanding of the company culture. Additionally, during orientation and onboarding, specific sessions should be dedicated to discussing and explaining these values and behaviors. Using examples and scenarios can help illustrate these concepts in practical terms, making them more relatable and easier to grasp. Moreover, integrating discussions on values and expected behaviors into various training programs—whether related to technical skills, compliance, or leadership development—ensures that these messages are consistently reinforced across different learning experiences.

Another important aspect is the role of leadership and management in modeling the organization's values. Senior leaders and managers should embody these values in their daily interactions and decision-making processes, serving as powerful examples for employees to emulate. It is equally important for leaders to communicate openly about the organization's values and share stories or anecdotes that highlight how these principles have positively impacted the company's success. Such transparency fosters trust and encourages employees to adopt similar behaviors.

Regular communication and reinforcement of values are also essential. Town hall meetings or all-hands sessions provide a platform to reiterate the organization's values and expected behaviors. During these meetings, leaders can discuss recent examples of employees effectively demonstrating these values, which reinforces their importance in the workplace. Additionally, incorporating messages about values and behaviors into internal newsletters, emails, and other communication channels helps keep these principles top of mind for all employees. Highlighting success stories or initiatives that exemplify the organization's culture can further enhance understanding and alignment.

Implementing **feedback mechanisms** is vital for assessing and promoting cultural alignment. Performance reviews should include an assessment of how well employees have adhered to the organization's values and expected behaviors. Constructive feedback should be provided to guide improvement, while recognizing positive contributions to the company culture reinforces desired behaviors.

Furthermore, anonymous surveys or feedback mechanisms allow employees to share their perceptions of the organizational culture. This feedback can identify areas for improvement and address any concerns, demonstrating that employee voices are valued. I hear business leaders reference a culture of feedback often, but many parts of your culture must be in place for that to be a reality. I dive much deeper into this topic in another book I've written on advanced HR strategies. It's worth the time investment.

Another critical element in cultural communication is ensuring transparency about unwritten rules. Facilitating discussions about these rules allows for open dialogue in the organization. Acknowledging that unwritten rules exist and explaining their rationale helps new hires and existing employees navigate the culture more effectively. Although some aspects of company culture may be informal, documenting key practices or norms that are essential for successful integration into the organization is beneficial. Sharing these documents with employees as part of their onboarding materials can help clarify expectations. It doesn't have to be more complicated than sitting down with your team and talking about your department's unwritten rules. For example, does a manager's closed door mean anger, stress, or just a tight deadline? Is it okay to open the door? Do employees wait for a regularly scheduled meeting to obtain feedback from the manager, or can they approach it at any time? How do they obtain time with the manager outside of regularly scheduled meetings? In the past, I've had a one-pager that turned into three pages of unspoken rules for our team. It was a game changer for bringing new hires into the group.

To further promote cultural alignment, organizations should initiate cultural integration initiatives. Encouraging employees to collaborate on cross-functional projects provides opportunities for them to observe and learn firsthand about different aspects of the organization's culture. Additionally, when discussions about diversity, equity, and inclusion are integrated into conversations about the organization's values and expected behaviors, these principles are reflected in all facets of company culture. This commitment to inclusivity fosters a more cohesive and engaged workforce.

Compliance and Paperwork

When onboarding new employees, organizations must ensure that several forms and documents are completed to meet legal compliance requirements, set clear expectations, and provide essential information about the workplace. This thorough process not only protects the organization but also facilitates a smooth transition for new hires into their roles. I've captured an overview of the necessary forms and documents commonly provided to new employees.

First and foremost, employment forms are critical for establishing the foundation of the employment relationship. The employment application is a standard form that collects personal information, employment history, and references from the new hire. Additionally, candidates typically submit a resume or curriculum vitae (CV) that outlines their educational background, work experience, skills, and accomplishments. The offer letter is another essential document that formally outlines the terms and conditions of employment, including the position title, start date, compensation, benefits, and any contingencies that may apply, such as background checks or drug tests. In some cases, an employment contract may be required, providing a more detailed agreement that includes confidentiality agreements, noncompete clauses, and specifics about job responsibilities and expectations.

Another crucial set of documents pertains to tax and payroll forms. The Form W-4, or Employee's Withholding Certificate, is used to determine the federal income tax withholding from the employee's paycheck, while state tax withholding forms serve a similar purpose at the state level, if applicable. New hires also typically complete a direct deposit authorization form, which allows the employer to deposit the employee's wages directly into their bank account, streamlining the payroll process. Furthermore, benefits enrollment forms are essential for helping new hires choose their benefits. Health insurance enrollment forms enable employees to select health coverage options for themselves and their dependents. Additionally, 401(k) or retirement plan enrollment forms are provided for those wishing to participate in employer-sponsored retirement savings plans, allowing them to select their contribution amounts. Other benefit enrollment forms may cover dental insurance, vision insurance, life insurance, disability insurance, and flexible spending accounts (FSAs) or lifestyle spending accounts (LSAs).

In addition to employment and benefits documentation, organizations should also provide company policies and agreements. The employee handbook is a comprehensive document that outlines company policies, procedures, expectations, and benefits. This includes vital information on vacation and sick leave policies, codes of conduct, and employee rights. A nondisclosure agreement (NDA) is often required to outline confidentiality obligations regarding the company's proprietary information. Additionally, a code of conduct or ethics policy sets forth expected ethical standards and behaviors in the organization.

Lastly, several other required documents help ensure safety and compliance in the workplace. New employees should provide emergency contact information, which includes details of individuals to contact in case of accidents or emergencies. The I-9 form is essential for verifying the employee's eligibility to work in the United States and must be accompanied by the required identification documents. Finally, acknowledgment forms should be signed to confirm that new hires have received and understood various company policies, such as harassment policies, safety protocols, and IT security policies.

Mandatory training sessions play a crucial role in the onboarding process because they help new hires understand essential policies, regulations, and safety protocols in the organization. These training sessions not only promote compliance but also foster a safe and respectful workplace culture. Here is an overview of common mandatory training sessions that organizations typically implement.

Safety training is a foundational component of onboarding, focusing on educating employees about workplace hazards, safety protocols, emergency procedures, and the correct use of safety equipment. Depending on the workplace environment, the topics covered in safety training may include fire safety, ergonomics, handling of hazardous materials, personal protective equipment (PPE), and evacuation procedures. The importance of this training cannot be overstated, as it ensures compliance with Occupational Safety and Health Administration (OSHA) regulations, significantly reduces the risk of workplace accidents, and promotes a safe work environment for all employees.

Another essential training session is anti-harassment and diversity training, which educates employees about appropriate workplace behavior, respectful communication, and the legal definitions of harassment, discrimination, and retaliation. This training covers various types of harassment, including sexual and racial harassment, and includes information on reporting procedures, the consequences of harassment, and the organization's commitment to maintaining a harassment-free workplace. The significance of this training lies in its ability to foster a respectful workplace culture, mitigate legal risks, and inform employees about their rights and responsibilities regarding workplace conduct.

Data protection and privacy training are also critical, particularly in an era in which data breaches and privacy concerns are prevalent. This training educates employees on the importance of safeguarding sensitive information, such as customer data, intellectual property, and employee records. Topics typically covered include data protection laws, such as the General Data Protection Regulation (GDPR) and the

California Consumer Privacy Act (CCPA), company policies on data handling, secure data storage practices, and protocols for responding to data breaches. This training is vital for ensuring compliance with data protection regulations, reducing the risk of data breaches or leaks, and protecting the organization's reputation and trustworthiness with stakeholders. Cybersecurity awareness training has become increasingly important as organizations face growing threats in the digital landscape. This training educates employees on identifying phishing attempts, recognizing malware, using secure passwords, and following best practices to protect digital assets. Topics often include common cybersecurity threats, secure remote work practices, data encryption, and employees' role in maintaining cybersecurity. The importance of this training lies in its ability to mitigate cybersecurity risks, safeguard sensitive information from cyber threats, and enhance the organization's overall resilience against potential cyberattacks.

To effectively implement these mandatory training sessions, organizations should consider several key strategies. First, training should be scheduled shortly after new hires join the organization, with refresher courses provided periodically to reinforce learning. Employing interactive methods, such as case studies, quizzes, and real-life scenarios, can engage employees and enhance retention of information.

Additionally, it is crucial to document training completion; requiring employees to acknowledge their participation through signed attendance sheets or online learning platforms fosters accountability.

Lastly, organizations should prioritize continuous improvement by soliciting feedback from employees to refine training content and delivery methods, ensuring that they remain relevant and effective over time. By incorporating these mandatory training sessions into the onboarding process, organizations not only comply with legal requirements but also cultivate a culture of safety, respect, and responsibility that benefits both employees and the organization.

Technology and Tools

Giving new hires necessary access to IT systems, software, and equipment is crucial for their productivity and seamless integration into the organization. A well-structured approach can facilitate a smooth onboarding experience. Here's a comprehensive guide to making sure new employees have everything they need to succeed from day one.

The first step is **pre-deployment preparation**, which begins with an IT needs assessment. This assessment is essential for determining each new hire's specific IT requirements based on their role, department, and responsibilities. Once these needs are identified, the organization can proceed to procure the necessary hardware—such as laptops, desktops, and mobile devices—as well as any software licenses required for the new hire's job functions.

Additionally, user accounts should be created for all necessary company systems, including email, network access, and any specialized software or applications they will use. On the **onboarding day**, it is important to provide a comprehensive welcome kit. This kit should include all necessary equipment, such as laptops and phones, along with setup instructions detailing how to connect to Wi-Fi and access company resources. To further support new hires, an IT orientation session should be conducted. During this session, new employees are introduced to IT policies, cybersecurity best practices, and the process for requesting technical support if needed.

Once the initial setup is complete, attention turns to **software and application access**. It is crucial to ensure that all required software and applications are installed on the new hire's devices. Along with access credentials, organizations should offer training sessions or materials to help new hires familiarize themselves with the essential software and applications they will be using regularly in their roles. **Network and email access** is also a vital component of the onboarding process. Employers must verify that new hires can connect to the organization's internal network securely, even when working remotely. Assistance should be provided for setting up company email accounts, including configuring email clients and understanding email protocols and usage guidelines.

Security is another critical aspect to consider. **Access controls** should be set up to grant appropriate permissions based on the new hire's role and responsibilities. This ensures that they have access to necessary files, folders, and shared drives while adhering to data security protocols. Additionally, organizations should provide cybersecurity training to educate new hires on identifying phishing attempts, using secure passwords, and protecting sensitive information.

Providing **technical support and troubleshooting** resources is essential for a successful onboarding experience. New hires should be informed about available IT support channels, including help desk contacts and ticketing systems. Furthermore, FAQs, knowledge bases, and self-help guides can empower new hires to resolve common technical issues independently.

Finally, establishing a **feedback mechanism** is crucial for continuous improvement. Organizations should solicit feedback from new hires regarding their IT setup experience. This feedback can be invaluable for identifying areas that need enhancement and refining the onboarding process for future hires. By following this structured approach, organizations can equip new employees with the necessary IT tools and knowledge to thrive, ultimately leading to enhanced productivity and a positive onboarding experience.

Training new hires on the specific tools and technology they will be using in their roles is essential for ensuring that they can perform their jobs effectively and contribute to the organization's overall success. A structured approach to this training can help new employees feel confident in their abilities and more quickly acclimate to their new environment. The first step in providing effective training is to identify training needs. This begins with conducting a comprehensive needs assessment to pinpoint the specific tools, software, and technology platforms that new hires will need to utilize in their roles. Understanding the key responsibilities and tasks associated with the new hire's position is critical for determining which tools and technologies are essential for their success. By aligning training with job responsibilities, organizations help new employees acquire the skills they need for their immediate job demands.

Once training needs are identified, the next phase involves developing training materials. This entails creating structured training modules or sessions that cover each tool or technology comprehensively. It is important to consider the varying skill levels of new hires when tailoring the content to ensure accessibility and relevance. Additionally, preparing user manuals, guides, or online resources can provide new hires with step-by-step instructions they can refer to while learning to use each tool or technology effectively.

When it comes to delivery methods, organizations should prioritize hands-on training sessions where new hires can interact with the tools and technology in a simulated or real-world environment. Demonstrations can also be highly beneficial, as these sessions showcase the features, functionalities, and best practices for utilizing each tool effectively. Supplementing hands-on training with online learning platforms or video tutorials can provide continuous learning opportunities and reinforce the concepts covered during in-person training. Incorporating practical exercises into training sessions is vital for enhancing learning retention. Presenting real-life scenarios or case studies that require new hires to apply their knowledge of the tools and technology allows them to solve problems and complete tasks in a meaningful context. Interactive simulations or role-playing exercises can further simulate typical job-related situations, providing new hires with the opportunity to practice using the tools and technology in a supportive environment.

To make sure new hires grasp the material, organizations should assess learning and provide feedback. Quizzes or assessments can gauge new hires' understanding of the tools and technology, allowing organizations to provide constructive feedback and remedial training as needed. Additionally, encouraging new hires to share their feedback on the training content, delivery methods, and overall learning experience can contribute to continuously improving training effectiveness.

Providing continuous support and resources is also critical for new hires' success. Organizations can offer ongoing support by granting access to technical experts, help desk services, or peer mentoring for troubleshooting and addressing questions related to the tools and technology. Maintaining a resource library or knowledge base with updated information, tips, and troubleshooting guides can be an invaluable asset for new hires as they navigate their roles.

Finally, integrating training with job shadowing can enhance the onboarding experience. Pairing new hires with experienced colleagues allows them to receive on-the-job training and practical insights into using the tools and technology in real-world scenarios. Moreover, incorporating feedback on the use of tools and technology into regular performance reviews promotes continuous improvement and skill development.

Socialization and Team Integration

Facilitating introductions with team members and key stakeholders is an essential aspect of the onboarding process that helps new hires build relationships, integrate into the organizational culture, and understand their roles in the broader context of the company. A structured approach to introductions can create a welcoming atmosphere and set the stage for collaborative teamwork.

To start, pre-onboarding preparation is crucial. Begin by identifying key stakeholders, which involves compiling a list of team members, department heads, and other influential individuals the new hire will interact with regularly. This list should also include those whose roles are critical to the new hire's success. Once key stakeholders have been identified, it's important to inform them about the new hire's background, role, and start date. This not only prepares the team for the new member's arrival but also encourages stakeholders to think about how they can contribute to a positive introduction. On the new hire's first day, as covered previously in the recruitment chapter, it's vital to organize onboarding day introductions. Hosting a formal or informal welcome session allows team members and stakeholders to introduce themselves and briefly describe their roles. To make this session more effective, create a structured agenda for introductions, ensuring that the new hire has the opportunity to meet with key stakeholders and team members across various departments or functional areas. This deliberate approach helps the new hire gain a holistic understanding of the organization.

Participation in **team meetings and huddles** is another effective strategy for facilitating introductions. Schedule the new hire to attend team meetings or departmental huddles, where they can introduce themselves and learn about ongoing projects and team dynamics. This interaction encourages team members and stakeholders to provide overviews of their roles and responsibilities, emphasizing how they collaborate in the organization. Such meetings not only help new hires acclimate to their team but also foster a sense of belonging.

In addition to group interactions, one-on-one meetings with key stakeholders are beneficial. Schedule dedicated meetings between the new hire and important individuals, such as supervisors, mentors, or colleagues who can provide guidance and support. Facilitating informal coffee chats or virtual meetings allows the new hire to ask questions, discuss career aspirations, and build rapport with team members in a relaxed setting.

For organizations with remote teams, virtual introductions are essential. Video conferencing platforms can facilitate introductions, ensuring that remote employees feel included. Virtual coffee breaks or informal gatherings foster team bonding in a remote work environment. Introducing the new hire to team collaboration tools, such as Slack or Microsoft Teams, allows them to engage in team discussions, share updates, and participate in group activities, enhancing their sense of connection.

After introductions have been made, it's important to provide follow-up and support. Sending follow-up emails or messages summarizing the introductions and providing contact information for team members and stakeholders reinforces these connections. A buddy system, in which an experienced colleague or mentor guides the new hire through their initial weeks, can also offer valuable support and help answer any questions they may have.

Finally, a feedback loop is crucial for continuous improvement. Encourage new hires to provide feedback on their introduction experience, including suggestions for enhancing future onboarding processes or team integration. This feedback not only helps refine the onboarding experience for future hires but also fosters a culture of openness and continuous learning in the organization. By proactively facilitating introductions with team members and key stakeholders, organizations foster a welcoming environment for new hires, promote collaboration, and accelerate their integration into the team and company culture. These efforts are essential for building strong relationships, enhancing communication, and, ultimately, contributing to the new hire's success and long-term engagement in the organization.

Social activities and team-building events for new hires are crucial for fostering camaraderie, building relationships, and integrating them into the organizational culture. A well-thought-out approach can significantly enhance the onboarding experience and create a sense of belonging in the team. The first step in effectively planning social activities is to understand preferences. It's essential to consider the interests and preferences of both the new hires and the existing team members when selecting activities. This understanding ensures higher participation rates and engagement levels.

Additionally, establishing a frequency for these social activities, such as monthly or quarterly events, can provide ongoing opportunities for team bonding. It's important to allocate a sufficient budget and resources for these activities, which may include venue rentals, catering options, and any necessary equipment or materials. Various types of social activities can help build relationships. A welcome lunch or dinner is an excellent place for new hires to meet team members in a relaxed setting, promoting open communication and connection. Team outings, such as bowling, mini-golf, or escape rooms, offer a fun environment for team members to work together and strengthen their bonds. Additionally, volunteer activities or community service projects allow teams to bond while making a positive impact on the community. For remote teams, virtual socials, such as online happy hours, games, or themed gatherings, can foster engagement despite geographical distances.

Team-building events are another effective way to promote collaboration among team members. Starting meetings or events with icebreaker activities can help new hires and existing members get to know one another, breaking down barriers and easing initial awkwardness. Incorporating team-building exercises into workshops or training sessions fosters collaboration and enhances problem-solving skills. Team challenges or competitions that require teamwork and communication can further reinforce these skills in a fun and engaging manner.

It's vital to ensure that all activities are inclusive and diverse. This involves being respectful of the diverse backgrounds, preferences, and abilities of all team members when planning events. I'm thrilled to see that we seem to be shifting away from the nonstop happy hours and evening team meals. I have greatly changed my relationship with alcohol and need work time to be separated from social and family time, so these are welcome shifts in work culture.

Additionally, rotating responsibilities for planning activities among team members can encourage participation and spark creativity, allowing everyone to contribute their unique ideas. Effective communication and engagement are essential in maximizing participation in social activities. Advance notice of upcoming activities allows new hires and team members to plan accordingly, increasing the likelihood of their attendance. Encouraging participation by emphasizing the value of these events in building relationships and strengthening teamwork can motivate team members to engage actively.

After events, implementing a feedback mechanism is critical. Soliciting feedback from participants, including new hires, about their experiences with social activities and team-building events allows organizations to gather valuable insights. This feedback can be used to improve future events and adapt to the team's needs. Remaining adaptable and flexible in organizing activities, considering feedback and changing circumstances, can enhance the overall effectiveness of the onboarding process.

Lastly, it's important to encourage leadership support for social activities. Involving leaders in these events demonstrates their commitment to team-building efforts and promotes a positive organizational culture. When leaders actively participate, it not only encourages team members to engage but also reinforces the organization's values of collaboration and unity.

Feedback and Continuous Improvement

Establishing a schedule for regular check-ins between new hires and their managers is essential for providing the necessary support, guidance, and feedback during the onboarding process. A structured approach to these check-ins can significantly enhance the new hire's integration and overall experience in the organization.

The initial check-in should occur within the **first week** of the new hire's start date. This meeting's primary purpose is to introduce the new employee to their manager, clarify expectations, and discuss initial goals and objectives. During this first meeting, managers should cover essential topics, such as a warm welcome and introduction to the team, an overview of the new hire's role and responsibilities, any initial tasks or projects they will undertake, and a chance to address any immediate questions or concerns. Scheduling this meeting within the first few days sets a positive tone and provides new hires with the guidance they need right from the start.

Following the initial meeting, **weekly check-ins** during the first month are crucial for monitoring progress, providing ongoing support, and addressing any challenges that may arise. These regular meetings help maintain open lines of communication and ensure that the new hire's integration remains on track. Key topics to cover during these weekly check-ins include progress on assigned tasks or projects, feedback on performance and areas for improvement, clarification of expectations and goals, and a discussion of any training needs or additional support required. This proactive approach can help identify and resolve issues before they escalate, fostering a supportive environment.

After the first month, managers should transition to **bi-weekly or monthly check-ins**, adjusting the frequency based on the new hire's progress and the level of support needed. These meetings continue to provide essential support while offering guidance on career development and discussions about long-term goals and objectives. Topics for these check-ins might include project updates and achievements, career development aspirations and opportunities, alignment of performance goals with team objectives, and feedback on team integration and collaboration. This ongoing dialogue is vital for helping new hires feel engaged and aligned with their team and organization.

In addition to regular check-ins, **quarterly or semiannual reviews** are important for evaluating achievements, discussing career progression, and setting future goals. These more formal performance reviews should be scheduled to reflect on accomplishments, address challenges, and plan for continued growth and development. During these reviews, managers should cover performance goals and achievements, provide feedback on strengths and areas for improvement, discuss career development aspirations, and ensure alignment with the organization's values and objectives. This structured evaluation process can help new hires see the path for their future in the company.

Effective **communication and follow-up** are critical components of the check-in process. Consistent communication between scheduled check-ins allows for ongoing support and feedback, which is essential for a successful onboarding experience. Additionally, documenting key discussion points, action items, and agreements during these meetings fosters accountability and facilitates follow-up on commitments made.

Finally, it's important for managers to demonstrate **flexibility and adaptability** in the check-in process. This means being open to adjusting the frequency and format of meetings based on the new hire's progress, workload, and evolving needs. Encouraging new hires to provide feedback on the check-in process allows organizations to continuously improve their communication and support mechanisms, creating a positive onboarding experience that fosters long-term success.

Using **surveys and feedback tools** to gather insights on the onboarding experience is a proactive strategy that enables organizations to understand new hires' perspectives and identify areas for improvement. This approach not only helps in enhancing the onboarding process but also contributes to overall employee satisfaction and engagement.

The first step in utilizing surveys effectively is **designing the survey** itself. Organizations should develop surveys that cover various aspects of the onboarding experience, including overall satisfaction with the onboarding process, feedback on training programs and materials, insights on team integration and support received from managers and colleagues, and evaluations of administrative processes, such as IT setup and resource access. It is also beneficial to include open-ended questions that allow new hires to provide specific suggestions or comments. A combination of multiple-choice questions, rating scales (like the Likert scale), and open-ended questions can gather both quantitative and qualitative feedback, creating a well-rounded view of the onboarding experience.

Timing and frequency are critical components in collecting effective feedback. Organizations should administer surveys at strategic intervals during the onboarding process—immediately after the first week, at the end of the first month, and quarterly or semiannually during the first year. Periodical follow-up surveys can also track ongoing satisfaction and identify areas for continuous improvement. This regularity ensures that feedback is timely and relevant, allowing organizations to make necessary adjustments as new hires acclimate to their roles.

Selecting the right **feedback tools and platforms** is also crucial for successful survey administration. Online survey tools like SurveyMonkey, Google Forms, or internal HR software platforms can collect anonymous feedback, which encourages new hires to provide honest insights without fear of repercussions. Anonymity is key to gathering candid feedback, as it fosters an environment where employees feel safe sharing their experiences.

Once the surveys are collected, organizations must focus on **analyzing and acting on feedback**. This involves thoroughly analyzing survey responses to identify trends, common themes, and specific areas of concern or satisfaction. The insights gained from this analysis should prioritize improvements in the onboarding process, addressing pain points and enhancing the overall employee experience. By translating feedback into actionable insights, organizations can create a more effective onboarding strategy that meets the needs of new hires.

The concept of **continuous improvement** is integral to this process. Organizations should close the feedback loop by sharing survey results with relevant stakeholders, including HR, managers, and leadership teams. Implementing actionable recommendations based on feedback not only optimizes the onboarding experience but also aligns it with organizational goals. This collaborative approach ensures that everyone involved in the onboarding process is aware of the insights gained and the changes being made.

Engagement and participation are essential to the success of the feedback process. Organizations should actively encourage new hires to participate in surveys by emphasizing the importance of their input in shaping future onboarding processes. Following up with new hires about how their feedback has influenced changes in the onboarding experience fosters a culture of transparency and continuous improvement, ultimately enhancing their sense of belonging and commitment to the organization.

Performance Management

Setting clear expectations regarding job responsibilities, performance standards, and goals from the outset is crucial for aligning new hires with organizational objectives and fostering a productive work environment. When new employees have a solid understanding of what is expected of them, they are more likely to integrate smoothly into the team and contribute effectively to the organization's success. To begin with, providing a detailed job description is essential. This document should comprehensively outline the roles of a new hire, responsibilities, and key duties. Early in the onboarding process, scheduling a meeting to discuss these responsibilities in detail helps ensure clarity on specific tasks, deliverables, and expectations. It's also important to explain how their role aligns with departmental or organizational goals. This context emphasizes the new hire's impact on the larger framework of the company and fosters a sense of belonging.

Next, establishing performance standards is critical for guiding new hires in their roles. Defining measurable performance metrics, or key performance indicators (KPIs), provides clear benchmarks for evaluation. These may include specific sales targets, project deadlines, or customer satisfaction ratings. Moreover, clarifying expectations regarding the quality and quantity of work is essential. New hires should understand standards for accuracy, efficiency, and customer service. Regular feedback sessions should be established to discuss performance against these standards, allowing for ongoing dialogue about areas for improvement.

When it comes to goals and objectives, setting SMART (specific, measurable, achievable, relevant, time-bound) goals is a practical approach. These goals should align with the new hire's role and career development aspirations. It's beneficial to outline both short-term objectives, such as quarterly goals, and long-term objectives, like annual targets, to provide a clear road map for success. Mutual agreement between the new hire and their manager on these defined goals is crucial, and adjustments should be made as necessary based on ongoing discussions.

Finally, fostering an environment of clarity and transparency is fundamental to setting expectations. Open communication should be encouraged, allowing new hires to ask questions, seek clarification, and discuss challenges related to their responsibilities, performance standards, and goals. Establishing a feedback mechanism where both parties can provide input on the effectiveness of the expectations set will enable necessary adjustments and improvements.

Conducting **initial performance reviews** for new hires is a pivotal step in their successful integration into the organization. These reviews serve as a checkpoint to assess progress, provide constructive feedback, and align expectations between the new hire and their manager. A well-structured approach to these reviews can foster a supportive atmosphere that encourages growth and collaboration. For many of my clients, we implement a sixty-day review process that allows the new hire to give feedback on their training and present any outstanding needs they may have for learning, technology, or social integration. This gives the manager (and HR) the opportunity to see their progress and offers a structured time for the leader to give feedback as well. This can be set up in your HR/payroll platform with automation, so it doesn't have to be yet another thing to remember to execute.

Preparation is the foundation of an effective performance review. Before scheduling the meeting, it's essential to gather pertinent information. This includes reviewing the new hire's job responsibilities, initial goals, and any quantitative or qualitative metrics established during onboarding. Collecting feedback from colleagues and stakeholders who have interacted with the new hire can provide a 360-degree view of their performance, highlighting various perspectives.

Setting the stage for the meeting is equally important. Selecting a suitable time and location conducive to a focused discussion is crucial; for remote teams, utilizing video conferencing tools can facilitate face-to-face interaction. Clearly communicating the purpose of the review is essential; emphasizing that it is a constructive process aimed at mutual understanding and improvement helps set the tone. Starting the meeting on a positive note by expressing appreciation for the new hire's contributions and efforts can create a supportive atmosphere.

During the performance review meeting, it's important to cover several discussion points comprehensively. Begin by reviewing the goals set during onboarding and assessing progress made toward achieving them. Discuss any accomplishments or challenges encountered along the way. Evaluating how well the new hire has adapted to their role responsibilities is also vital, as it identifies strengths and areas needing improvement. Integrating into the discussion feedback received from colleagues and stakeholders provides a well-rounded view of the new hire's performance, highlighting notable observations and commendations.

When it comes to providing constructive feedback, balance is key. Acknowledge achievements while addressing areas that need improvement, using specific examples to illustrate points effectively. Discussing opportunities for skills development or additional training can support the new hire's growth in the role and organization.

Collaboratively setting new or revised goals for the upcoming period ensures that these goals are SMART—specific, measurable, achievable, relevant, and time-bound. Encouraging dialogue during the performance review is essential. Actively listening to the new hire's perspective allows them to share insights, challenges, and suggestions for improvement. Addressing any concerns or misunderstandings promptly fosters an environment where open communication is valued and encouraged.

Following the review, it's crucial to document the outcomes. Summarizing the discussion points, agreements reached, and action items identified serves as a reference for future reviews and development discussions. Documentation should include noted strengths, areas for improvement, and agreed-upon goals. As a result, both the manager and the new hire have a clear record of their conversation.

Finally, follow-up communication is vital to providing the new hire with ongoing support. After the performance review, following up to provide any additional resources or support needed to achieve the agreed-upon goals reinforces the commitment to their success. Maintaining ongoing communication lets the new hire know that they are valued and aligns them with organizational expectations, promoting a culture of continuous improvement and engagement. If you'd like my consulting firm's free 5-point rating scale that will help you kick start this process, go to saltandlightadvisors.com/fivepointratingscale to download. It will help you define expectations, ensure consistency across reviews, and make performance discussions easier – so take advantage of the freebie!

Long-Term Onboarding

Extending onboarding beyond the initial ninety days is crucial for ongoing support, development, and retention. This extended onboarding period plays a significant role in facilitating a smoother transition into the organization and fostering a deeper sense of belonging among new hires. One of the key benefits of extended onboarding is continued integration. While the initial phase introduces new hires to the organization's culture, values, and norms, ongoing onboarding allows them to develop deeper relationships with their colleagues. This is essential for understanding the company's unique dynamics. Additionally, extended onboarding encourages team collaboration and provides networking opportunities that enhance teamwork, leading to a more cohesive work environment.

Continuous learning and development is another vital aspect of extended onboarding. Providing ongoing training and development opportunities enables new hires to continuously improve their skills and knowledge, ensuring that they remain relevant and capable of meeting evolving job requirements. This focus on growth not only benefits the employees but also positions the organization to adapt to changing market conditions. Furthermore, extended onboarding helps new hires understand their potential career paths in the organization. Discussions about career development opportunities, skill-building initiatives, and potential advancement paths are critical during this phase.

Performance improvement is also a significant advantage of extended onboarding. Regular feedback sessions that extend beyond the initial onboarding period allow managers to offer ongoing guidance and support. This helps new hires address performance gaps, refine their skills, and excel in their roles. Moreover, continued discussions about goals and expectations create alignment with organizational objectives, enabling necessary adjustments as priorities shift or the new hire's role evolves.

The impact of extended onboarding on engagement and retention cannot be overstated. By investing in extended onboarding, organizations demonstrate their commitment to new hires' success, contributing to higher levels of engagement, job satisfaction, and loyalty. Effective extended onboarding programs can significantly reduce early turnover rates, help new hires feel valued and integrated, and lead to longer tenure and lower recruitment costs. Furthermore, extended onboarding plays a role in organizational adaptation. It helps new hires navigate changes in the organization, such as restructuring, new leadership, or shifts in business priorities, ensuring that they remain aligned with the company's evolving strategies. This adaptability is essential in a fast-paced business environment where change is constant.

Implementing an effective extended onboarding program involves several key implementation tips. A structured approach is necessary, as is an onboarding plan that outlines clear milestones and objectives extending beyond the initial ninety days. Establishing regular feedback loops and performance reviews will help monitor progress, address concerns, and celebrate achievements.

Lastly, organizations should regularly evaluate the effectiveness of their extended onboarding programs, adjusting based on feedback and evolving organizational needs.

Career development is a cornerstone of employee engagement, satisfaction, and retention. When organizations prioritize the growth of their employees, they not only foster a more motivated workforce but also create a culture that attracts and retains top talent. Let's dive into how organizations can effectively provide information on career paths, development opportunities, and long-term goals to support their employees' professional growth.

Career path exploration is the first step in supporting employee development. Organizations should define clear career paths that outline potential roles, responsibilities, and progression opportunities. This clarity provides employees with a road map for advancement in the organization, empowering them to visualize their future. An easy way to do this is to map out each role and the gaps in skills or what it takes to grow into the next role. I create this for my clients in a simple graphic (thank you, Canva, for making my life easier), and their team members love it. Additionally, offering job shadowing opportunities allows employees to observe and learn from colleagues in different roles. This firsthand experience can provide valuable insights into various career paths, helping employees make informed decisions about their professional journeys. Furthermore, access to career counseling or mentoring programs can facilitate discussions about career aspirations. These programs enable employees to receive guidance tailored to their individual goals, ultimately leading to personalized development plans that align with their ambitions.

Next, organizations must provide **development opportunities** to enhance employees' skills and knowledge. Regular training sessions, workshops, and seminars covering a wide range of topics—from technical skills to leadership and soft skills—are essential. Such initiatives not only foster professional growth but also signal to employees that their development is valued. Supporting employees in obtaining relevant certifications or attending courses that align with their career goals further contributes to their professional development. Moreover, assigning stretch assignments or challenging projects can broaden employees' experiences, allowing them to develop new skills while showcasing their potential.

Aligning **long-term goals** with employee aspirations is another critical component of effective career development. Organizations should encourage employees to set SMART (specific, measurable, achievable, relevant, time-bound) goals that reflect both their personal career aspirations and the organization's objectives. Performance reviews should be utilized as valuable opportunities to discuss these long-term goals, track progress, and identify any development needs. Incorporating succession planning discussions into this process can help organizations identify high-potential employees and prepare them for future leadership roles, ensuring a robust talent pipeline.

Providing **resources and support** is essential for fostering career development. Structured career development programs that include mentorship, coaching, and access to career planning tools and assessments can significantly enhance employees' growth experiences. Promoting internal mobility by advertising job openings internally encourages employees to explore new roles in the organization, facilitating smooth transitions between departments or functions. This not only helps retain talent but also allows employees to acquire diverse experiences that enrich their career trajectories.

Organizations must also cultivate a **continuous learning culture**. This involves creating an environment where employees are encouraged to seek new knowledge, share expertise, and contribute to their professional growth. Regular feedback and recognition are critical components of this culture. Providing constructive feedback not only helps employees identify areas for improvement but also motivates them by acknowledging their achievements and reinforcing their career development efforts.

Finally, a **personalized approach** to career development can significantly enhance the employee experience. Individual development plans (IDPs) based on employees' career aspirations, strengths, and areas for growth allow for tailored support. These plans should be reviewed and adjusted regularly to reflect changing goals and organizational needs to help employees remain engaged and aligned with their career trajectories.

Metrics and Evaluation

Measuring the success of an onboarding program is essential to ensure that new hires integrate smoothly into the organization and become productive contributors. By evaluating specific metrics, organizations can gain valuable insights into the effectiveness of their onboarding processes and identify areas for improvement. Here are key metrics to consider when assessing the success of onboarding.

Time to productivity is a critical measure that assesses how long it takes for new hires to reach full productivity in their roles from their start date. This metric involves tracking the time required for new hires to complete their training, become proficient in job tasks, and start contributing effectively to team projects. A shorter time to productivity indicates that the onboarding process is effective in equipping new hires with the necessary skills and knowledge to perform their roles efficiently. It reflects the organization's ability to facilitate a smooth transition into the new hire's responsibilities, thereby enhancing overall productivity.

Retention rates provide another vital metric, measuring the percentage of new hires who remain with the organization after a specified period, typically six months to one year. To calculate this metric, organizations should compare the number of new hires who stay employed against those who leave, whether voluntarily or involuntarily, within the retention period. Higher retention rates suggest that the onboarding program successfully engages new hires, aligns with their expectations, and supports their integration into the organizational culture. This metric is crucial for understanding how well the organization nurtures its talent and fosters a sense of belonging among new employees.

New-hire satisfaction is another important metric that assesses new employees' satisfaction with their onboarding experience and initial impressions of the organization. Organizations can collect this data through surveys or interviews, gathering feedback on various aspects of the onboarding process, including the quality of training, support received, and overall satisfaction. Positive new-hire satisfaction ratings indicate that the onboarding program meets expectations, enhances engagement, and fosters a positive perception of the organization. When new hires feel satisfied with their onboarding, they are more likely to become committed employees.

Feedback from **managers and team members** provides a valuable perspective on new hires' readiness, integration into the team, and contributions to team dynamics. Gathering this feedback through performance reviews, team meetings, or informal discussions can help evaluate new hires' collaboration, communication skills, and overall impact on team morale. Positive feedback from managers and team members is an indicator of effective integration and alignment of new hires with team goals and organizational culture. It reflects the new hire's ability to work harmoniously on their team, enhancing both individual and collective performance.

Performance and goal achievement metrics evaluate new hires' performance against predefined goals, targets, or key performance indicators (KPIs) established during the onboarding process. Organizations should compare new hires' performance metrics, project outcomes, or achievement of training objectives with the expectations set during onboarding. Achieving or exceeding performance goals demonstrates that new hires have successfully applied the knowledge and skills gained during onboarding. This metric is essential for assessing the long-term effectiveness of the onboarding process in driving performance.

Finally, tracking **diversity and inclusion metrics** related to new hires is vital for making sure that the onboarding process supports organizational diversity initiatives. This includes analyzing demographic representation, retention rates among diverse groups, and results from inclusion surveys. By collecting and analyzing this data, organizations can ensure that their onboarding processes foster a welcoming and inclusive workplace culture. Enhancing diversity and inclusion through effective onboarding not only supports organizational growth and innovation but also improves overall employee engagement and satisfaction.

Continuous improvement of the onboarding process is essential for organizations aiming to create a seamless and effective experience for new hires. By utilizing data and feedback, organizations can identify strengths, areas for enhancement, and opportunities to optimize the onboarding experience. A systematic approach to achieving continuous improvement includes several key steps. The first step in this process is collecting data and feedback. Implementing regular surveys and feedback mechanisms is vital to gathering insights from new hires, managers, and other key stakeholders. Organizations can utilize online surveys, focus groups, or one-on-one interviews to capture both qualitative and quantitative feedback. In addition to subjective insights, quantitative performance metrics—such as time to productivity, retention rates, and new-hire satisfaction scores—provide a clear gauge of the onboarding process's effectiveness. Moreover, soliciting input from managers and team members regarding new hires' integration, performance, and alignment with team goals enriches the feedback pool.

Once data has been collected, the next step is to analyze it and identify trends. Reviewing survey results, performance metrics, and feedback allows organizations to identify trends and common themes, as well as areas that require improvement. Benchmarking current data against industry standards enables organizations to assess their onboarding program's performance relative to their peers. Conducting a root cause analysis can also help uncover the underlying reasons for any challenges or issues identified during the onboarding process, leading to a deeper understanding of the factors at play.

With data analysis complete, organizations can move on to identifying improvement opportunities. Prioritizing areas that require immediate attention or have the potential to significantly enhance the onboarding experience is crucial. Addressing specific pain points identified by new hires—such as clarity of job roles, training effectiveness, or team integration—can lead to meaningful improvements. Additionally, researching and incorporating best practices from industry leaders or successful peers can further enhance the program's effectiveness.

The next step involves implementing changes and testing. Organizations should develop actionable plans to address identified improvement opportunities, outlining specific steps, responsibilities, and timelines for implementation. Testing new initiatives or changes on a smaller scale—such as with a subset of new hires or specific departments— allows for assessment of effectiveness before broader implementation. Adopting an iterative approach to refining onboarding processes enables organizations to make incremental improvements based on ongoing feedback and results. Monitoring and evaluation are critical components of continuous improvement. Organizations must continuously monitor the implementation of improvements to track progress and gather real-time feedback from stakeholders. Evaluating the impact of changes through updated performance metrics, surveys, and feedback mechanisms provides a comprehensive view of the onboarding process's effectiveness. Remaining flexible to adapt strategies based on ongoing data analysis and feedback allows for continuous alignment with organizational goals and evolving employee needs.

Finally, communicating improvements is essential for maintaining transparency and engagement throughout the organization. Updates and improvements to the onboarding process should be communicated clearly to all stakeholders, including new hires, managers, HR teams, and senior leadership. Celebrating successes and improvements achieved through continuous improvement efforts reinforces a culture of innovation and employee-centric practices.

Case Studies and Best Practices

Successful onboarding programs play a crucial role in integrating new hires into an organization and setting the stage for their long-term success. Here are a few exemplary onboarding programs implemented by leading organizations.

Google is renowned for its comprehensive onboarding process, affectionately known as Noogler orientation. This program immerses new hires, referred to as Nooglers, into Google's unique culture while equipping them with the tools and resources needed for success. One of the key features is the warm welcome extended to Nooglers, which includes personalized gifts, access badges, and introductions to teams and mentors.

Extensive training sessions cover Google's products, technologies, and internal systems, complemented by workshops that focus on teamwork and innovation. Additionally, ongoing support is facilitated through regular check-ins with managers and mentors, encouraging Nooglers to explore different roles and projects to find their best fit in the organization.

The impact of Google's onboarding program is profound, contributing to high levels of employee satisfaction, engagement, and retention rates. It helps new hires integrate quickly into the company culture and aligns their individual goals with Google's mission of organizing the world's information and making it universally accessible and useful.

Zappos, the online shoe and clothing retailer celebrated for its exceptional customer service, takes a distinctive approach to onboarding that emphasizes cultural fit and employee happiness. New hires participate in a month-long training program known as The Offer, during which they learn about the company's core values, culture, and customer service philosophy. A key feature of the program is hands-on learning, in which employees spend time working in various departments, including customer service, to gain firsthand experience of the company's operations.

Zappos also places a strong emphasis on building relationships and encouraging new hires to connect with colleagues and leaders through mentorship and social activities. This approach fosters a strong sense of belonging and commitment among employees, aligning them with the company's customer-focused culture. The success of the Zappos onboarding program is evident in its positive impact on employee loyalty and the company's reputation for outstanding customer satisfaction.

Airbnb offers an onboarding program that centers around welcoming new hires into its innovative and diverse culture, preparing them to contribute to the company's mission of creating a world where anyone can belong anywhere. New employees participate in Airbnb Welcome, a week-long orientation that introduces them to the company's mission, values, and community-driven culture.

To foster collaboration and innovation, employees engage in cross-functional projects and team-building exercises. Airbnb encourages continuous learning through Airbnb University, which provides courses on leadership, technology, and personal development. The impact of Airbnb's onboarding program is significant, supporting employee growth, creativity, and adaptability. It enables new hires to embrace the company's values of inclusivity and hospitality, thereby contributing to Airbnb's global success and positive impact on communities worldwide.

These case studies highlight how successful companies—like Google, Zappos, and Airbnb—prioritize onboarding as a strategic initiative to align new hires with organizational culture, values, and goals. By investing in comprehensive onboarding programs that emphasize training, cultural immersion, and ongoing support, these organizations achieve high employee engagement, retention, and performance, ultimately driving their continued success in competitive markets.

One of my favorite personal onboarding experiences was when I was scheduled to start a new role the week after my fortieth birthday. My new employer knew this because I had asked to push the start date as I would be in Vegas with my best friends celebrating. When I arrived in my hotel room, I had a bottle of champagne and some chocolates in my room from my new boss and the head of HR. I was blown away. It wasn't anything huge but very meaningful to me. That same organization (which was fully remote) had us all meet in-person once a quarter at different locations around the US centered around where team members lived. The team member that was closest to the chosen spot picked the hotels and a few activities as well as the meeting locations. Even though neither of these instances had anything to do with my day-to-day tasks with this organization, it definitely made an impact on how I felt about being a part of this team.

We have already covered several aspects of onboarding process in the Hiring & Recruitment chapter, but let's cover some of the aspects briefly again. One of the best practices to consider is **preboarding preparation**. This phase involves sending personalized welcome communications before the new hire's first day, like what I mentioned for my fortieth birthday. These communications can include welcome emails or packages that provide valuable information about the company, the team, and specific role expectations. Additionally, offering access to necessary tools, systems, and resources allows new hires to familiarize themselves with the organization in advance, setting a positive tone for their arrival. It can be formal or informal, but anything that shows your new hire that you are excited to have them join will increase the odds of them showing up the first day and showing up excited to be the newest member of your team.

Establishing a **structured onboarding plan** is also essential. A well-organized onboarding checklist or timeline outlines key activities, training modules, and introductions during the first weeks and months. Furthermore, aligning clear goals and expectations with the new hire's role helps them understand how their contributions will drive overall company success.

Cultural integration is another crucial component of an effective onboarding program. Immersing new hires in the organization's culture through orientation sessions, values workshops, and introductions to key cultural influencers fosters a sense of belonging. Pairing new hires with experienced employees or mentors through **mentorship programs** can provide guidance on navigating cultural nuances and professional development opportunities. Moreover, **continuous feedback and support** systems are vital. Regular check-ins between new hires and their managers allow for timely feedback, addressing questions, and fostering alignment with goals. Encouraging new hires to provide feedback on their onboarding experience also promotes continuous improvement of the process.

Training and development are paramount in onboarding. Providing **role-specific training** ensures that new hires understand their job responsibilities, processes, and tools necessary for success. Offering career development opportunities through workshops, certifications, and learning platforms can also facilitate skill enhancement and growth. To promote socialization and team integration, organizations should facilitate introductions to team members and key stakeholders, fostering collaboration and professional relationships. Social events, team-building exercises, and networking opportunities can help new hires feel more connected to their colleagues and the company culture.

Innovative approaches to onboarding can further enhance the experience for new hires. **Technology integration** plays a critical role in modern onboarding processes. For example, virtual onboarding tools, such as video conferencing, virtual tours, and online platforms, can effectively engage geographically dispersed teams or remote workers. Mobile-friendly onboarding apps allow new hires to access training modules and updates anytime, anywhere, making the onboarding experience more accessible and user-friendly. Additionally, incorporating **gamification** into training modules and onboarding activities can enhance engagement and knowledge retention. By creating challenges or quizzes related to company culture and values, organizations can motivate new hires while rewarding successful completion.

Personalized experiences are also essential for effective onboarding. Offering customized onboarding pathways based on new hires' backgrounds, experiences, and learning preferences can enhance engagement and learning outcomes. Simulations or role-playing exercises can provide hands-on experience, better preparing new hires for real-world challenges they may encounter. Furthermore, focusing on inclusion and diversity is crucial in modern onboarding practices. Incorporating diversity and inclusion training into onboarding programs promotes awareness and sensitivity, fostering inclusive behaviors among new hires. Introducing new hires to employee resource groups (ERGs) or affinity networks can further support diverse communities in the organization.

Finally, measuring the effectiveness of onboarding initiatives is vital for continuous improvement. Utilizing data analytics to track key metrics, such as time to productivity, retention rates, and employee satisfaction scores, can provide insights into the impact of onboarding efforts. By fostering a culture of continuous improvement, organizations can refine and optimize their onboarding processes over time, remaining relevant and effective in meeting the needs of both employees and the organization as a whole.

Onboarding is more than a checklist—it's a strategic investment in employee success and retention. By structuring onboarding over the first ninety days, incorporating training, and fostering social integration, small businesses can ensure new hires become productive, engaged team members. Next, we'll explore how disciplinary actions play a role in maintaining workplace standards and performance.

CHAPTER 3

Disciplinary Actions and Employee Relations

Employee discipline isn't just about punishment, it's about maintaining consistency, fairness, and workplace culture. Small business owners often struggle with how to address performance or behavior issues without creating resentment. This chapter provides a structured approach to disciplinary actions, from verbal warnings to terminations, ensuring compliance with employment laws while protecting your company culture.

Disciplinary Actions

Effective management of disciplinary actions is vital for maintaining workplace order and ensuring fair treatment of employees. To begin with, it is essential to establish clear policies that outline documented procedures for disciplinary actions. Organizations should develop and communicate these policies so that employees are fully aware of the expected standards of behavior and the potential consequences for failing to adhere to them. Consistency and fairness are paramount in applying disciplinary actions across the organization. This approach helps prevent claims of favoritism or discrimination, as it means similar infractions result in similar consequences.

Implementing a progressive discipline system is another critical aspect of effective disciplinary management. This system typically involves a series of steps, including verbal warnings, written warnings, suspensions, and, if necessary, termination. Such a framework allows employees the opportunity to correct their behavior before more severe actions are taken. It is crucial to maintain detailed records of each step in the disciplinary process, including the nature of the infraction, the employee's response, and the actions taken. Proper documentation is essential for defending against potential wrongful termination claims, as it provides a clear record of the disciplinary actions taken.

Fairness and due process must also be central to any disciplinary action. Conducting a thorough investigation before taking action is crucial; this includes gathering evidence, interviewing witnesses, and allowing the employee an opportunity to respond to any allegations. Providing employees with a chance to present their side of the story fosters transparency and helps create fairness in the process.

Furthermore, compliance with employment laws is non-negotiable. Employers must ensure that disciplinary actions do not disproportionately affect employees based on race, gender, age, disability, or other protected characteristics, thereby minimizing the risk of discrimination claims. Additionally, consideration must be given to whether an employee's behavior may be related to a disability or other protected status, and reasonable accommodations should be made when required by law. First, we'll cover the types of warnings, and then we'll cover the how-to and some key considerations for administering later in the chapter.

Types of Employee Disciplinary Actions

Verbal Warning

A verbal warning is a formal yet initial discussion between a supervisor and an employee regarding a specific behavior or performance issue. Though often informal in tone, it is essential to communicate clearly the nature of the issue, its potential consequences, and the supervisor's expectations for improvement. This approach allows the employee to understand and address the concern without documentation in their personnel record, often making it an ideal first step in handling minor infractions. A well-delivered verbal warning underscores the importance of the issue while encouraging a constructive response from the employee. Even though this is called a *verbal* warning, I like to follow up with an email recapping what we discussed to make sure the employee has clarity *and* to have a documentation foundation if it's needed later.

Written Warning

A written warning is a formal, documented notice provided to the employee that outlines the specific misconduct or performance issue and details the expected changes in behavior. This step often follows a verbal warning when the issue persists or the infraction is more severe. By formally recording the warning, both the employee and the organization have a record of the incident, ensuring clarity and accountability. Written warnings convey the seriousness of the behavior and serve as a clear reminder that improvement is required to avoid further disciplinary action. It's great to tie in the company values to provide alignment and clarity during this step in the process.

Suspension

Suspension involves the temporary removal of an employee from their duties, often without pay, to underscore the gravity of a serious infraction. This action allows the employee time to reflect on their behavior and signals to the organization that certain behaviors will not be tolerated. Suspension can also allow the company to investigate the situation further, especially if immediate removal from the work environment is warranted. By temporarily separating the employee from the organization, suspensions emphasize the critical need for corrective action and signal the consequences of continued misconduct. Keep in mind that if the suspension is without pay and the employee has company benefits that include payroll deductions, you will need to proactively address what the employee needs to do to maintain their benefits (like paying the entire premium by the fifteenth of the month by check, due to the HR office, or something similar). If you allow the employee to utilize any paid time off, that may cover the amount of the benefits premium.

Demotion

A demotion reduces an employee's rank, responsibilities, or pay and is often a measure taken when performance consistently falls short of job requirements despite prior corrective actions. Unlike termination, demotion allows the employee to remain with the organization while taking on responsibilities more aligned with their demonstrated capabilities. This measure also preserves the organization's investment in the employee's training and experience, providing them a chance to contribute in a role better suited to their strengths. By reducing responsibilities, a demotion signals that improvement is essential while allowing the organization to retain valuable knowledge and skills. I have seen only one successful demotion at an employer (between where I've worked and my clients) in the last twenty years of my career, so this isn't a decision to take lightly.

Termination

Termination is the final step in the disciplinary process, representing a permanent end to the employment relationship due to serious or repeated misconduct. It is reserved for situations in which the employee's behavior severely breaches company standards or previous disciplinary actions have failed to yield improvement. Termination not only addresses the immediate issue but also serves as a strong reminder to all employees of the importance of adhering to organizational values and standards. This decisive action underscores the organization's commitment to maintaining a productive, respectful, and safe work environment.

Importance of Employee Disciplinary Actions

Disciplinary actions are critical for maintaining order in an organization. By enforcing company policies and standards, these measures help create a respectful and predictable workplace. Consistent application of discipline reduces instances of disruptive behavior, promotes professionalism, and cultivates a stable environment where all employees know the boundaries. This structured approach to order and discipline is foundational to building a workplace that values cooperation, mutual respect, and a shared commitment to the organization's mission. Fair and consistent disciplinary actions foster a culture of trust in the workplace. When employees see that all individuals are held to the same standards, they are more likely to respect the organization's policies and trust its management. Ensuring consistency in disciplinary actions also prevents perceptions of favoritism, which can erode morale and productivity. By applying these measures uniformly, organizations strengthen their commitment to equality, creating a work environment where each employee knows they will be treated fairly.

Disciplinary actions safeguard the organization's integrity by addressing behaviors that could damage its reputation or operations. Whether it's a performance issue or a conduct violation, disciplinary measures reinforce the values that are critical to the company's long-term success. Employees, customers, and stakeholders alike benefit when the organization is seen to uphold its standards rigorously and hold employees accountable for their actions. This commitment to integrity builds trust and confidence in the organization's brand and mission.

Disciplinary actions also play a crucial role in driving productivity and performance by holding employees accountable for meeting established standards. By addressing behaviors that hinder productivity, managers encourage employees to meet or exceed expectations, which supports overall organizational effectiveness. Additionally, by focusing on corrective actions, disciplinary measures help employees identify areas for improvement, fostering a proactive and solution-oriented work environment that emphasizes continuous improvement.

Well-documented disciplinary actions provide the organization with a critical layer of legal protection. In cases of disputes or claims of wrongful termination, a record of prior actions and communications shows that the organization can demonstrate its adherence to a fair and consistent process. This documentation serves as evidence that actions were taken for legitimate reasons, reducing the risk of legal complications. Properly managed disciplinary processes thus protect the organization from potential lawsuits and ensure compliance with labor laws and regulations.

Discipline, when applied constructively, can also serve as a valuable developmental tool. By providing feedback and highlighting areas for improvement, disciplinary actions guide employees in addressing performance gaps and realigning with company standards. This approach not only helps employees grow but also increases their engagement and satisfaction as they succeed in the organization. By reducing turnover and increasing retention, constructive discipline contributes to a more cohesive, skilled workforce. Employee disciplinary actions are essential tools that promote a well-ordered, productive, and positive workplace. Addressing issues promptly and fairly allows organizations to uphold their standards, protect their reputation, and foster a work environment where employees can thrive.

Promoting Fairness in the Process

Consistent application of disciplinary actions is foundational to fairness in the workplace. By holding every employee accountable to the same standards, the organization communicates that its policies and procedures apply equally to all, regardless of position or tenure. This uniform approach helps prevent accusations of favoritism and bias, fostering a sense of equality and inclusivity. When employees observe that the organization's rules are enforced evenly, they're more likely to respect and trust management, knowing that everyone is expected to adhere to the same behavioral and performance standards.

Transparency in disciplinary procedures allows employees to understand precisely what is expected of them and what the consequences will be for violations. A transparent system outlines clear steps for infractions and gives employees insight into how the organization approaches issues fairly and consistently. This openness builds trust in management by reducing fears of arbitrary decisions, as employees know what actions lead to disciplinary consequences.

Trust in the system is essential for morale and for reinforcing an environment where employees feel valued and respected. Effective documentation and communication in disciplinary actions provide a factual and reliable record of each step taken. By maintaining accurate records, the organization can support its decisions with clear evidence, which is crucial if disputes arise, or questions of fairness are raised. Due to this approach, disciplinary actions are based on documented facts rather than subjective assessments, reinforcing fairness and objectivity. Clear, well-maintained records also protect both the organization and the employee, as they provide a verifiable account of the issue, response, and resolution.

Ensuring Safety

Addressing unsafe behaviors through disciplinary actions is critical to creating a secure workplace. When employees disregard safety protocols or engage in risky behaviors, they endanger not only themselves but also their colleagues and the organization as a whole. Disciplinary actions for safety violations underscore the organization's commitment to maintaining a safe work environment, emphasizing that safety is non-negotiable.

Swift and fair responses to safety breaches help reduce the likelihood of accidents and injuries, demonstrating to employees that their well-being is a top priority. Disciplinary actions reinforce the importance of adhering to safety protocols, sending a clear message that these rules are not optional. Consistently enforcing safety measures encourages employees to prioritize safe practices in their daily tasks, which ultimately contributes to a culture of safety.

When employees know that noncompliance will result in disciplinary action, they're more likely to follow protocols carefully, which significantly reduces the potential for hazardous situations and helps create a proactive safety culture in the organization. Disciplinary actions are essential for preventing workplace violence and managing aggressive behaviors. Addressing incidents swiftly can prevent escalation, protecting both employees and the organization from potential harm. Zero tolerance for violent or aggressive behavior, demonstrated through immediate disciplinary measures, helps maintain a secure and respectful work environment. This approach reassures employees that they are safe at work, as the organization has procedures in place to address harmful behavior promptly and effectively.

Enhancing Efficiency

Disciplinary actions serve as effective tools for addressing and correcting performance-related issues. By setting clear standards and communicating consequences for failing to meet those standards, organizations encourage employees to align their efforts with performance expectations. This emphasis on improvement helps boost productivity, as employees become more aware of their impact on overall team and organizational success.

Disciplinary actions also reinforce that maintaining high performance is essential for individual and collective efficiency, supporting a productive and high-functioning workforce. Addressing disruptive behavior through disciplinary actions is vital for preserving a focused and efficient work environment. Disruptions, such as tardiness, gossip, or noncompliance with policies, can negatively impact the productivity and morale of the entire team. By setting boundaries for acceptable behavior and enforcing them, disciplinary actions minimize distractions and allow employees to concentrate on their tasks.

This proactive approach to managing disruptive behavior ensures the organization operates smoothly and all team members can work in an environment conducive to productivity. Disciplinary measures clarify what is expected from employees regarding performance and behavior, reducing uncertainty. When employees know exactly what is required to succeed and what actions will result in consequences, they can work more effectively and with greater confidence. This clarity promotes a more organized and efficient workflow, as employees are less likely to waste time second-guessing their responsibilities. Consistent enforcement of expectations fosters a culture of accountability and high standards, which benefits the organization and its employees alike.

Supporting Organizational Culture

Disciplinary actions play an essential role in upholding the organization's core values and standards. By addressing behaviors that conflict with these values, disciplinary actions demonstrate the organization's commitment to its principles. This alignment reinforces a cohesive culture where employees understand and embody the organization's values, creating a more unified and mission-driven workforce. As employees see that management upholds these standards consistently, they're more likely to internalize and support the organization's values, contributing to a stronger and more positive culture.

Disciplinary actions are a key component in fostering a culture of accountability. When employees are held responsible for their actions, they develop a sense of ownership over their behavior and its impact on the organization. This accountability promotes higher engagement, as employees feel more invested in meeting expectations and contributing positively to the team. Knowing that they are answerable for their conduct encourages employees to maintain professionalism, which enhances overall morale and cultivates a culture where individuals are committed to their roles and to each other.

Constructive disciplinary actions serve as valuable learning opportunities for employees, guiding them in understanding and correcting their mistakes. By framing disciplinary actions as a chance for growth rather than punishment, organizations can encourage employees to develop professionally and improve their performance. This approach supports long-term career development, as employees learn to take responsibility, adapt to feedback, and refine their skills. Encouraging growth through constructive discipline not only benefits the individual employee but also strengthens the organization by fostering a workforce capable of continuous improvement.

Over my tenure in HR, I've seen employees respond to discipline in a few different ways. A person who is secure in themselves and desires to grow may take the feedback, internalize it, and apply it. This is the ideal outcome. Others may resent the delivery of the information or begin to question their teammates as to who turned them in, reported any behavior, or went behind their back. Other employees may not be able to receive feedback or are not open to change and either "quiet quit" or begin actively looking for other jobs outside of the department or company. Any of these responses are normal behaviors. The important part of consistent disciplinary action is to stay on top of the situation as the leader or HR manager and continue to address any continued performance issues and set clear expectations for behavior.

Employment Laws and Regulations Governing Employee Discipline

Employee discipline is guided by a framework of federal, state, and local laws that uphold fair treatment, prevent discrimination, and protect workers' rights. These laws ensure that disciplinary actions are lawful, transparent, and consistent with workplace policies while respecting employees' rights and promoting ethical standards.

Labor Laws

Fair Labor Standards Act (FLSA)

The FLSA sets the groundwork for wage and hour regulations, covering critical aspects, such as minimum wage, overtime pay, and child labor restrictions. When dealing with disciplinary actions related to pay discrepancies or deductions, organizations must adhere to FLSA guidelines to avoid legal issues. For instance, if a disciplinary measure involves a suspension without pay, the employer must comply with the FLSA's regulations to prevent potential violations related to wage and hour requirements. The FLSA's protections ensure that employees are compensated fairly, even in disciplinary situations, underscoring the importance of maintaining lawful pay practices.

National Labor Relations Act (NLRA)

The NLRA protects employees' rights to organize, discuss work conditions, and engage in collective bargaining. Disciplinary actions that interfere with these rights, such as punishing employees for discussing wages or forming unions, are prohibited under the NLRA. This law emphasizes that employees must feel secure in their ability to advocate for fair treatment without fear of retaliation. When disciplinary actions are considered, organizations must remain cautious not to infringe upon these rights, as violations can lead to legal repercussions and weaken trust between management and the workforce.

Anti-Discrimination Laws

Title VII of the Civil Rights Act of 1964

Title VII prohibits discrimination based on race, color, religion, sex, or national origin, ensuring that disciplinary actions are applied equitably across all protected categories. Employers must take care to avoid disciplinary measures that appear biased or disproportionately affect specific groups. Disciplinary actions under Title VII must be well-documented and based solely on objective behavior or performance criteria. The goal is to maintain an inclusive workplace where employees feel respected and confident that disciplinary measures are free from discriminatory intent.

Americans with Disabilities Act (ADA)

The ADA protects individuals with disabilities from discrimination and mandates reasonable accommodations where necessary. Any organization that takes disciplinary actions against employees with disabilities must consider reasonable adjustments to accommodate their needs. For example, if an employee with a disability struggles to meet specific performance metrics, an employer should provide that accommodation before initiating disciplinary action. This approach ensures that disciplinary actions are fair and respects the ADA's mandate for inclusivity and accessibility in the workplace.

Age Discrimination in Employment Act (ADEA)

The ADEA safeguards employees aged forty and older from age-based discrimination so that disciplinary actions do not disproportionately impact older workers. Employers must be careful that disciplinary decisions are based on objective criteria rather than stereotypes related to age, such as assumptions about an older employee's adaptability. By maintaining age-neutral disciplinary practices, organizations can support an equitable workplace and avoid potential age discrimination claims.

Workplace Safety Regulations

Occupational Safety and Health Act (OSHA)

OSHA mandates that employers provide a safe work environment and address safety violations promptly. When disciplining employees for unsafe behaviors, employers must do so in alignment with OSHA standards. Additionally, OSHA prohibits retaliation against employees who report unsafe conditions. Therefore, when safety-related disciplinary actions are necessary, they should focus on reinforcing safety protocols without discouraging employees from voicing safety concerns.

This approach helps maintain a secure environment while supporting employees' rights to a safe workplace.

State-Specific Safety Regulations

In addition to OSHA, many states have specific safety and workers' compensation laws that impact disciplinary practices, particularly in industries with unique safety requirements. Employers must comply with both federal and state safety regulations, as states may have additional requirements beyond OSHA. For instance, disciplinary actions related to workplace injuries or incidents may need to follow specific state guidelines to avoid violations of local laws. Observing these regulations is essential for guaranteeing that safety-related disciplinary actions are lawful and respectful of employees' rights.

Privacy Laws

Employee Privacy Rights

The Electronic Communications Privacy Act (ECPA) and related privacy laws regulate how employers monitor employee communications. When disciplinary actions involve electronic communications, such as email or internet use, employers must handle these cases in compliance with privacy protections. For instance, any surveillance or monitoring should be disclosed and transparent to avoid legal breaches. Disciplinary actions based on monitored communications must balance organizational interests with respect for individual privacy rights, fostering a respectful and legally compliant work environment.

State Privacy Laws

State-specific privacy laws can impose additional restrictions on how employers gather, use, and disclose employee information, impacting disciplinary procedures. Some states have strict regulations regarding employee surveillance, personal data collection, and electronic monitoring. Organizations operating in these states must ensure that disciplinary actions involving personal data are managed carefully, as failure to comply with state privacy laws can lead to legal consequences and damage to employee trust.

Employment Contracts and Agreements

Contractual Obligations

Employment contracts, collective bargaining agreements, and individual agreements often include terms governing disciplinary actions. Employers must adhere to these agreements, as they may specify processes for handling disciplinary measures, such as requirements for advance notice, documentation, or appeals. Deviating from these terms can expose the organization to breach of contract claims. Clear, consistent adherence to contractual obligations in disciplinary matters helps maintain trust, reduces conflict, and supports a structured approach to managing performance and conduct.

Whistleblower Protection Laws

Whistleblower Protection Act

The Whistleblower Protection Act shields employees who report illegal or unethical practices in their organization from retaliatory disciplinary actions. Employers are prohibited from disciplining or terminating employees who report misconduct in good faith, even if it exposes flaws in the organization. This law encourages transparency and ethical conduct by safeguarding employees who bring concerns to light. Employers must approach disciplinary matters involving potential whistleblowers carefully to avoid unintended retaliation and ensure legal compliance.

Ethical Standards in Disciplinary Practices

Fairness in disciplinary actions means treating all employees equally, regardless of rank, background, or personal relationships. This principle helps prevent favoritism and fosters a respectful workplace culture. Equitable treatment requires that all disciplinary actions be based on objective criteria so that employees feel valued and respected. Consistent, fair treatment also builds employee morale, as it reinforces the idea that everyone is subject to the same rules, creating a balanced environment that promotes mutual respect. Establishing clear, objective criteria for disciplinary actions is essential to maintaining an unbiased approach. When disciplinary measures are based on specific, documented behaviors or performance issues, it reduces the influence of subjective judgments. Objectivity in discipline promotes fairness and makes sure actions are justified, helping prevent potential biases and avoid disputes. By grounding disciplinary practices in transparent, observable criteria, the organization builds credibility and supports a just workplace.

Transparency in disciplinary policies and procedures helps employees understand expectations and consequences. When employees are informed of the behaviors or performance issues that lead to disciplinary actions, they are more likely to adhere to company standards. Transparent communication builds trust, as it reassures employees that they are judged based on clear guidelines. This approach fosters accountability and empowers employees to take responsibility for their actions, knowing that the process is open and understandable.

Documenting each disciplinary action and its underlying reasons provides a clear record that supports both the employer's decisions and the employee's rights. When there is proper documentation, organizations can trust that disciplinary actions are fact-based and defendable if contested. Maintaining thorough records reinforces the credibility of the disciplinary process and protects against potential legal challenges. It also supports fairness by providing a consistent reference for evaluating similar incidents, helping uphold an equitable approach across the organization.

Consistent application of disciplinary measures across similar situations is vital for maintaining fairness and credibility. When disciplinary actions vary without reason, it undermines the organization's integrity and damages employee morale. Uniformity in application fosters a reliable environment where employees trust that rules will be applied evenly. This consistency is essential to establishing a dependable and equitable disciplinary process, helping the organization retain credibility and maintain a positive workplace culture.

Why These Elements Matter

Upholding ethical standards in disciplinary actions is crucial for creating a workplace where employees feel respected and valued. Fairness, transparency, and consistency reinforce these standards, ensuring that disciplinary actions are both justified and perceived as just. Employees are more likely to trust management and feel committed to the organization when disciplinary practices reflect ethical principles. This ethical foundation supports a strong organizational culture, fostering long-term engagement and reinforcing positive relationships between employees and leadership. Adhering to principles of fairness, transparency, and consistency is essential for minimizing legal risks, particularly in cases involving discrimination, wrongful termination, or retaliation. Courts and regulatory bodies closely examine disciplinary practices, and organizations with well-documented, fair processes are better positioned to defend against legal claims. By following these principles, an organization reduces its liability and enhances its reputation as a fair and compliant employer, supporting both legal security and business continuity.

When employees perceive the disciplinary process as fair, transparent, and consistent, they are more likely to trust management and engage positively in the workplace. A fair disciplinary process fosters respect, improving communication and collaboration between management and staff. This supportive environment enhances employee morale, helping to attract and retain talent. In a positive work environment, employees feel secure and empowered to contribute to the organization's success, driving higher productivity and supporting long-term organizational goals.

Verbal Warnings

Verbal warnings serve as the initial step in addressing minor infractions, providing employees with an opportunity to recognize and correct their behavior or performance without formal consequences. A verbal warning is informal yet purposeful, highlighting an issue that needs improvement while showing the employee that the organization values corrective support over immediate discipline. This form of feedback is often used for minor issues and emphasizes the importance of meeting organizational standards before problems escalate further.

When to Issue a Verbal Warning

Verbal warnings are typically reserved for minor infractions that, while noteworthy, do not justify formal disciplinary action. These can include repeated tardiness, isolated errors in performance, or minor lapses in following company policies. The goal is to address these issues early to prevent them from developing into larger concerns. For instance, an employee who occasionally arrives late may benefit from a verbal reminder rather than a written reprimand, with the expectation that they can adjust their behavior moving forward. When an infraction occurs for the first time or is relatively minor, a verbal warning serves as a measured response. It allows the organization to address the issue informally, giving the employee a fair chance to correct the behavior without formal documentation. A verbal warning is often appropriate before escalating to a written warning, especially if the employee has not previously exhibited a pattern of problematic behavior. This approach shows employees that the organization values personal growth and improvement, supporting a positive work culture.

How to Issue a Verbal Warning

Before issuing a verbal warning, it's essential to gather relevant information about the issue, including specifics about the behavior or performance in question. As a result of this preparation, the conversation is based on facts, and the warning aligns with company policies. Reviewing these policies also helps HR and managers maintain consistency, ensuring that the warning is both fair and appropriate to the situation. It is important to conduct verbal warnings in a private and confidential setting to preserve the employee's dignity. This setting also enables open communication, allowing the employee to ask questions or express any misunderstandings. The warning should be specific and objective, describing the exact behavior or performance issue without judgment.

Additionally, managers should clarify the expected changes and outline what behavior or performance standards are required moving forward. Actively listening to the employee's perspective shows respect and can help resolve misunderstandings, fostering mutual respect and collaboration. Even though verbal warnings are informal, documenting the conversation is best practice. Noting the date, the issue discussed, and any agreed-upon steps can provide useful context if future actions become necessary. This documentation also supports fairness and consistency, helping HR track progress and maintain a record for future reference.

Follow-Up

After issuing a verbal warning, it is crucial to monitor the employee's progress to ensure that improvements are made. This can involve checking in on their attendance, productivity, or adherence to company policies, depending on the issue. Monitoring progress demonstrates to the employee that the organization values improvement and supports their success. If the employee needs additional help meeting expectations, managers should offer resources or support, such as training or mentorship. Addressing obstacles proactively helps create a supportive work environment, empowering the employee to make positive changes. Setting a follow-up meeting to review the employee's progress can reinforce the organization's commitment to their improvement. This meeting provides an opportunity for additional feedback, celebrating improvements or addressing lingering issues, which helps maintain open communication and fosters an environment of support and accountability.

Key Considerations

Maintaining a respectful and professional tone is essential, as the goal is to correct behavior, not to chastise. Professionalism helps ensure that the employee feels supported rather than reprimanded, reinforcing a constructive approach to discipline. Consistency is key to maintaining fairness. Applying verbal warnings consistently across similar situations avoids perceptions of favoritism and upholds the organization's commitment to equal treatment. A constructive approach frames the warning as an opportunity for improvement, focusing on positive outcomes rather than punishment. This approach encourages employees to see discipline as a chance to grow, which can foster a stronger connection to the organization and its values. By issuing verbal warnings thoughtfully, organizations can address minor infractions effectively, providing employees with a clear opportunity to improve without escalating to formal discipline.

Written Warnings

Written warnings are formal documents used to address more serious infractions or repeated issues that have not been corrected following a verbal warning. A written warning serves as an official record of the issue, outlining the behavior or performance problem and specifying the changes needed. This formalized step communicates the importance of compliance and signals that more severe actions may follow if the behavior continues. Written warnings are an essential tool for HR, providing both a corrective path for the employee and a documented record for the organization.

When to Issue a Written Warning

Written warnings are generally issued when an employee has failed to correct issues following a verbal warning or has repeatedly violated policies. For instance, if an employee continues to arrive late despite a previous verbal warning, a written warning may be warranted. This escalation underscores the seriousness of the issue, indicating that the organization expects corrective action. Written warnings are also appropriate for moderate infractions that go beyond minor issues. These can include ongoing performance issues or more significant breaches of company policies. A written warning signals that the issue is serious. And when formal documentation is required, the employee is more likely to understand the importance of resolving the problem.

Process of Issuing a Written Warning

Preparing a written warning requires gathering all relevant documentation, including prior verbal warnings and performance records, to ensure that the warning is based on a clear history of issues. Reviewing company policies at this stage helps maintain consistency and compliance, supporting a fair approach to discipline. When a standard format is used, written warnings are consistent and contain all necessary elements. This includes the date, the employee's details, a description of the infraction with specific examples, previous discussions, and an outline of expectations. Clearly stating the required changes and potential consequences establishes a structured improvement plan, providing the employee with a road map to correct the issue. A private meeting allows for respectful and confidential delivery of the written warning. During the meeting, the manager should review the document's contents, explain the details of the infraction, and clarify expectations. Giving the employee an opportunity to provide feedback demonstrates respect and can help resolve misunderstandings. Obtaining the employee's signature indicates that they have been informed of the issue and the consequences, reinforcing transparency in the disciplinary process.

Documentation and Follow-Up

Filing the written warning in the employee's personnel file is crucial, as it provides a clear record of the disciplinary history. This documentation helps HR track progress and supports any future actions if the behavior continues. Documenting details of the meeting, including the date, attendees, and main points discussed, reinforces transparency and accountability. This record serves as a reference for future actions and helps prevent misunderstandings. After issuing the written warning, monitoring the employee's performance is essential to ensure compliance. Continued support, as outlined in the action plan, helps reinforce the organization's commitment to the employee's improvement. Scheduling follow-up meetings allows for additional feedback, demonstrating that the organization is invested in the employee's success.

Key Considerations

Professionalism is essential during the written warning process to create a constructive and respectful environment. By maintaining a positive and supportive tone, managers help employees focus on improvement rather than feeling penalized. Consistency in the application of written warnings across similar cases is vital to maintaining a fair and unbiased approach. Fairness builds trust in the disciplinary process, reinforcing that employees are treated equitably. Detailed documentation is crucial for effective written warnings, as it prevents misunderstandings and provides a clear record for potential future actions. Clarity in documentation strengthens the organization's ability to defend its actions if questioned. By following a structured process for written warnings, organizations can effectively address serious or repeated issues, providing employees with a clear understanding of expectations and a chance to improve.

I had a client at one point who skipped over the verbal warning and jumped straight into a final written warning. The manager was very frustrated and for good cause (the employee was regularly skipping a vital step in their workflow that was causing major problems downstream for others). The employee, who felt ambushed and undervalued (and offended), gave their two weeks' notice just one week after receiving the written warning. The resignation could have been avoided if the manager had shared feedback verbally (and heard the employee's side of the story) prior to going straight to a written warning. The employee had recently been contacted by another organization and because of the discomfort in the process, they chose to accept an interview and later received a job offer, causing them to quit. Progressive disciplinary actions may seem like an "HR thing," but they truly give employees a chance to improve before escalating discipline.

Suspensions: Understanding When and How to Implement Them

Suspension is a significant disciplinary action used in response to serious infractions or ongoing issues that require immediate attention but do not necessarily warrant termination. This disciplinary measure serves as both a means of signaling the seriousness of an issue and an opportunity for further investigation or corrective action. When used judiciously, suspensions help uphold organizational standards, promote workplace safety, and maintain professional integrity.

Circumstances for Employee Suspensions

Suspension is particularly appropriate in cases involving serious misconduct that violates company policies, laws, or ethical standards. Such infractions may include theft, harassment, acts of violence, substance abuse on the job, or severe breaches of safety protocols. These behaviors present immediate risks to other employees and to the organization, necessitating swift action to prevent further harm. Although termination may ultimately be warranted, suspension can serve as an interim measure, allowing time for the organization to thoroughly review the situation. By addressing serious misconduct promptly with a suspension, the organization demonstrates its commitment to a safe and respectful work environment. When allegations arise that require thorough investigation, suspending the employee involved can help preserve the integrity of the process. For example, if the employee's continued presence might interfere with an investigation into misconduct or their interactions with colleagues might create workplace tensions, a temporary suspension can allow the investigation to proceed impartially. This approach is particularly important in cases where the alleged misconduct could disrupt the workplace or influence other employees. By temporarily removing the employee, the organization safeguards the investigative process, ensuring that it can proceed without bias or influence.

In cases of persistent performance issues in which prior corrective measures, such as verbal or written warnings, have failed, suspension can emphasize the seriousness of the situation. For example, if an employee consistently fails to meet critical performance metrics despite having an improvement plan, a suspension can serve as a firm reminder that improvement is essential. This period allows the employee to reflect on their performance and recognize the organization's expectations, potentially motivating them to make necessary changes before further disciplinary action is taken.

Suspension can also be a step in a progressive disciplinary framework and be employed after prior warnings have failed to yield improvement. For employees with repeated policy violations despite prior interventions, suspension highlights the escalating nature of disciplinary actions and clearly indicates that further infractions may lead to termination. Utilizing suspension as part of a structured discipline process enables the organization to document its efforts to support employee improvement, reinforcing a fair and consistent approach to behavior management.

Implementing a Suspension

Before issuing a suspension, HR should review the company's disciplinary policies to ensure compliance with established guidelines and consistency with past practices. This includes gathering relevant documentation, such as records of prior warnings, performance assessments, or incident reports. The suspension must align with labor laws to avoid legal issues. Consulting legal counsel may be advisable in complex cases so that all actions are compliant and defensible, particularly if there is a history of prior infractions. A private meeting should be scheduled to discuss the suspension with the employee in a respectful and confidential setting. During the meeting, the specific reasons for the suspension, its duration, and any applicable conditions should be explained clearly. A formal written notice should also be provided, detailing the misconduct or performance issues, the suspension's start and end dates, and any conditions for return. If applicable, this notice may outline required steps for the employee during the suspension, such as attending training or counseling. When the employee signs this document as acknowledgment, not necessarily agreement, they are being fully informed of the disciplinary action.

Throughout the suspension period, HR or management should monitor any conditions set forth, such as training completion, to ensure that the employee understands and complies with expectations. Additionally, giving the employee a point of contact allows them to address any questions or concerns, maintaining professional communication. This engagement is particularly useful if the suspension is prolonged or the employee must meet requirements before returning, as it keeps them connected and informed without breaching confidentiality.

Upon the employee's return, reintegration is essential so that they feel supported in meeting expectations. A meeting should be scheduled to discuss their progress, address any lingering concerns, and outline steps for moving forward. Reviewing the employee's performance after suspension helps confirm that they understand and are committed to the required standards. Offering additional support, such as mentoring or resources, can help the employee transition smoothly back into their role and reaffirm the organization's commitment to their success.

Key Considerations

Consistency in applying suspensions across the workforce is vital to maintaining fairness. When employees observe that suspensions are handled equitably, without favoritism, they are more likely to view the disciplinary process as just. Consistency also helps protect the organization from claims of bias, as it demonstrates that the same standards apply to all employees, regardless of their position or personal relationships in the organization.

Fairness in implementing suspensions supports a positive workplace culture where employees trust that disciplinary actions are based solely on behavior or performance. Thorough documentation of the suspension process is essential for tracking disciplinary history, supporting HR decisions, and addressing any future disputes. This documentation should include records of all communications related to the suspension, the specific reasons behind the action, and any follow-up meetings or conditions. Maintaining detailed records safeguards the organization by providing an objective account of the disciplinary process, supporting legal compliance, and helping the organization defend its decisions if questioned.

Adherence to labor laws and regulations regarding suspensions is paramount to avoid legal challenges. Laws governing suspensions vary by jurisdiction, so HR should be familiar with relevant regulations. For instance, certain cases may involve wage and hour laws if an employee's suspension is unpaid, while other cases may raise concerns regarding discrimination or retaliation. Consulting legal counsel as needed helps ensure that the organization's approach is compliant and reduces the risk of legal disputes, protecting both the organization and its reputation.

Best Practices

When there is a well-defined suspension policy, employees understand the conditions and consequences of this disciplinary action. By outlining these details in the employee handbook or other accessible resources, the organization sets clear expectations, which can deter behaviors that might otherwise lead to suspension. Clear policies also support HR and management by providing a reference for consistent, fair implementation, enhancing the credibility of the disciplinary process.

While suspensions are a serious consequence, they should be framed as an opportunity for the employee to reflect and improve. Emphasizing the constructive aspects of a suspension can encourage employees to assess their behavior, make necessary changes, and return to work with a renewed commitment to meeting organizational standards. This approach reinforces the organization's investment in employee growth and development, showing that the goal of discipline is to support positive change rather than solely punitive measures. Offering resources or assistance to help the employee address the issues leading to suspension can greatly aid in their successful reintegration. Counseling, training, or mentoring may be particularly helpful in cases involving performance or behavioral issues. By supporting employees through the suspension and return process, the organization fosters an environment where discipline is part of a broader effort to help employees succeed, creating a more engaged and dedicated workforce.

By carefully following these guidelines, organizations can implement suspensions effectively, ensuring fairness, transparency, and alignment with company policies. Structured, supportive suspensions contribute to a balanced disciplinary process that upholds standards while reinforcing the organization's commitment to employee improvement.

Demotions: Managing with Sensitivity and Fairness

Demotions are a challenging yet sometimes necessary step in addressing performance or alignment issues. When handled thoughtfully, a demotion can offer an employee a fresh start in a role that better matches their abilities or the organization's current needs. By approaching demotions with transparency, empathy, and support, HR and management can create a respectful process that fosters a constructive transition.

When an employee consistently fails to meet their role's performance standards despite receiving feedback, coaching, and performance improvement plans, a demotion may be the most appropriate solution. Repeatedly missing key performance metrics, struggling to fulfill essential job duties, or showing a steady decline in job performance can impact team dynamics and overall productivity. In these cases, a demotion allows the organization to place the employee in a role better suited to their current skills while preserving morale and maintaining team standards. This approach is less punitive than termination and can provide the employee with an opportunity to contribute effectively in a different capacity.

In some cases, an employee's skills may no longer align with the demands of their current role. This misalignment often occurs when a position's requirements evolve over time or when an employee is promoted into a role that requires capabilities they are not prepared to meet. For instance, a manager who excels at operational tasks but struggles with strategic decision-making may benefit from being in a role where their strengths can shine. Demoting an employee in such cases isn't about penalizing them but about realigning their responsibilities to match their skill set, thereby enhancing their success and preserving their value in the organization.

Behavioral issues that affect an employee's effectiveness in a leadership or higher-level role may also necessitate demotion. Poor leadership style, difficulty managing teams, or failure to embody company values can hinder both team morale and performance. By reassigning the employee to a role with fewer supervisory responsibilities, the organization addresses the behavior in a constructive way. A demotion can allow the individual to refocus on their responsibilities while providing additional coaching to support positive behavior changes. At the same time, demotion preserves their employment and protects the work environment.

Organizational restructuring, downsizing, or changes in business strategy may require adjustments to existing roles, including demotions. For instance, in a department that's downsizing, some employees may need to shift to different roles to align with a leaner operational structure. In such cases, demotions are not a reflection of the employee's performance but rather a result of shifting business needs. By communicating openly and offering support, HR can help employees navigate these changes and find their place in the newly structured organization.

When an employee lacks the necessary qualifications or fails to keep pace with industry advancements, a demotion may be a way to realign their role with their current capabilities. For instance, a technical employee who hasn't updated their skills may struggle in a role requiring the latest expertise. Rather than focusing solely on the shortfall, a demotion in this context provides the employee with a role that matches their skills and potentially offers training opportunities to regain necessary competencies. This approach allows for constructive career realignment and gives employees time to develop the qualifications needed for future advancement.

Handling Demotions with Sensitivity and Fairness

Steps for Handling Employee Disciplinary Actions

1. **Document the issue**

   - Record the date, infraction details, and any past related incidents.

   - Maintain consistency with company policies and past cases.

2. **Hold a private meeting**

   - Address concerns confidentially with the employee.

   - Listen to their perspective and clarify expectations.

3. **Issue a verbal or written warning**

   - Verbal warnings for first-time/minor infractions.

   - Written warnings for repeat offenses or moderate concerns.

4. **Develop an improvement plan**

   - Outline specific actions required for improvement.

   - Establish a 30/60/90-day follow-up plan.

5. **Follow up and document**

   - Schedule follow-up meetings to track progress.

- If improvement occurs, close the case with documentation.

- If issues persist, escalate to suspension or termination.

Before deciding to demote an employee, it's essential to assess all aspects of the situation to determine if a demotion is indeed the best course of action. Exploring alternative solutions, such as additional support, training, or temporary role adjustments, sometimes mitigates the need for demotion. Reviewing company policies ensures that the process aligns with organizational standards and complies with legal guidelines. A well-prepared approach shows respect for the employee and reinforces that the decision is grounded in fairness and necessity.

Demotion discussions should always be conducted in a private, face-to-face meeting to respect the employee's dignity. During this meeting, HR or the manager should clearly explain the reasons for the demotion, using specific examples related to performance, behavior, or organizational changes that led to the decision. This explanation should be factual and free from personal criticism, focusing on the business needs and the employee's best interests. Approaching the conversation with empathy and support, acknowledging the employee's contributions, and reinforcing the organization's commitment to their success in the new role can help ease the transition.

After the discussion, HR should provide a formal written notice detailing the demotion, including new role responsibilities, any changes in compensation or benefits, and the effective date. It's crucial to communicate these changes transparently to avoid misunderstandings. Outlining expectations for the new role, along with any necessary training or resources, helps the employee adapt to their updated responsibilities. This clarity fosters a smoother transition and reinforces the organization's commitment to a constructive and fair process.

Support and Transition

Supporting the employee as they transition to their new role is vital for their confidence and long-term success. Assistance may include additional training to address skill gaps, mentorship from a colleague experienced in the new position, or a structured onboarding process tailored to the updated role. This support demonstrates the organization's investment in the employee's development and helps build resilience as they adjust to the change, reinforcing a culture of growth and adaptability.

Regular check-ins with the employee are important to gauge their adjustment and address any challenges they may face. These meetings provide opportunities to assess their progress, offer constructive feedback, and reaffirm the organization's commitment to their success. Regular monitoring also helps HR and management identify any additional support the employee may need to thrive, underscoring the organization's proactive approach to employee well-being. A demotion can be a valuable opportunity for growth if framed constructively. Encouraging the employee to view demotion as a chance to develop strengths or acquire new skills can promote a positive outlook. Highlighting potential future advancement or skill acquisition in the new role can help the employee set meaningful goals and maintain motivation. This approach reinforces the organization's support for their professional journey, turning a challenging situation into a foundation for growth and success.

Key Considerations

Making demotion practices fair across the organization is critical to maintaining trust and credibility. Applying demotions consistently according to clear standards helps avoid perceptions of favoritism or discrimination. It is essential for HR to adhere to a uniform approach when handling similar cases, ensuring that employees trust the organization's commitment to equitable treatment. Fairness in the demotion process not only supports morale but also reinforces the integrity of the organization's disciplinary practices.

Thorough documentation of the demotion process is essential for HR and legal purposes. Detailed records should include the reasons for the demotion, any prior warnings or feedback, the communication process, and the support measures provided to the employee. Maintaining accurate documentation provides transparency and protects the organization by creating a record that supports the decision if questioned. It also allows HR to review patterns or trends, offering insights that may inform future HR strategies.

Adhering to labor laws and regulations regarding demotions is crucial to avoid potential legal issues. This includes understanding the implications for compensation, benefits, and employment rights. In some cases, consulting with legal counsel may be necessary to ensure that the demotion aligns with both company policies and legal standards. Legal compliance supports the organization's risk management efforts and guarantees that the demotion process respects employees' rights, protecting both the organization and its employees.

Best Practices

Transparency is vital for maintaining trust and understanding throughout the demotion process. Clearly communicating the reasons for the demotion and the criteria used to make the decision helps the employee feel respected and valued, even during challenging transitions. Transparency supports the organization's reputation for fair practices and fosters a culture where employees feel secure in the organization's integrity. Providing career counseling or guidance can help the employee navigate their new path and explore future opportunities inside or outside the organization. By supporting the employee's career goals, the organization demonstrates a commitment to their success and development.

Career counseling also empowers the employee to focus on skill-building and promotes a forward-thinking approach to their career. Framing the demotion as an opportunity for realignment and personal growth helps the employee view it as a constructive step rather than a punishment. Emphasizing that the decision was made in the interest of both the employee and the organization encourages a positive outlook. This approach reinforces a culture that values development, demonstrating that the organization is committed to helping employees succeed in roles that align with their strengths.

By handling demotions with sensitivity, fairness, and professionalism, organizations can minimize the negative impact on morale and support a respectful transition. Following these guidelines helps maintain a constructive work environment, ensuring that the demotion process is not only fair and legally sound but also supports the employee's ongoing development and growth.

Conducting Thorough and Unbiased Investigations

A well-structured and impartial investigation is essential for addressing allegations of misconduct or performance issues. An objective and fact-based investigation not only helps uncover the truth but also reinforces employee trust in organizational fairness and transparency. Here's a detailed guide to each step in the process:

Initiate the Investigation

Clearly defining the scope of the investigation is the first step in creating accuracy and relevance. Identifying the nature of the allegations, such as specific misconduct or performance issues, sets the stage for the entire process. It's crucial to establish which areas will be examined and which individuals may be involved or affected, as this helps prevent the investigation from becoming overly broad or losing focus. A clear scope enables the investigator to remain focused on relevant information and avoid unnecessary detours, ultimately leading to a more efficient and effective investigation.

Selecting an impartial investigator is essential for maintaining the investigation's integrity. The investigator should be a neutral party, free from personal or professional conflicts with the individuals involved. This may mean appointing an HR professional, a member of management, an external consultant, or a legal advisor with experience in handling similar cases. The investigator must also have a deep understanding of applicable laws, company policies, and best practices to ensure that the investigation is thorough, legally compliant, and conducted with sensitivity. Choosing the right investigator helps build trust in the process and reinforces organizational commitment to fairness.

Plan the Investigation

An investigation plan is a road map that outlines each step, producing a systematic and organized process. The plan should detail the specific actions, such as gathering evidence, interviewing witnesses, and reviewing documents, to maintain focus and efficiency. Setting a realistic timeline for completing the investigation helps manage expectations and avoids unnecessary delays, which can reduce stress for those involved.

A well-structured plan also serves as a reference point for keeping the investigation on track, supporting a consistent and comprehensive approach. Notifying the involved parties is an important step that reinforces transparency while safeguarding confidentiality. Informing the employee under investigation about the allegations provides them with the opportunity to prepare for the process and understand their rights. Confidentiality is critical in these situations, as it protects the integrity of the investigation and the privacy of everyone involved. By emphasizing confidentiality, the organization promotes trust and prevents potential reputational damage or undue influence over the investigation's outcome.

Gather Evidence

Gathering relevant documents, such as emails, performance reviews, and disciplinary records, provides the factual basis for the investigation. These materials form the foundation of the evidence and offer concrete insights into the alleged issues. Securing all evidence prevents tampering or loss, which is essential for maintaining accuracy and integrity. Comprehensive and well-organized evidence also helps the investigator analyze details effectively, resulting in a more informed and credible outcome.

Interviews with the employee involved and any witnesses are critical to understanding the situation from multiple perspectives. Interviewing the accused employee allows them to respond directly to the allegations and share their side of the story. Witness interviews can provide additional context and corroborate information. Conducting these interviews in a fair and unbiased manner is essential to avoid influencing responses or injecting assumptions. Accurate documentation of interviews, whether through written notes or audio recordings, supports transparency and ensures that statements are recorded faithfully, which is vital for the investigation's credibility.

Analyze Evidence

Analyzing the evidence requires a careful and objective review of all findings. The investigator should look for patterns, corroborating details, and any inconsistencies among the pieces of evidence. Evaluating each piece critically helps establish whether the allegations are substantiated. This step requires patience, as a thorough analysis helps prevent misinterpretations and supports an informed and balanced conclusion. Objective evaluation of evidence reinforces the integrity of the investigation and means decisions are based on facts rather than assumptions.

Remaining objective throughout the investigation is vital for maintaining fairness and impartiality. Avoiding bias means withholding judgment until all evidence has been analyzed and basing conclusions solely on factual information. Consulting legal counsel, if needed, helps ensure that the investigation follows legal standards, particularly in cases involving potential violations of employment laws. Objectivity throughout the process upholds organizational values, demonstrating a commitment to fair treatment for all employees.

Make a Decision

Based on the analysis, the investigator should reach a conclusion regarding the validity of the allegations. Determining whether the issues are substantiated and assessing the severity of any findings allows the organization to make informed decisions about next steps. Preparing a detailed report that includes evidence, interview summaries, and the basis for any conclusions provides a clear and documented account of the investigation, supporting transparency and accountability.

If the findings indicate misconduct or performance issues, the investigator should recommend appropriate disciplinary actions or improvement plans. In addition to addressing the specific case, the investigator may suggest preventive measures, such as policy updates or additional training, to help prevent similar issues in the future. Providing well-considered recommendations supports a proactive approach, reinforcing the organization's commitment to a positive and compliant work environment.

Communicate Outcomes

Communicating the outcome of the investigation to the employee involved is essential for closure. The investigator or HR professional should explain the decision clearly, including any disciplinary actions and the reasons behind them. Offering support resources, such as counseling or career development options, if applicable, can help the employee cope with the outcome and reinforce that the organization values their well-being, regardless of the investigation's findings. Informing relevant managers and HR personnel about the investigation's outcome leads to appropriate follow-up actions. Coordinating with these parties supports a consistent response and upholds the investigation's integrity.

All documentation related to the investigation should be securely filed for future reference, maintaining confidentiality and supporting legal compliance. This ensures that records are accessible if needed while safeguarding sensitive information.

Review and Improve

After the investigation is completed, a post-investigation review provides valuable insights into the effectiveness of the process. Assessing whether the investigation was fair, efficient, and consistent with organizational standards allows HR to identify strengths and potential areas for improvement. Gathering feedback from involved parties, when appropriate, adds further perspective, contributing to a culture of continuous improvement. Using insights from the review to refine procedures or policies enhances the organization's investigative practices.

Adjustments may include updating protocols, adding resources, or providing additional training. Offering training to employees and managers on handling misconduct or performance issues helps prevent misunderstandings and promotes a supportive environment. Investing in process improvements demonstrates the organization's commitment to fairness, reinforcing trust and supporting a culture where issues are addressed thoughtfully and professionally.

By following these steps, organizations can conduct investigations that are thorough, fair, and compliant with legal and ethical standards. A structured approach to investigating misconduct or performance issues reinforces the organization's dedication to accountability and supports a respectful, professional workplace culture.

Ensuring Clarity and Legal Protection in the Disciplinary Process

Detailed documentation is the backbone of a fair and legally sound disciplinary process. Every interaction, decision, and action taken must be accurately recorded to provide transparency, uphold employee rights, and protect the organization. Thoughtful, consistent documentation strengthens the disciplinary process, reinforcing trust, accountability, and effective communication between HR, management, and employees. Here's why meticulous documentation is essential and how to implement it at every step.

Importance of Detailed Documentation

Documentation offers a structured and transparent account of each action taken during the disciplinary process, creating a clear record that reflects fairness and diligence. By keeping detailed records, HR and management can reference the disciplinary journey, from initial warnings and meetings to evidence gathering and final outcomes. This clarity ensures that each case is handled with consistency, reinforcing that organizational standards and procedures are applied fairly across the board.

Documenting each step also minimizes the risk of ambiguity, helping prevent misinterpretations that can arise due to memory lapses or subjective perceptions. Objective documentation provides a factual basis for every action, showcasing that disciplinary steps are driven by evidence and unbiased reasoning. By recording issues, attempted solutions, and the rationale for any disciplinary measures, HR can demonstrate the impartiality of the process. Detailed documentation also helps employees understand exactly what behavior is expected, the areas needing improvement, and the potential consequences of continued issues. When employees have a clear record of what's required, disputes are less likely to arise, as employees understand both the organizational expectations and the support available to them.

Compliance with employment laws and regulations is critical for organizations, especially when disciplinary actions are involved. Comprehensive records serve as proof that the organization has followed all necessary steps, safeguarding itself from claims of unfair treatment or wrongful termination. Should legal disputes arise, detailed documentation provides a solid defense, showing that the organization adhered to due process, considered alternative solutions, and communicated openly with the employee. Well-maintained records can be vital in court proceedings, reinforcing the organization's commitment to lawful and fair practices. Documentation acts as a continuous thread that ties together every communication with the employee, providing a reliable reference for past interactions, warnings, feedback, and agreements. When there is a comprehensive record, all parties are on the same page regarding expectations, actions taken, and any improvements or recurring issues. Detailed records also provide continuity in management, serving as a valuable reference point in performance evaluations or in any similar issues that arise in the future. By maintaining clear documentation, HR and managers can ensure consistency, allowing them to address issues effectively and fairly over time.

Implementing Effective Documentation

Every interaction with the employee throughout the disciplinary process should be meticulously documented. For verbal warnings, record the date, time, and specifics of what was discussed, noting the employee's response and any agreed-upon actions. Written warnings should be comprehensive, detailing the nature of the issue, supporting evidence, and required corrective actions. Include specific dates, expectations, and signatures to create a clear, formal record that supports the process. Recording each interaction reduces ambiguity and provides an unbiased, factual account of the disciplinary process.

Collecting and securely storing all relevant evidence, including emails, performance reports, and witness statements, is crucial for establishing the foundation of the disciplinary process. Detailed notes taken during meetings or interviews should capture key points, decisions made, and any necessary follow-up actions. Maintaining these records in an organized manner enables easy access when needed, whether for future evaluations or legal proceedings. Comprehensive records provide continuity and context, ensuring that HR and management have a thorough understanding of each case's background.

Adhering to organizational disciplinary procedures is essential for maintaining a consistent and fair approach. Documentation should follow established policies so that each step of the disciplinary process is handled according to company standards. Promptly updating records to reflect any new developments is equally important, as it keeps documentation accurate and current.

A consistent approach not only enhances transparency but also reinforces organizational credibility, as employees recognize that discipline is applied impartially and in alignment with policy. Protecting the confidentiality of disciplinary documentation is vital for upholding employee privacy and maintaining trust in the organization. All records should be securely stored, with access restricted to authorized personnel only. Following organizational policies for document retention and secure disposal is also critical for maintaining records for an appropriate period and disposing of them responsibly when no longer needed. Confidential storage upholds the integrity of the disciplinary process and prevents unauthorized access to sensitive information.

Detailed documentation at every step of the disciplinary process is essential for clarity, fairness, and legal protection. By meticulously recording all actions, evidence, and communications, organizations ensure transparency, accountability, and consistency in managing disciplinary issues. This approach not only supports a well-managed workplace but also creates a solid foundation for addressing potential disputes or legal challenges, reinforcing the organization's commitment to ethical practices and employee rights.

Guidelines for Effectively and Respectfully Communicating Disciplinary Actions

Effectively communicating disciplinary actions is a key responsibility in HR and management, as it directly impacts employee morale, trust, and the overall work environment. A well-managed conversation about disciplinary actions can preserve dignity, demonstrate fairness, and reinforce organizational standards. Here are guidelines to help ensure that disciplinary actions are communicated professionally and respectfully.

Preparation

Before the conversation, it's essential to thoroughly review all documentation related to the disciplinary issue. This includes previous warnings, specific evidence, and any feedback already provided to the employee. Understanding the situation in detail enables you to present facts accurately and answer any questions with confidence. When you review documentation, you're aware of the context and history, which is essential for a fair and consistent approach. This preparation reinforces that the disciplinary action is based on objective information rather than personal judgment.

Choose a time and a location that ensures privacy and minimize interruptions. A private setting demonstrates respect for the employee's confidentiality and protects their dignity, while an uninterrupted environment allows for a focused discussion. Planning the meeting thoughtfully also gives the employee the time and space to respond and ask questions without feeling rushed, reinforcing that the organization values a respectful and thorough approach.

Clear and Direct Communication

Clearly articulate the nature of the disciplinary action, referencing specific behaviors or performance issues. Providing concrete examples and documented instances helps the employee understand precisely what behaviors are problematic and why they need to change. This specificity minimizes ambiguity, making it easier for the employee to recognize and correct the issues.

By grounding the conversation in clear, factual examples, you reinforce fairness and transparency in the disciplinary process. Avoid using technical jargon or overly complex terms, as these can create confusion and obscure the main message. Using straightforward, simple language helps the employee fully understand the issue and expectations moving forward. Clear language also minimizes the risk of misunderstandings, allowing both parties to engage in a productive and constructive conversation. When the message is easily understood, it's easier for the employee to take action.

Maintain Professionalism

Approach the conversation with a calm and objective demeanor, focusing on the facts and avoiding any display of frustration or personal biases. Maintaining composure demonstrates professionalism and sets a respectful tone for the conversation, which helps the employee remain receptive to the feedback. By staying focused on the specific issue, you reinforce the organization's commitment to a fair and unbiased process, emphasizing that the goal is improvement rather than punishment.

Show respect and empathy by addressing the employee with courtesy and acknowledging their perspective. Listening to their side, even if disciplinary action must be taken, shows that you value them as an individual. Respectful communication fosters a more positive environment and can reduce defensive reactions, making the employee more likely to accept feedback constructively. This approach demonstrates that the organization cares about its employees' well-being and values respectful treatment, even in challenging conversations. A wise mentor once shared this advice with me, and it applies to both work and personal situations: we want to respond, but we do not want to react. In short, that's the difference between being emotional in a situation and objective (or more focused on logic). While we all have feelings and want to use compassion, in a situation like a disciplinary action, we want to respond to the employee but not react.

Explain the Rationale

Clearly explaining the reasons behind the disciplinary action helps the employee understand why the behavior or performance issue is unacceptable. Discussing their actions' impact on the team and organization reinforces the importance of maintaining standards and promotes accountability. Providing context also helps the employee see the bigger picture, which can make the feedback feel more constructive than punitive. Reference any prior warnings, feedback, or improvement plans related to the issue, emphasizing that the current disciplinary action is part of a consistent effort to support the employee's success. By showing a documented history of attempts to address the issue, you reinforce that the disciplinary process is fair and the employee has been given multiple opportunities to improve. This consistency helps the employee recognize that the organization is committed to their growth and has taken a measured approach.

Outline Next Steps

Clearly outline the expectations moving forward, including any specific actions the employee needs to take to address the issue. Providing a timeline for improvement and specifying available resources, such as training or mentorship, supports a structured approach to improvement. This clarity helps the employee understand exactly what is expected, increasing the likelihood of positive change and reducing the chance of misunderstandings. Explain the potential consequences if the issue persists or if there are additional infractions. Being up-front about the possible outcomes emphasizes the seriousness of the situation while allowing the employee to make informed decisions. Outlining consequences also sets clear boundaries, reinforcing the organization's standards and encouraging the employee to take corrective actions seriously.

Offer Support

Offering resources, such as additional training, mentoring, or access to counseling services, demonstrates the organization's commitment to helping the employee succeed. Providing support encourages the employee to view the disciplinary action as a chance to grow rather than a punishment. This support reinforces that the organization values their development and is invested in their success, which can lead to improved morale and engagement.

Invite the employee to ask questions, share their perspective, or provide feedback on the issue. A two-way conversation promotes mutual understanding, allowing any misunderstandings to be addressed in real time. Encouraging dialogue also reinforces that the organization values open communication and respects the employee's input, making it more likely that they will feel respected and receptive to the disciplinary feedback.

Document the Conversation

Documenting key points from the conversation, including what was discussed, the employee's response, and any agreed-upon actions, is essential for accurate recordkeeping. Detailed notes provide a factual account of the meeting, supporting transparency and protecting the organization in case of future disputes. Thorough documentation also reinforces that the organization takes the disciplinary process seriously and values accountability at every stage. After the meeting, provide a written summary of the discussion, outlining the disciplinary action, expectations, and any agreed-upon steps. Sending this summary ensures that the employee has a clear record of the conversation. It also allows them to refer to the expectations if needed. Requesting that the employee acknowledge that they received the document helps confirm that they understand the disciplinary action and expectations, promoting clarity and accountability.

Maintain Confidentiality

Confidentiality is critical when handling disciplinary actions, as it protects the employee's dignity and maintains trust in the organization. Sharing details of the disciplinary action only with those who need to know prevents potential damage to the employee's reputation and morale. By keeping these matters private, the organization reinforces its commitment to respecting employees' privacy and upholding a professional and supportive work environment. I have (unfortunately) known many leaders and even a few HR professionals who discussed employee matters liberally with others. This is a quick way to be viewed as a gossip and someone to not trust, which will damage credibility and your leadership impact in the future.

Follow Through

Regularly checking in with the employee to assess their progress shows that the organization is committed to their improvement and invested in helping them succeed. These follow-ups provide an opportunity to give feedback on their development, reinforcing the importance of meeting the established expectations. Monitoring progress also helps HR and management gauge the effectiveness of the disciplinary action, allowing for timely adjustments if needed.

If the issue continues or if there are notable improvements, reassess the situation to determine whether additional actions or support measures are necessary. Regular reevaluation ensures that the disciplinary approach remains relevant and any adjustments are made to align with the employee's progress. This flexibility demonstrates the organization's commitment to a fair and supportive process, adapting as needed to support the employee's growth.

Reflect and Learn

Reflecting on the disciplinary action process after it's complete allows HR and management to identify areas for improvement in handling similar situations in the future. Gathering feedback and assessing the effectiveness of the approach can help refine communication strategies and enhance consistency. This reflective approach promotes continuous improvement and reinforces a culture of learning and development in HR practices.

Effectively and respectfully communicating disciplinary actions involves careful preparation, clear and direct communication, professionalism, and genuine support. By adhering to these guidelines, organizations can handle disciplinary situations with sensitivity and fairness, supporting a positive and respectful work environment. These practices uphold organizational values, foster trust, and help employees understand expectations while feeling respected and valued.

A Structured Approach to Employee Development and Accountability

Progressive discipline is a systematic approach to managing employee performance and behavior issues through a series of escalating steps. This method provides employees with clear feedback, opportunities to correct issues, and a fair path toward improvement. By addressing issues incrementally, progressive discipline promotes fairness, maintains morale, and fosters a supportive work environment. Below is an in-depth look at the concept, benefits, and steps involved in a progressive discipline system.

Progressive Discipline

Progressive discipline involves a structured process in which disciplinary measures escalate based on the severity or recurrence of the behavior or performance issue. It provides employees with multiple opportunities to improve before more severe actions, such as suspension or termination, are considered. This approach supports a fair, transparent, and consistent disciplinary process that benefits both the organization and the employee.

Step	Purpose	Example Infraction
Step 1: Verbal Warning	Address minor infractions and correct behavior early	Tardiness, minor policy violations
Step 2: Written Warning	Document ongoing issues and set clear improvement expectations	Repeated absences, underperformance
Step 3: Suspension	Provide a serious consequence and time for reflection	Workplace misconduct, safety violations
Step 4: Termination	Final step when prior attempts fail, remove employee	Severe policy breach, uncorrected behavior

1. Initial Warning

The initial warning is used to address minor infractions or performance concerns, allowing the organization to address issues early. Typically informal, this verbal warning communicates the problem and sets clear expectations for improvement. The purpose is to give the employee a chance to understand the concern without formal consequences, signaling that the organization is invested in their success. It provides the opportunity to correct behavior before it becomes a documented issue, helping the employee feel supported and motivated to meet standards.

2. Written Warning

When an issue persists or is more serious, a written warning is warranted. This formal document outlines the behavior, references previous discussions, states expectations for improvement, and specifies the consequences if the problem continues. The written warning ensures that the employee is aware of the seriousness of the issue while providing a documented record for future reference. It emphasizes the organization's commitment to fair practices by giving the employee a clear, structured path to improvement.

3. Final Written Warning

A final written warning is issued if issues persist despite previous warnings or if a serious concern needs to be addressed immediately. This warning specifies consequences and includes an improvement plan with a timeline, giving the employee one last opportunity to address the issue. By setting specific, measurable goals, the final written warning reinforces that the organization has taken a fair approach and provides a last chance to avoid more severe actions, underscoring the seriousness of the situation.

4. Suspension or Demotion

For repeated infractions or serious behavior issues, suspension or demotion can be used as a step before termination. Suspension provides a temporary break for the employee to reflect on their actions, while demotion adjusts their responsibilities to better suit their skill set. This approach allows the employee to regroup and reassess, offering them a final opportunity for improvement. Suspension or demotion also demonstrates that the organization is willing to make adjustments to help the employee succeed while maintaining high standards.

5. Termination

Termination is the final step in the progressive discipline process, taken only after other measures have been exhausted or if the behavior is egregious enough to warrant immediate removal. This step signifies that the employee's behavior or performance is fundamentally incompatible with the organization's expectations. By following a structured approach with ample documentation, the organization can demonstrate that termination was a fair and considered decision, protecting both the organization and its employees.

Benefits of Progressive Discipline

Progressive discipline offers a variety of benefits, promoting a balanced approach to managing behavior and performance while upholding organizational standards and supporting employee development. A progressive discipline process provides a consistent framework for addressing issues, ensuring that all employees are treated fairly. Clear expectations are communicated at each stage, helping employees understand the behaviors required and the consequences for failing to meet those expectations. This clarity and structure foster trust, showing employees that the organization values consistency and is committed to equitable treatment.

Progressive discipline offers employees multiple chances to correct behavior or improve performance, reinforcing that the organization is invested in their growth. Each step provides constructive feedback, allowing employees to understand specific areas for improvement and how they can meet organizational standards. This supportive approach reduces the likelihood of turnover, as employees feel encouraged and valued rather than penalized.

Each step in progressive discipline creates a documented history of the employee's performance, communications, and actions taken to address issues. This recordkeeping is essential for legal compliance, as it provides evidence that the organization has made good-faith efforts to support the employee. Documentation also supports objective decision-making, showing that the disciplinary process is fair, structured, and consistently applied.

A progressive discipline approach helps ensure that all employees are subject to the same standards, reducing the risk of bias. By following a standardized process, HR and management can approach disciplinary actions objectively, basing decisions on documented behavior rather than personal judgments. This consistency reinforces trust and fairness in the organization and helps prevent discrimination claims.

Rather than focusing solely on punishment, progressive discipline encourages employees to grow and improve their skills and behavior. This approach aligns with a positive organizational culture, where feedback is intended to help employees reach their potential. When employees feel supported, they are more likely to engage with improvement plans and strive to meet expectations, benefiting both their personal development and the organization's success. By providing opportunities for positive change, progressive discipline helps maintain respectful and professional relationships between employees, HR, and management. It demonstrates that the organization values each employee's contribution and is committed to helping them succeed. This approach builds trust, showing employees that the organization prioritizes their growth and well-being and doesn't just enforce rules.

Employee Performance Improvement Plans (EPIPs)

An employee performance improvement plan (EPIP) is a formal, structured document created to help employees address and resolve performance or behavioral issues. It provides clear goals, specific timelines, and necessary resources, giving employees a road map for improvement.

The EPIP highlights areas where an employee falls short, outlines what's required to meet performance standards, and guides them in achieving success. When effectively implemented, an EPIP not only supports individual growth but also reinforces organizational values and standards, contributing to a productive and cohesive work environment.

An EPIP's main purpose is to address specific performance issues while giving the employee a structured opportunity to improve. It typically includes defined goals, measurable outcomes, a timeline, and supportive resources, all of which help the employee understand what's needed to meet job expectations. This structured approach benefits both the employee and the organization by managing performance issues fairly with clear criteria for success.

Components of an Employee Performance Improvement Plan

An EPIP starts with a detailed description of the specific performance or behavioral issues that need improvement. This section outlines what the employee is struggling with, whether it's missed deadlines, poor-quality work, or difficulty in collaboration. By articulating the problem clearly, the organization ensures that the employee understands precisely what areas need attention, creating a foundation for targeted improvement.

The EPIP sets measurable and realistic goals that the employee must meet to demonstrate improvement. These goals should be specific and relevant to the employee's role, such as increasing sales by a certain percentage or reducing errors in reporting. By setting achievable goals, the EPIP encourages the employee to make meaningful progress and enables HR to assess their development objectively.

The action plan outlines the specific steps the employee needs to take to meet their performance goals. It might include tasks like attending training, completing projects, or working closely with a mentor. This road map provides structure, and the employee knows exactly how to address their performance issues. An action plan helps transform broad improvement goals into manageable tasks, making the journey to success more attainable.

The EPIP specifies a realistic time frame for the improvement process, often over thirty, sixty, or ninety days. Milestones and deadlines are included to allow for regular check-ins, giving both the employee and management a clear schedule for assessing progress. A defined timeline keeps the process focused, providing structure and urgency that helps motivate the employee to meet their goals.

A key part of an EPIP is identifying any resources or support needed to help the employee improve. This might include access to training programs, feedback sessions, or guidance from a mentor. By offering support, the organization demonstrates a commitment to the employee's success, empowering them with the tools they need to succeed. The EPIP outlines specific methods for evaluating progress, such as performance reviews, task assessments, or feedback from colleagues. This structured evaluation allows for regular assessment and keeps the process transparent. As a result, the employee has a fair chance to meet expectations. Regular evaluations help both the employee and management stay aligned on progress and adjust the plan if needed.

If the employee does not meet the improvement goals within the specified timeline, the EPIP outlines potential consequences. These could include further disciplinary action, reassignment, or termination. By clearly stating the consequences, the organization emphasizes the importance of improvement and ensures that the employee understands the potential outcomes of failing to meet expectations. Many people perceive EPIPs as documentation to cover an employer as they prepare to terminate the employee. Ultimately, that is true if the employee doesn't meet the outlined requirements in the EPIP. So, it's up to the employee as to the true purpose of the document; they can apply the necessary changes or not, meaning they improve, or they don't and are terminated. While it's a big decision to end employment, it is truly as simple as that.

How an EPIP Can Help Employees Improve Their Performance

An EPIP provides a structured opportunity for employees to address performance issues constructively. When implemented thoughtfully, it clarifies expectations, supports development, and helps maintain positive workplace relationships. An EPIP provides employees with a clear understanding of what is expected of them and the specific areas where they need to improve. This clarity reduces ambiguity and helps employees focus on the changes required to succeed. When expectations are outlined clearly, employees can prioritize their efforts effectively, making it easier to meet the organization's standards.

The structured nature of an EPIP, with specific goals and deadlines, helps employees concentrate their efforts on prioritized tasks. By breaking down improvement goals into manageable steps, the EPIP increases the likelihood of successful outcomes. This focused approach enables employees to concentrate on one aspect at a time, making the improvement process less overwhelming and more achievable.

An EPIP also identifies resources and support mechanisms, such as training programs, mentorship, or feedback sessions, to help employees reach their goals. Providing these resources empowers employees to improve, showing them that the organization is invested in their success. This support reinforces the organization's commitment to helping employees grow, fostering a positive culture of development.

Regular check-ins and feedback sessions are integral to an EPIP, promoting open communication between the employee and their manager. These conversations allow the employee to understand their progress, address challenges, and seek guidance, fostering a supportive and transparent environment. With open communication, the employee feels supported. Meanwhile, management has an opportunity to address potential obstacles in real time.

An EPIP provides a systematic way to track the employee's progress toward meeting improvement goals. Monitoring progress allows for timely adjustments to the plan if necessary, ensuring that the employee stays on the right path. Regular monitoring also gives the employee a sense of accountability and provides HR with the data needed to make fair decisions.

Implementation: Guidelines for Creating and Implementing Effective EPIPs

Creating an EPIP requires careful planning and thoughtful execution to make it both fair and effective. Here's a step-by-step guide to implementing a successful EPIP.

1. Define the Purpose of the EPIP

Clearly outline the purpose of the EPIP and the specific performance issues it aims to address. With this objective statement, both the employee and management understand why the EPIP is necessary and what it seeks to achieve. By setting a clear purpose, the organization provides a foundation for a focused and purposeful improvement process.

2. Document Specific Performance Issues

Identify and document the exact performance or behavioral issues that need improvement, using specific examples and evidence. Avoid vague language and be explicit about the concerns, ensuring that the employee fully understands the areas requiring attention. Specificity reduces the risk of confusion and helps the employee take actionable steps.

3. Set Clear, Measurable Goals

Define specific, measurable, achievable, relevant, and time-bound (SMART) goals for improvement. For example, increasing sales by 15 percent within sixty days or completing a project with minimal errors by a set date provides clear targets. SMART goals allow for objective assessment of progress, making it easier to evaluate success at each stage.

4. Develop an Action Plan

Outline the steps required to achieve the goals, including any tasks, responsibilities, or resources needed. A detailed action plan provides a road map for the employee, giving them clear instructions on how to address their performance issues. This guidance helps them know precisely what actions to take, making the improvement process less daunting.

5. Establish a Realistic Timeline

Set a reasonable time frame for the EPIP, including milestones and deadlines for specific tasks or reviews. A well-defined timeline keeps the process manageable, allowing for regular progress assessments. Thanks to realistic deadlines, the employee has enough time to make improvements while maintaining a sense of urgency.

6. Identify Support and Resources

Determine what resources, training, or support the employee will need to succeed. Providing access to these resources demonstrates the organization's commitment to their development. When employees have the tools needed to improve, they are more likely to meet the plan's goals and feel supported.

7. Schedule Regular Check-Ins

Plan for frequent meetings to review progress, offer feedback, and adjust the plan if needed. Regular check-ins foster ongoing communication and provide opportunities for timely intervention if the employee encounters challenges. These meetings also reinforce accountability, helping the employee stay engaged in their improvement journey.

8. Provide Constructive Feedback

During check-ins, offer clear, specific, and actionable feedback. Recognize areas where the employee is excelling and highlight areas that need further improvement. Constructive feedback provides a balanced perspective, encouraging the employee to focus on progress while addressing weaknesses.

9. Document Progress and Feedback

Maintain detailed records of all meetings, feedback, and progress assessments. Documenting each step creates a clear record of the employee's performance journey and the efforts made to address concerns. This documentation is critical for transparency and supports future decision-making.

10. Evaluate Outcomes

At the end of the EPIP, assess whether the employee has met the defined goals. Reviewing performance data, supervisor feedback, and other relevant information helps determine the EPIP's success. A thorough evaluation provides insight into whether further action or support is needed.

11. Communicate Final Decisions

Clearly communicate the outcome of the EPIP, discussing whether the goals were met and outlining any remaining issues or next steps. Providing closure to the EPIP process ensures transparency and reinforces accountability.

12. Adjust and Follow Up

If the employee has shown improvement but still needs further development, consider extending the EPIP or creating a new plan. When there is additional support, the employee continues to progress. And that improvement reinforces the organization's commitment to their growth.

Appeals and Grievances: Upholding Fairness and Employee Rights

Employees' ability to appeal disciplinary actions or file grievances is a cornerstone of a fair and respectful workplace. These processes offer employees a structured way to voice concerns about disciplinary actions or workplace conditions, fostering a transparent, positive environment. Below is an exploration of employee rights, legal protections, and best practices for handling appeals and grievances.

Employee Rights

When it comes to disciplinary actions and grievances, employees have fundamental rights that uphold fairness and due process in the workplace. These rights empower employees to appeal disciplinary decisions or file grievances when they believe they have been treated unfairly. These rights also help build a workplace culture rooted in respect and accountability.

Employees generally have the right to challenge disciplinary actions they feel are unjust or improperly administered. This right to appeal provides a path for employees to seek a fair assessment of their situation, ensuring that their voice is heard. Appeals typically follow an established procedure, such as filing a written request within a specified time frame. Employees must also provide supporting documentation, like relevant evidence or witness statements, to strengthen their case. An appeals committee or higher-level management reviews the request objectively, leading them to modify, reverse, or confirm the disciplinary action. The process underscores the importance of fair hearing and representation, with some cases allowing for union or legal representation, especially in unionized settings. This system gives employees confidence that disciplinary actions are subject to fair review and promotes trust in organizational procedures.

Employees may also file grievances to address concerns related to workplace conditions, management practices, or perceived policy violations. Grievances allow employees to formally raise issues they believe violate employment standards, creating a documented trail that holds the organization accountable for addressing these concerns. Employees should follow established channels, such as reporting grievances to their supervisor or HR, and must provide detailed information, including dates, incidents, and supporting evidence. The grievance process involves an investigation by the organization to gather facts, interview relevant parties, and review documentation. Based on the findings, the organization may implement corrective actions, revise policies, or apply other remedies.

Employees have the right to confidentiality and protection from retaliation throughout the process, ensuring a safe environment for voicing concerns. Various employment laws, including anti-discrimination laws, labor laws, and workplace safety regulations, protect employees' rights to appeal and file grievances. For unionized employees, collective bargaining agreements may provide additional protections and specify procedures for filing grievances. Legal safeguards reinforce that employees have the right to challenge unfair treatment without fear of retribution. Staying informed of these laws and agreements allows HR and management to handle appeals and grievances in a compliant and respectful manner, protecting both the employee's rights and the organization's integrity.

For appeals and grievances to be effective, organizations must communicate the procedures clearly. Employees should be informed of their rights to appeal and file grievances, including the steps involved and the available protections. Documentation throughout the process provides transparency and a complete record, reinforcing that the organization is committed to a fair and systematic approach. Prompt resolution of appeals and grievances maintains a positive work environment, demonstrates respect for employee concerns, and builds trust between employees and management.

Process for Handling Appeals

Handling appeals and grievances requires a structured approach to maintain fairness, transparency, and compliance. Following established procedures helps organizations address concerns effectively and uphold employee rights. Developing and documenting clear policies for handling appeals and grievances is the foundation of a fair process. These policies should be outlined in the employee handbook or policy manual and communicated to employees during onboarding and through periodic reminders. Clearly documented procedures help employees understand how to raise concerns and reassure them that their appeals will be managed systematically.

A straightforward process for submitting appeals or grievances, such as a designated form or email address, makes it easier for employees to initiate their requests. Promptly acknowledging receipt of the appeal or grievance with a formal response reassures employees that their concerns are taken seriously. This acknowledgment should include an estimated timeline for resolution, providing employees with a sense of transparency and respect.

An initial review of the appeal or grievance helps determine whether it falls within the scope of the company's policies and procedures. This assessment also allows HR or management to clarify any details with the employee to fully understand the issue. By thoroughly assessing the situation, the organization ensures that each concern receives the appropriate attention and response.

Assigning a neutral investigator, such as a senior manager, HR representative, or external consultant, results in an unbiased review of the appeal or grievance. To avoid any conflicts of interest, this individual should have no prior involvement with the issue at hand. By designating an impartial investigator, the organization reinforces its commitment to a fair and objective process. A comprehensive investigation involves gathering all relevant information, interviewing involved parties, and reviewing documentation. Guaranteeing confidentiality during this process protects the privacy of everyone involved and guards against potential retaliation. A thorough and impartial investigation provides the necessary foundation for an informed decision, upholding the integrity of the process.

After reviewing the findings, the investigator makes an informed decision based on the collected evidence. Documenting the findings in a report that outlines the investigation process, the evidence, and the final decision provides a transparent and accountable record. This documentation is crucial for demonstrating that the process was thorough and fair.

Communicating the decision to the employee clearly and in a timely manner, along with the rationale behind it, demonstrates respect and transparency. If applicable, providing constructive feedback and discussing any actions taken as a result of the appeal or grievance reinforces the organization's commitment to fairness and supports the employee's understanding of the outcome. Once a decision is made, any necessary changes, such as policy adjustments or corrective measures, ensure that the resolution is effective. Monitoring the situation after implementation allows the organization to confirm that the resolution fully addresses the issue and prevents further problems. This follow-through strengthens the organization's credibility and helps maintain a positive work environment.

Maintaining detailed records of the appeal or grievance process—including submissions, communications, investigation reports, and decisions—supports transparency and accountability. Regularly reviewing these records helps HR identify patterns or areas where policies may need improvement, supporting continuous improvement in organizational practices. Soliciting feedback from employees and other stakeholders on the appeal and grievance process provides valuable insights into potential improvements. When this feedback is used to revise policies and procedures, the process remains fair, transparent, and responsive to employee needs.

Regular updates demonstrate the organization's commitment to providing an effective and supportive environment for raising concerns. Staying informed about relevant labor laws, anti-discrimination laws, and other regulations ensures that the organization's approach to appeals and grievances remains compliant. Consulting legal counsel, when necessary, helps address complex issues and reinforces that the organization's actions are aligned with legal standards. This attention to compliance protects both the employee's rights and the organization's interests.

Role of Managers and HR in the Disciplinary Process

Managers and HR play distinct but interconnected roles in addressing employee performance and behavior issues. Managers are on the front lines, identifying and addressing issues as they arise, while HR provides the structure, support, and oversight necessary to ensure a fair and legally compliant disciplinary process. Together, they help create a positive and productive work environment.

Manager Responsibilities

Managers are responsible for identifying performance or behavior issues early, initiating disciplinary actions when necessary, and guiding employees through improvement. Their actions directly impact employee morale, productivity, and workplace culture. Managers have a duty to monitor employee performance continuously, observing both achievements and areas needing improvement. Through regular performance evaluations, daily interactions, and feedback from other team members, managers can spot patterns that may indicate potential issues. Observing early signs—such as declining productivity, frequent absences, or noticeable behavioral changes—can prevent problems from escalating. Proactively addressing these signs also allows managers to provide support sooner, fostering an environment where issues are addressed constructively. Additionally, encouraging open communication creates a space where employees feel comfortable discussing challenges, which can help managers understand and address issues before they worsen.

When issues arise, it's essential for managers to follow the organization's disciplinary policies precisely. Adhering to established guidelines ensures consistency, protecting both the organization and the employee. Managers must gather all relevant evidence to support any disciplinary action, which includes performance records, witness statements, or relevant communication. Documenting these findings creates a transparent record and helps maintain objectivity. Managers must clearly explain the expectations that weren't met and the potential consequences, issuing warnings as appropriate. Starting with verbal or written warnings demonstrates a fair approach, giving the employee a chance to correct their actions. By handling the disciplinary process with objectivity and fairness, managers reinforce trust and maintain a respectful workplace.

Once disciplinary actions are initiated, managers must continue to support the employee, providing guidance on improving their performance or behavior. Offering resources, such as training, coaching, or mentoring, shows the employee that the organization is invested in their growth. Managers should provide regular, constructive feedback, recognizing improvements while pointing out remaining challenges. Open lines of communication allow employees to ask questions and seek clarity, which can reduce anxiety and help them feel supported. If a performance improvement plan (EPIP) is necessary, managers work collaboratively with the employee to set clear goals and establish a road map for improvement. Monitoring progress through check-ins demonstrates commitment to the employee's success.

Managers must handle disciplinary matters privately, respecting the employee's confidentiality and dignity. Supporting employees' professional development throughout the process encourages a positive outlook and can lead to lasting improvement.

HR Responsibilities

The HR department plays a vital role in overseeing the disciplinary process, ensuring legal compliance, and supporting managers and employees. HR helps establish fair policies, provides training, and offers guidance throughout the disciplinary process. HR is responsible for developing, maintaining, and communicating company policies related to employee discipline. These policies must align with legal standards and best practices, resulting in fairness and consistency.

HR also monitors compliance during disciplinary actions, confirming that policies are followed, documentation is complete, and employees' rights are protected. HR stays updated on relevant labor laws and industry regulations, including anti-discrimination, privacy, and workplace safety standards—so that disciplinary actions comply with legal requirements. In complex cases, HR may consult with legal professionals to make sure actions are legally sound, protecting the organization from potential liability and safeguarding employee rights.

HR is essential in training managers on how to handle disciplinary issues effectively and fairly, covering topics like documentation, communication, and adherence to company policies. This training helps managers handle situations objectively and confidently. HR also assists managers in decision-making by providing guidance on appropriate disciplinary actions, procedures, and consequences. Reviewing disciplinary documentation guarantees accuracy, completeness, and compliance, reinforcing the consistency of the process. In cases of disputes, HR acts as a mediator, keeping the disciplinary process constructive and focused on resolving issues while upholding fairness.

HR is a resource for employees during the disciplinary process, addressing concerns and grievances related to disciplinary actions. HR ensures that employees understand their rights and have access to the grievance process if needed. They verify that disciplinary actions are proportionate, and employees are treated fairly, allowing employees to respond to allegations.

HR may also offer counseling, employee assistance programs, or career development opportunities to help affected employees. Additionally, HR monitors the impact of disciplinary actions on employee morale, making sure that appropriate support is in place to maintain a positive work environment. HR is responsible for following established procedures and timelines, overseeing warnings and investigations, and implementing EPIPs.

HR reviews the outcomes of disciplinary actions for fairness and alignment with company policies while also monitoring whether issues have been resolved effectively. It also maintains detailed records of each disciplinary action, including incident documentation, communications, and outcomes, which are essential for legal compliance and future reference. This oversight means that the disciplinary process is handled fairly, consistently, and in a way that supports the organization's values.

Together, managers and HR form a cohesive team that upholds the integrity of the disciplinary process, creating a fair and respectful work environment. Managers identify and address issues while providing support and feedback, and HR monitors legal compliance, offers guidance, and mediates disputes. By working in tandem, managers and HR can address performance and behavior issues effectively, contributing to a positive, productive workplace culture.

Training for Managers: Ensuring Effective Disciplinary Practices, Conflict Resolution, and Productive Communication Skills

Training managers in disciplinary practices, conflict resolution, and communication is essential to creating a supportive, consistent, and legally compliant workplace. These skills empower managers to address issues fairly, build trust with their teams, and reduce conflicts.

Effective Disciplinary Practices

Training in disciplinary practices provides managers with the skills needed to handle employee issues consistently and fairly. Consistency is crucial in maintaining trust within the team, as employees are more likely to perceive fairness when managers apply disciplinary actions without favoritism or bias. Well-trained managers are equipped to handle disciplinary issues without letting personal preferences influence their decisions, helping create a respectful and professional environment. Additionally, training ensures that managers understand legal implications, including labor laws, anti-discrimination regulations, and internal company policies, which reduces the risk of costly disputes or lawsuits.

Equipped with proper documentation skills, managers can record each step of the process accurately, protecting both the organization and the employee. By understanding how to document effectively, managers provide a reliable record that supports fair and transparent discipline.

Conflict Resolution

Conflict resolution training prepares managers to handle workplace conflicts before they escalate, promoting a harmonious work environment. Managers learn techniques for de-escalating tense situations so that issues are addressed quickly and constructively. These skills enable managers to identify underlying problems and negotiate solutions, fostering a positive relationship with employees.

Skilled conflict resolution builds trust between managers and employees by showing that management is committed to fair and open communication. With training, managers are better equipped to tackle conflicts with a problem-solving approach, helping employees feel heard and respected. The ability to address issues constructively helps maintain team cohesion and improves morale.

Communication Skills

Effective communication is at the heart of successful management. Training in communication skills enables managers to convey information clearly and transparently, which helps employees understand expectations, receive constructive feedback, and navigate disciplinary actions with confidence. Clear communication reduces the risk of misunderstandings that can cause unnecessary stress or conflict, especially during disciplinary or feedback sessions.

Managers also learn how to communicate with empathy, creating a supportive environment that addresses both employee needs and organizational goals. Empathetic communication fosters employee engagement and satisfaction, as it makes employees feel valued and respected. When managers can communicate effectively, employees are more likely to feel motivated and supported in their roles.

Benefits of Training Managers

Well-trained managers are more adept at handling disciplinary actions and conflicts in a way that fosters positive relationships. This training helps managers navigate challenging situations without damaging employee morale, which is crucial for maintaining a healthy work environment. By managing issues effectively, managers build trust, leading to stronger, healthier relationships with their teams.

Managers who are skilled in disciplinary practices and conflict resolution contribute to a more productive and motivated team. Employees feel more secure and engaged when they know that managers will address issues fairly and supportively. When employees perceive management as fair and supportive, they are more likely to put forth their best efforts, improving overall team performance and productivity.

Proactive management training reduces turnover and absenteeism by equipping managers to address issues before they escalate. Employees are more likely to remain with a company when they feel that their concerns are addressed, and they work in a supportive environment. When managers understand how to provide support effectively, employees feel valued, which leads to greater job satisfaction and commitment to the organization.

Employee Awareness: Educating Employees About Disciplinary Policies and Procedures

Educating employees about disciplinary policies ensures a transparent and fair work environment where employees understand what is expected of them and the consequences of not meeting those expectations. This knowledge empowers employees to align their behavior with company standards and reduces misunderstandings.

Clear knowledge of disciplinary policies helps employees understand what is expected regarding behavior and performance, reducing ambiguity. When employees know the rules, they can better align their actions with organizational standards, promoting a positive work culture. Awareness of potential consequences also helps employees understand the importance of adhering to company rules, reducing the likelihood of policy violations. Educating employees about these policies creates a proactive environment where they are more likely to take ownership of their actions and make informed decisions that align with company expectations.

Transparency about disciplinary policies fosters a sense of fairness and builds trust between employees and management. Employees who understand the disciplinary process are more likely to view it as fair, as they know how decisions are made and they understand the criteria for disciplinary actions. This clarity prevents employees from feeling blindsided if disciplinary measures are needed. Informed employees are less likely to interpret actions as arbitrary or unfair, which reduces tensions and creates a more harmonious workplace.

Educated employees are less likely to dispute disciplinary actions due to misunderstandings or lack of awareness. Knowing the procedures and the reasons behind disciplinary decisions helps mitigate conflicts and grievances, as employees recognize the fairness of the process. Awareness of disciplinary policies also encourages self-management, as employees who understand the consequences of their actions are more likely to proactively adhere to company policies. This self-regulation fosters a culture of responsibility and reduces the need for frequent interventions.

Transparency about disciplinary policies helps build trust between employees and management, fostering a positive workplace culture. When employees feel informed and included in the process, they are more likely to trust organizational decisions. This trust encourages employees to be accountable, as they understand the importance of meeting expectations. Educating employees about policies reinforces personal responsibility, which contributes to a culture where everyone strives to meet high standards. Including disciplinary policies in onboarding programs ensures that new hires understand expectations and procedures from the start, supporting a smooth integration into the organization. This proactive approach helps new employees understand their responsibilities and align with organizational values early on, reducing the risk of policy violations. By setting clear expectations from the beginning, onboarding programs lay a strong foundation for success and help new hires feel confident and informed in their roles.

Educating employees about disciplinary procedures helps protect the organization from potential legal disputes. Employees who understand their rights and the procedures are less likely to claim unfair treatment, as they recognize that the organization's actions align with established policies. Clear communication also promotes ethical behavior by setting guidelines for acceptable conduct. Employees who are aware of the standards and potential consequences are more likely to act responsibly and uphold company values.

Understanding disciplinary policies empowers employees to take proactive steps to avoid violations and seek clarification if needed, which boosts their engagement. Empowered employees feel more confident and motivated to contribute positively to the organization, leading to higher morale.

Additionally, reducing anxiety by helping employees understand the disciplinary process creates a more supportive environment. Employees who feel secure in their roles are more likely to be productive and engaged, contributing to a positive work culture. Educating employees about disciplinary policies and procedures is essential for fostering a fair, transparent, and positive work environment. It ensures that employees understand expectations, encourages compliance, and reduces the likelihood of conflicts or legal issues.

Preventive Measures: Proactive Management to Prevent Disciplinary Issues

Proactive management practices are essential in preventing disciplinary issues and maintaining a constructive work environment. By offering regular feedback, providing effective coaching, and fostering a supportive culture, managers can prevent performance concerns from escalating. These strategies not only reduce the need for disciplinary actions but also enhance employee engagement, motivation, and long-term organizational success.

Regular feedback is a foundational aspect of proactive management, allowing employees to continuously understand their strengths and areas for improvement. By providing ongoing feedback, managers can address concerns before they become significant issues, preventing small challenges from escalating into more serious problems. This continuous improvement approach also helps employees stay aligned with organizational goals, reinforcing that feedback is a supportive tool rather than punitive.

Frequent and constructive feedback reduces misunderstandings, as employees have a clear sense of expectations and are better equipped to adjust their performance. Coaching empowers employees by focusing on developing the skills and competencies needed to excel in their roles. Through targeted support and training, managers help employees overcome specific challenges and build on their strengths, reducing the likelihood of performance issues requiring formal discipline. Effective coaching instills confidence, as employees feel supported in navigating workplace demands. When employees have the tools to succeed, they are more likely to engage in positive behaviors, fostering a proactive culture that minimizes the need for disciplinary actions.

A positive work environment is essential for fostering employee engagement and reducing the potential for disciplinary issues. Engaged employees are more motivated and committed to organizational goals, leading to better performance and fewer behavioral problems. An open and supportive atmosphere also encourages employees to communicate about challenges, allowing managers to address issues early.

When employees feel safe and valued, they are more likely to seek guidance, which enables managers to provide support before issues escalate, maintaining a harmonious and productive workplace. Proactive management includes setting clear expectations around roles, responsibilities, and standards. When employees understand what is required of them, they are more likely to meet expectations and avoid behaviors that might lead to disciplinary actions. Clearly communicating company policies and procedures further reinforces these expectations, promoting a culture of accountability. Transparency helps prevent violations, as employees have a solid understanding of the organization's rules and the consequences of not meeting them.

Positive reinforcement through recognition and rewards encourages employees to continue exhibiting desirable behaviors. By celebrating successes, managers can reinforce the importance of alignment with organizational values, motivating employees to perform well and avoid negative behaviors. Regular recognition boosts morale and fosters a supportive environment where employees feel appreciated and motivated to contribute positively. High morale and motivation help prevent performance problems and behavior issues, leading to a more harmonious work environment.

Proactive managers address potential issues early, which prevents them from escalating into more serious problems. By recognizing and addressing minor concerns promptly, managers can guide employees toward improvement without resorting to disciplinary measures. Taking a supportive approach to early intervention demonstrates a commitment to employee development and well-being, building trust and encouraging employees to seek assistance when needed. This approach fosters a culture where employees feel supported and are less likely to engage in behaviors requiring formal discipline.

Training and development opportunities equip employees with the skills and knowledge needed to meet performance expectations. Training enables employees to stay updated on best practices, reducing the likelihood of performance issues. Additionally, investing in employees' career growth signals the organization's commitment to their success, fostering a positive environment. Employees who see opportunities for advancement are more engaged and motivated, making them less likely to exhibit behaviors that could lead to disciplinary problems.

Clear Policies: The Need for Well-Communicated Policies and Expectations

Clear, well-communicated policies regarding behavior and performance are essential for fairness, consistency, and alignment with organizational goals. These policies provide a road map for employee conduct, promote a transparent workplace culture, and protect the organization from legal risks. Clear policies establish uniform standards that ensure that all employees are held to the same expectations. This consistency prevents perceptions of favoritism and helps managers apply disciplinary actions fairly. When employees know that everyone is subject to the same rules, they feel more secure in the fairness of the organization's practices. Equitable treatment, reinforced by clearly communicated policies, helps maintain trust and boosts morale, as employees understand the rules and potential consequences of their actions. Clearly defined policies eliminate ambiguity, helping employees understand what is required regarding behavior and performance.

When expectations are articulated well, employees are more likely to adhere to company standards, as there's little room for confusion about their responsibilities. This clarity also prevents misunderstandings that can lead to disciplinary problems, as employees are aware of both the rules and the consequences of noncompliance. Clear communication of expectations supports a culture of accountability and proactive engagement.

Well-defined policies provide employees with clear guidelines on acceptable behavior and performance expectations, making it easier to hold employees accountable for their actions. Managers can measure employee performance objectively against these standards, ensuring that feedback is based on specific criteria rather than subjective assessments. This objectivity in evaluations and disciplinary actions supports fair treatment and helps employees understand how their performance aligns with organizational expectations. Clear policies encourage open dialogue between employees and management because employees feel more comfortable seeking clarification when they understand the rules. This transparency also sets the stage for constructive feedback, as employees can align their performance with organizational goals proactively.

Open communication channels allow employees to feel informed and empowered, contributing to a work environment where expectations are clear, and feedback is welcomed. When employees know what is expected and understand the consequences of not meeting those expectations, it reduces the potential for misunderstandings or conflict. This clarity fosters a harmonious work environment where employees feel supported and are less likely to experience confusion about their roles. A clear understanding of roles and responsibilities also enhances engagement and motivation, as employees feel confident in their contributions and know how their work aligns with organizational goals.

Well-communicated policies are vital for the successful onboarding of new employees. Including policies in the onboarding process helps new hires understand the organization's standards and their responsibilities from the beginning. This early introduction to expectations helps them integrate smoothly into the company culture. Ongoing training also reinforces policies and expectations, which keeps employees informed and aligned with evolving goals and standards.

Clear policies enable the organization to comply with legal and regulatory requirements, reducing the risk of legal issues related to employee behavior and performance. Well-defined policies also provide a foundation for documenting disciplinary actions and performance evaluations, which is essential for protecting the organization in legal disputes. When employees understand the policies and their rights, they are less likely to claim unfair treatment, further reducing legal risks.

Well-communicated expectations align individual performance with organizational goals, as employees understand how their work impacts the company's overall success. This alignment improves productivity, as employees are motivated to meet performance standards. Clear policies also streamline decision-making, reducing the need for frequent oversight, which enhances operational efficiency and allows managers to focus on strategic activities.

Cultural Considerations: Embracing Diversity and Inclusion in Disciplinary Practices

In a diverse workplace, cultural differences can significantly influence how disciplinary actions are perceived and received. Managers and HR professionals must adopt culturally sensitive approaches that respect these differences, fostering an inclusive work environment where all employees feel understood and valued.

Each culture has unique norms and values that influence perceptions of authority, communication styles, and conflict resolution. For instance, in some cultures, maintaining harmony is paramount, and indirect communication is preferred to avoid confrontation. In contrast, other cultures value direct feedback and individual accountability, viewing discipline as a straightforward way to address issues. Recognizing these differences helps managers tailor their approach to disciplinary actions, ensuring that cultural norms are respected.

Lastly, attitudes toward authority vary widely, with some cultures holding strong respect for hierarchical structures, while others may emphasize egalitarian values, which may affect how discipline is perceived. A nuanced understanding of these factors can guide managers to apply discipline in ways that align with employees' cultural expectations.

Cultural sensitivities also shape how disciplinary actions are perceived. For example, while public reprimands might be acceptable and even expected in some cultures, they can be perceived as humiliating or overly harsh in others. Employees from different backgrounds may also interpret disciplinary actions differently. Some might see them as constructive feedback and opportunities for growth, while others could perceive them as personal criticisms or attacks. Furthermore, cultural expectations regarding support during the disciplinary process can vary; some employees may expect a more empathetic and supportive approach, while others might anticipate a straightforward, results-oriented response. Understanding these perceptions allows managers to implement respectful disciplinary actions, reducing the risk of misunderstandings and negative reactions. Implementing culturally sensitive disciplinary practices shows respect for employees' diverse backgrounds and promotes inclusivity. This not only helps build trust but also creates a positive work environment where employees from all cultures feel valued.

Tailoring communication styles to fit cultural norms ensures that feedback is understood as intended, reducing the chances of misinterpretation and improving the effectiveness of the disciplinary process. Furthermore, a culturally sensitive approach creates fairness and equity by acknowledging that different backgrounds may influence how discipline is perceived. Doing so helps avoid unintended biases. This fairness reinforces a sense of justice in the organization, supporting an inclusive culture where diverse perspectives are respected.

To promote cultural sensitivity in disciplinary practices, organizations should provide cultural awareness training for managers and HR personnel, enabling them to understand how cultural differences impact expectations and perceptions. Customized communication approaches, such as indirect feedback where appropriate, can help align disciplinary actions with cultural norms. Inclusive policies that consider cultural differences offer a framework for addressing diverse needs and make policies accessible to all employees. Establishing feedback mechanisms allows employees to voice concerns or suggest improvements, providing insights into how disciplinary practices can be more culturally inclusive. Consulting with cultural experts or advisors can also enhance the effectiveness of disciplinary actions, as they bring valuable knowledge on culturally appropriate practices.

Global Considerations: Adapting Disciplinary Practices for a Global Workforce

In a globalized workforce, disciplinary practices must be adaptable to respect cultural differences and meet the requirements of varying legal contexts. A flexible, regionally tailored approach ensures that disciplinary actions are effective, compliant, and culturally appropriate across different locations. Cultural norms around authority, communication, and conflict resolution vary significantly across regions. For example, in cultures with strong hierarchical structures, employees may view disciplinary actions as necessary for maintaining order, while in more egalitarian cultures, top-down directives might be met with resistance. Understanding these cultural dynamics is essential for delivering disciplinary actions in ways that resonate with local employees.

Communication styles also play a role; some cultures prefer a nuanced approach to feedback, valuing subtlety, while others expect direct, clear communication. Recognizing cultural attitudes toward discipline allows managers to frame disciplinary actions as constructive opportunities for growth rather than criticisms, fostering a supportive global work culture.

Labor laws and regulations vary widely across countries, affecting the structure and procedures of disciplinary actions. For instance, certain jurisdictions have strict rules on documentation, procedural fairness, and employee rights, while others may have more lenient requirements. Some countries provide employees with robust rights to appeal disciplinary actions, whereas others offer limited legal recourse. Understanding these legal differences is essential as HR navigates local compliance requirements and avoids potential legal disputes.

Termination procedures also differ, with some countries mandating extensive documentation and severance packages, while others allow for more streamlined processes. Adapting disciplinary actions to local legal contexts guarantees that the organization operates within regulatory boundaries and respects employees' rights. To make disciplinary actions effective and compliant across different regions, organizations should stay informed about local labor laws and regulations, which may impact requirements for documentation, notice periods, and employee rights. Cultural sensitivity training equips managers with the skills to handle disciplinary actions in ways that respect cultural differences. As a result, practices are both effective and respectful.

Customizing communication styles to align with cultural preferences—such as using indirect feedback where needed—helps disciplinary messages resonate with employees. Local legal experts can provide guidance on navigating complex employment laws so that practices are legally sound. Implementing global consistency with local flexibility allows organizations to maintain a unified framework while adapting to cultural and legal nuances. Additionally, seeking feedback from local teams helps organizations understand how disciplinary practices are perceived and enables adjustments for greater relevance.

Case Studies and Best Practices: Learning from Organizational Approaches to Discipline

Organizations approach disciplinary practices in diverse ways to align with their values, industry requirements, and workforce needs. Through case studies of companies like Google, Walmart, Uber, Patagonia, and Amazon, we see the importance of balancing structure, flexibility, cultural sensitivity, and transparency in handling discipline. These examples highlight successful strategies and lessons learned, illustrating the impact of tailored disciplinary practices.

Case Study: Google

Background: Google, widely recognized for its open and inclusive work culture, faced challenges in aligning disciplinary practices with its value of transparency and employee support.

Disciplinary Approach:

- **Open Dialogue**: Google fosters an environment where employees are encouraged to discuss issues openly and provide feedback, which helps address potential disciplinary issues early. This approach to open communication allows managers and employees to resolve minor issues collaboratively, often preventing the need for formal disciplinary actions.
- **Employee Support**: Google also integrates support systems, including counseling and mentorship, to help employees meet performance expectations. This emphasis on development makes employees feel valued and reinforces the organization's commitment to improvement over punishment.

Successes:

- **Prevention of Escalation**: By creating a culture of open communication, Google is often able to resolve problems informally, reducing the frequency of severe disciplinary actions.
- **Employee Retention**: The supportive approach promotes high employee satisfaction and loyalty, contributing to lower turnover and a highly engaged workforce.

Lessons Learned:

- **Clarity and Documentation**: While Google's open culture is effective, there were instances when the lack of formal documentation led to misunderstandings. Clear documentation is necessary to avoid perceptions of unfairness and ensure consistency in disciplinary actions.

- **Balancing Openness with Structure**: Google recognized the need to balance its open culture with structured disciplinary processes. Integrating formal procedures provides a framework that aligns with both organizational values and the need for consistency.

Case Study: Walmart

Background: As a global retail leader with a diverse workforce, Walmart requires consistent and standardized disciplinary processes to manage its vast employee base effectively.

Disciplinary Approach:

- **Standardized Procedures**: Because Walmart implements uniform disciplinary procedures across its numerous locations, employees receive consistent treatment. From verbal and written warnings to termination protocols, these structured steps help uphold fairness across regions.
- **Training for Managers**: Walmart invests in training managers on handling disciplinary actions in a fair, policy-compliant manner, equipping them to manage issues with confidence and sensitivity.

Successes:

- **Consistency**: Standardized procedures allow Walmart to maintain fairness and equity across all locations, creating a unified approach to discipline.

- **Improved Manager Competency**: Training prepares managers to address disciplinary matters, improving their ability to handle sensitive issues effectively.

Lessons Learned:

- **Local Adaptation**: Walmart found that while standardization was effective, some degree of flexibility was needed to respect regional and cultural differences.
- **Employee Feedback**: Recognizing the value of employee feedback, Walmart identified the need to incorporate input from employees in refining its disciplinary process, ensuring that it remains fair and responsive to workforce needs.

Case Study: Uber

Background: Uber faced significant public scrutiny over its handling of harassment and discrimination complaints, prompting a major overhaul of its disciplinary practices.

Disciplinary Approach:

- **Overhaul of Practices**: In response to these challenges, Uber redefined its disciplinary framework, introducing clear reporting mechanisms, thorough investigations, and revised protocols for handling misconduct.
- **External Oversight**: Uber engaged external consultants to review and improve its practices to help them meet ethical standards and address past shortcomings.

Successes:

- **Enhanced Transparency**: The overhaul increased transparency. Employees became more confident in reporting issues, knowing that the disciplinary process was clear and equitable.
- **Improved Practices**: External expertise helped Uber establish best practices, aligning its disciplinary policies with industry standards and legal requirements.

Lessons Learned:

- **Importance of External Review**: Uber's case underscored the value of external assessments in identifying and rectifying gaps in disciplinary practices.
- **Cultural Shifts**: Uber recognized the need to foster a positive culture that supports ethical behavior, understanding that a supportive culture is integral to effective discipline.

Case Study: Patagonia

Background: Patagonia, known for its commitment to social and environmental responsibility, aimed to integrate disciplinary practices that aligned with its positive organizational culture.

Disciplinary Approach:

- **Empowerment and Responsibility**: Disciplinary actions were framed as opportunities for personal growth, with employees encouraged to take responsibility for their actions.
- **Holistic Approach**: Patagonia integrated disciplinary actions with broader development programs, such as coaching and ongoing feedback, which emphasized employee growth rather than punishment.

Successes:

- **Positive Culture**: This approach reinforced Patagonia's supportive culture, contributing to high employee engagement and satisfaction.
- **Effective Resolution**: Many issues were resolved through development-focused feedback, reducing the need for formal discipline.

Lessons Learned:

- **Need for Clear Boundaries**: While empowering employees was beneficial, Patagonia realized the necessity for formal procedures to address serious issues, ensuring that expectations were clear.
- **Balancing Development with Discipline**: Patagonia learned that combining development opportunities with a clear disciplinary framework is essential for sustaining an effective and orderly workplace.

Case Study: Amazon

Background: Known for its fast-paced, high-performance culture, Amazon required a disciplinary system that would sustain productivity without diminishing employee morale.

Disciplinary Approach:

- **Data-Driven Decisions**: Amazon uses performance data to identify and address issues, allowing for data-backed disciplinary actions that focus on specific performance metrics.
- **Structured Escalation**: Amazon's structured approach to discipline includes clear steps, from verbal warnings to termination, providing transparency and consistency.

Successes:

- **Efficient Resolution**: The data-driven approach allows Amazon to quickly identify and address performance issues, helping maintain productivity.
- **Clear Process**: Structured escalation provides clarity, allowing employees to understand the disciplinary process and expectations at each stage.

Lessons Learned:

- **Human Element**: While data is useful, Amazon recognized the need for empathy and balance to maintain morale, showing employees that disciplinary actions consider the human impact.
- **Communication**: Amazon found that clear, ongoing communication throughout the disciplinary process was crucial, as it provided employees with context and opportunities to address concerns.

Best Practices: Managing Disciplinary Actions with Fairness and Effectiveness

Managing disciplinary actions requires a structured, fair, and consistent approach to ensure that all employees feel respected and that the organization maintains a positive, compliant, and productive work environment. By following these best practices, HR and management can handle disciplinary issues effectively while reinforcing organizational values and integrity.

Establish Clear Policies and Procedures

Clear, documented policies provide a foundation for consistent and fair disciplinary practices. Disciplinary procedures should be included in the employee handbook and accessible to all employees. When there is a well-defined disciplinary process, everyone understands the expectations and possible consequences for noncompliance. Applying these procedures consistently across the workforce helps avoid perceptions of favoritism so that all employees feel they are treated fairly. Regular communication, especially during onboarding and periodic training, reinforces these standards, keeping policies top of mind and fostering a culture of accountability.

Provide Clear Expectations

Setting clear expectations about job performance and behavior is essential in helping employees understand what is required of them. Detailed job descriptions and specific performance standards offer employees a clear view of their responsibilities, reducing ambiguity and aligning their actions with company goals. Measurable standards allow both employees and managers to objectively assess performance, making it easier to recognize when improvement is needed. By telling employees exactly what is expected, organizations empower them to succeed and reduce the likelihood of misunderstandings or disciplinary issues.

Maintain Detailed Documentation

Thorough documentation of disciplinary actions is essential for transparency, fairness, and legal compliance. Each step, from verbal warnings to formal reprimands, should be recorded, including details of the infraction, the actions taken, and any agreed follow-ups. This recordkeeping helps maintain consistency and provides a clear trail of events that can be referenced if further action is necessary. Documentation also protects the organization by demonstrating that each action was handled objectively and in accordance with established policies, which is crucial if disputes arise.

Conduct Fair Investigations

A fair investigation is the cornerstone of an effective disciplinary process. Investigations should be thorough, gathering relevant evidence, such as witness statements, performance data, and documentation related to the issue. Impartiality is key, as investigations must be conducted without bias or assumptions, ensuring that findings are based solely on facts. A fair investigation builds trust in the disciplinary process, reinforcing that the organization is committed to treating employees with respect and objectivity.

Implement Progressive Discipline

Progressive discipline provides a structured approach to handling disciplinary issues, giving employees opportunities to improve before facing severe consequences. This approach typically includes verbal warnings, written warnings, and suspension, with termination as a last resort. By outlining clear steps for improvement and providing resources, such as training or mentorship, progressive discipline helps employees understand that the organization is invested in their development. This approach also emphasizes the importance of constructive feedback, which encourages positive changes in behavior and performance.

Focus on Fairness and Transparency

Transparency is critical in disciplinary actions, as it helps employees understand why decisions are made and the steps involved. Communicating the reasons for disciplinary actions and involving the employee by allowing them to share their side of the story fosters a sense of respect and fairness. When employees feel included in the process, they are more likely to view disciplinary actions as constructive and fair, which supports a positive organizational culture and reinforces trust between management and staff.

Use Constructive Feedback

Constructive feedback provides specific, actionable guidance to help employees improve. Feedback should clearly outline what went wrong and what steps the employee can take to meet expectations. Offering support and guidance—such as access to resources or additional training—reinforces the organization's commitment to helping employees succeed. Constructive feedback not only helps correct behavior but also encourages personal and professional growth, enhancing employee morale and engagement.

Ensure Legal Compliance

Legal compliance is a critical component of the disciplinary process, as it protects the organization from potential legal liabilities. Organizations must adhere to relevant labor laws, anti-discrimination regulations, and workplace safety standards. Consulting legal counsel to review policies and procedures helps keep the organization compliant and prepares it to handle complex issues. By prioritizing legal compliance, organizations reinforce their commitment to fair treatment and protect themselves against potential disputes.

Train Managers and Supervisors

Training managers on effective disciplinary practices, conflict resolution, and communication skills is essential for consistency and fairness. Well-trained managers are better equipped to address issues constructively and apply disciplinary procedures uniformly across the organization. When managers consistently apply policies, they reinforce a sense of fairness and make sure that employees know what to expect. Training also helps managers build strong, respectful relationships with their teams.

Communicate Disciplinary Actions Effectively

Respectful communication is vital when addressing disciplinary actions. Managers should explain the nature of the disciplinary action, the reasons behind it, and any required follow-up actions in a clear, professional, and empathetic manner. Respectful communication helps employees feel valued, even in challenging situations, which can prevent resentment and foster a positive attitude toward improvement. This approach also ensures that employees fully understand expectations and makes it easier for them to take corrective action.

Offer Appeals and Grievances Processes

Providing a clear process for appeals and grievances demonstrates the organization's commitment to fairness. Employees should be informed of their right to appeal disciplinary actions or raise grievances if they believe a decision was unfair. A fair and transparent review process, potentially involving a neutral third party, reinforces trust in the organization. With this approach, all employees feel heard, and disciplinary actions are just and unbiased.

Monitor and Review

Regularly reviewing disciplinary policies and practices ensures that they remain relevant, effective, and aligned with current best practices. Gathering feedback from employees and managers offers valuable insights into areas where the process could be improved while also fostering transparency. Regular reviews help the organization adapt to changes in laws or workplace dynamics, supporting continuous improvement in the disciplinary process.

Foster a Positive Work Environment

A positive work environment can prevent many issues that lead to disciplinary actions. Proactive measures, like regular feedback, coaching, and team-building activities, help address potential issues before they escalate. Building a supportive culture where employees feel valued and motivated to meet performance expectations reduces the likelihood of disciplinary problems. When employees feel supported and recognized, they are more engaged, productive, and committed to the organization's success.

Evaluating and Improving Disciplinary Systems: Ensuring Fairness, Compliance, and Effectiveness

Evaluating the effectiveness of disciplinary systems is essential for maintaining a fair, compliant, and efficient process. By using employee feedback, performance metrics, and compliance audits, organizations can identify areas for improvement and refine their disciplinary practices to align with both legal standards and organizational goals. Gathering employee feedback provides insights into how the disciplinary system is perceived and experienced. Surveys, polls, and focus groups offer a mix of quantitative and qualitative data, helping HR understand areas where the system is effective or where improvements are needed. Anonymous feedback channels encourage honest input, allowing employees to express concerns or suggestions without fear of retaliation. This feedback helps the organization build a disciplinary process that employees view as fair and transparent.

Performance metrics, such as resolution times, recurrence rates, and compliance with corrective actions, offer a quantitative measure of the system's effectiveness. Shorter resolution times suggest a more efficient process, while low recurrence rates indicate that disciplinary actions address root causes effectively. Monitoring turnover rates among disciplined employees can reveal the system's impact on retention, helping HR refine processes to retain talent while addressing behavioral issues.

Regular internal audits ensure that disciplinary actions are administered consistently and in accordance with policies and legal standards:

- Policy reviews and legal compliance checks with experts help organizations stay updated on current regulations, reducing the risk of legal disputes.
- Compliance audits support a disciplined, structured approach that protects both the organization and employees.
- Evaluating outcomes provides insights into the effectiveness of disciplinary actions in achieving behavior changes.
- Assessing the success rates of performance improvement plans and other corrective measures reveals which actions are most effective.
- Analyzing the broader impact of disciplinary actions on team morale helps the system support both individual and organizational goals.

Managers' insights provide practical perspectives on the disciplinary system's strengths and weaknesses. Evaluating the effectiveness of training programs for managers ensures that they are equipped to handle disciplinary issues fairly. Furthermore, training programs can be adjusted based on manager feedback to help HR address gaps and strengthen the support system for both managers and employees. Regular reviews of disciplinary records result in thorough and consistent documentation, providing a reliable reference for future decisions.

By implementing the additional following evaluation methods, organizations can refine their disciplinary systems, remaining fair, efficient, and aligned with legal standards and organizational goals:

- Trend analysis helps HR identify recurring issues, offering insights into systemic concerns that may require changes to policies or procedures.
- Comparing disciplinary practices with industry standards helps organizations stay competitive and adopt best practices.
- External reviews by consultants or industry experts provide an objective assessment, ensuring that the system aligns with both organizational and industry expectations.
- Post-discipline surveys allow organizations to assess employee satisfaction with the process. Including questions about the disciplinary system in broader satisfaction surveys helps HR gauge its overall impact on workplace morale, providing insights into improvements that support a positive organizational culture.
- When an organization stays updated on legal changes, the disciplinary system remains compliant with employment laws. Engaging legal professionals to review the system regularly ensures adherence to current standards, reducing the risk of legal challenges.
- Establishing a continuous feedback loop allows organizations to refine their disciplinary systems based on ongoing insights.
- Developing action plans to address identified weaknesses guarantees that the system evolves to meet the changing needs of both the workforce and legal landscape, maintaining fairness and effectiveness.

Strategies for Evolving Disciplinary Policies and Procedures

To create effective, fair, and legally compliant disciplinary policies, organizations must adopt a continuous improvement approach. This involves regularly evaluating policies, gathering feedback, adapting to regulatory changes, and implementing data-driven adjustments. By creating a responsive and dynamic system, organizations can manage disciplinary actions with integrity and maintain a positive workplace culture.

Perform Regular Policy Reviews

Scheduled policy reviews are essential for maintaining up-to-date and relevant disciplinary practices. Organizations should establish a regular review schedule, such as annual or biannual reviews, to assess and refine their disciplinary policies and procedures. These reviews allow HR and management to consider evolving organizational needs, legal requirements, and industry trends. During these reviews, feedback from employees, managers, and HR staff should be carefully considered to identify areas for improvement. Additionally, benchmarking against industry standards keeps policies in line with best practices, keeping the organization competitive and compliant. A structured review process strengthens the disciplinary system and reinforces the organization's commitment to fairness and transparency.

Incorporate Feedback Mechanisms

Effective disciplinary systems incorporate feedback from employees and managers to create fair, clear, and well-understood policies. Organizations can gather insights through surveys and polls that assess employees' perceptions of the disciplinary process and identify areas where adjustments may be needed. Focus groups offer deeper insights by allowing employees and managers to discuss their experiences and provide specific suggestions. To encourage open feedback, anonymous channels can be established, enabling employees to express their opinions without fear of repercussions. This feedback is invaluable for HR and management, offering a clear view of how disciplinary policies are perceived and how they can be improved to foster a fair and inclusive workplace.

Adapt to Legal and Regulatory Changes

Disciplinary policies must adapt to changes in employment laws and regulations to remain compliant and effective. HR departments should stay informed of legal updates by subscribing to newsletters, joining industry associations, and attending relevant seminars. Regular consultations with legal experts ensure that policies align with current regulations, reducing the risk of legal disputes. When changes to laws occur, HR should review policies and adjust procedures accordingly, communicating these updates to employees and managers. This proactive approach demonstrates the organization's commitment to legal compliance, protecting both the company and its workforce.

Analyze Disciplinary Data

Data analysis plays a critical role in understanding the effectiveness of disciplinary policies and identifying areas for improvement. Regularly reviewing data on disciplinary actions, including trends, outcomes, and recurrence rates, provides insights into the system's strengths and weaknesses. By identifying patterns, such as repeated infractions in a specific department or common issues among employees, HR can pinpoint areas where policies may need refinement or additional support. Data-driven insights allow HR to implement targeted adjustments, enhancing the disciplinary process's efficiency and effectiveness while addressing root causes of recurring issues.

Train and Develop Staff

Continuous training for managers, supervisors, and employees is essential to maintaining a fair and effective disciplinary process. Managers should receive ongoing training in disciplinary practices, communication skills, and conflict resolution to handle issues professionally and sensitively. Employees should be well-informed about disciplinary policies, ensuring that they understand their rights and responsibilities. Skills development in empathy, documentation, and objective evaluation supports fair and constructive handling of disciplinary actions. Through regular training, organizations create a knowledgeable workforce that is better equipped to uphold company values and foster a positive culture.

Implement a Continuous Improvement Process

A feedback loop that incorporates insights from evaluations, data analysis, and employee feedback helps create a responsive and evolving disciplinary system. Action plans based on these insights provide a structured approach to addressing identified weaknesses, with specific steps for implementing improvements. By regularly monitoring the effectiveness of changes, HR can achieve desired outcomes and make further modifications as needed. A commitment to continuous improvement reinforces an adaptable disciplinary system that remains fair, transparent, and relevant.

Foster a Positive Work Environment

Proactive management practices that prioritize feedback, coaching, and support can prevent many issues from escalating into disciplinary actions. Managers should engage employees through regular check-ins, recognizing achievements and addressing potential concerns early. Recognition programs and access to resources that support skill development can boost morale, creating an environment where employees feel valued and motivated. Open communication channels enable managers to discuss performance expectations openly and address issues before they become disciplinary matters, supporting a harmonious and productive workplace.

Engage in External Audits

External audits provide an objective assessment of disciplinary policies, offering a fresh perspective on areas for improvement. Independent consultants or auditors can evaluate policies to make sure they align with industry standards, regulatory requirements, and best practices. Benchmarking studies compare the organization's policies with those of similar companies, identifying gaps and opportunities for enhancement. Engaging external experts brings additional expertise and ensures that disciplinary policies are reviewed with impartiality, supporting a comprehensive and unbiased approach to improvement.

Leverage Technology

Utilizing HR software and tools can streamline disciplinary processes, reduce administrative burden, and improve documentation accuracy. Technology enables HR to track disciplinary actions efficiently, manage records securely, and access historical data for trend analysis.

Data analytics offer insights into disciplinary patterns and outcomes, helping HR make informed policy adjustments. Automation can create consistency by standardizing steps in the disciplinary process, from issuing warnings to tracking improvement plans. Leveraging technology creates a more efficient, data-driven disciplinary system that supports fairness and transparency.

Communicate Changes Effectively

Clear communication is essential when implementing changes to disciplinary policies, as it ensures that employees and managers understand new expectations and procedures. Updated documentation should be accessible to all employees, ideally accompanied by training sessions to explain the changes in detail. Providing opportunities for employees and managers to ask questions and offering feedback on the updates fosters understanding and encourages buy-in. By clearly communicating changes, HR keeps the workforce informed and aligned with the organization's commitment to a fair and evolving disciplinary process.

Implementing continuous improvement strategies in disciplinary policies and procedures is essential for maintaining a fair, compliant, and adaptable system. By regularly reviewing policies, incorporating feedback, analyzing data, and leveraging technology, organizations can create a dynamic disciplinary framework that supports organizational goals and values. Effective communication, external assessments, and a proactive approach to training further enhance the system, ensuring that it remains relevant, legally sound, and aligned with the organization's commitment to a positive work environment. Through these strategies, organizations can address issues with integrity, foster trust, and support employee growth, contributing to long-term success and a strong organizational culture.

When handled correctly, disciplinary actions can improve workplace performance and prevent bigger issues down the line. By applying fair, consistent policies and keeping documentation, small businesses can protect themselves while supporting employees in improving. The next chapter will focus on navigating employee terminations, when necessary, and how to do them legally and respectfully.

CHAPTER 4

Terminations

No business owner enjoys letting an employee go, but sometimes it's necessary for the health of the organization. Whether an employee is underperforming, violating policies, or the business is forced to make cuts, terminations must be handled professionally and legally. This chapter walks through how to prepare for and conduct terminations while minimizing risk and maintaining professionalism.

Terminating an employee is a significant decision with potential legal, ethical, and emotional impacts. It is essential to handle terminations thoughtfully and professionally, adhering to company policies and labor laws. In the last twenty years, I've been a part of hundreds of employee separations, layoffs, and reductions in force. They are tough, formative moments on both sides of the table. By following a structured process, organizations can provide a fair, legally compliant, and respectful transition while upholding the dignity of all involved.

Preparation

Before proceeding with a termination, HR should thoroughly review the organization's policies and procedures outlined in the employee handbook, employment contracts, and any relevant HR guidelines. Termination protocols vary among companies, and adhering to the correct process is critical for consistency and legal compliance. Familiarity with the appropriate steps and contractual obligations also supports a fair process, ensuring that the termination aligns with organizational standards and prevents potential legal repercussions.

By understanding the organization's guidelines, HR can approach the termination confidently, knowing that each step is backed by established procedures. Termination decisions must be carefully evaluated for compliance with applicable labor laws, including anti-discrimination regulations, contractual obligations, and any union agreements. HR must verify that the termination aligns with legal standards to mitigate risks of wrongful termination claims or other legal disputes. In some cases, consulting legal counsel may be advisable to confirm compliance, especially in complex situations. This thorough review helps protect both the organization and the employee, reinforcing that the decision is based on legal grounds and fair practices.

Accurate and thorough documentation is essential for any termination process. Collecting all relevant performance records, disciplinary actions, and incident reports provides a clear record of the issues leading to termination. Reviewing these documents allows HR to ensure that termination is warranted and all prior corrective actions have been exhausted. This documentation serves as an objective record that supports the decision and provides evidence in the event of a dispute. A well-documented termination process helps demonstrate fairness, transparency, and compliance with organizational policies.

Termination Decision

Assessing the reasons for termination is essential to determine whether termination is the most appropriate course of action. Reviewing the causes—such as performance issues, behavioral problems, or organizational changes—guarantees that all relevant factors are considered. For performance-based terminations, it is important to confirm that prior support, such as training or performance improvement plans, was provided. Considering alternative actions, like additional training or temporary role adjustments, can sometimes resolve issues without resorting to termination. This comprehensive evaluation supports a fair and reasoned decision-making process.

Seeking advice from HR professionals—and, if necessary, legal counsel—ensures that the termination is handled appropriately, and potential risks are minimized. HR expertise can help the organization comply with policies, while legal counsel can offer insights into potential liabilities or compliance concerns. This consultation is particularly important if the termination is sensitive or the employee is part of a protected class, where additional legal considerations may apply. Consulting with professionals reinforces the organization's commitment to a fair and legally sound approach. Not to mention, these decisions are oftentimes emotional ones, so having an external, unbiased party review the situation and weigh in ensures the right decision is made for everyone involved.

Preparation for the termination meeting is critical for keeping the conversation respectful and focused. Managers and HR should plan what they will say, choosing clear and concise language that conveys the decision professionally. The meeting should outline the reasons for termination, along with any next steps, such as paperwork or final payments. Preparing documentation in advance, including the termination letter, final paycheck, and information on benefits or severance (if applicable), helps facilitate a smooth transition and reduces the likelihood of misunderstandings.

Conducting the Termination Meeting

Holding the termination meeting in a private, confidential setting demonstrates respect for the employee's dignity. This approach allows for an honest and undisturbed discussion, minimizing disruptions and maintaining confidentiality. By protecting privacy, HR and management show sensitivity to the employee's emotions and create a respectful environment, which can make a difficult situation less distressing. Private settings also prevent potential negative impacts on other employees, who might otherwise be affected by witnessing the termination.

Clear communication during the termination meeting is essential to prevent misunderstandings. The reasons for termination should be communicated directly, using factual, objective information without personal criticism. Presenting the termination letter and any relevant documentation further reinforces transparency and helps the employee understand the final paycheck details, benefits continuation, or severance arrangements.

Communicating openly and respectfully reinforces the organization's commitment to fairness and professionalism throughout the termination process. Allowing the employee to ask questions or express concerns during the meeting demonstrates respect and compassion. HR and management should actively listen, offering clear answers to the best of their ability. Support options, such as information on unemployment benefits or career counseling, can help mitigate the emotional impact and provide the employee with resources for their next steps. This supportive approach can reduce tension, helping the employee leave on a more positive note and maintaining the organization's reputation for compassion.

I could write one entire book on termination meetings I've either led or have been witness to and how they were executed, including things said before, during, and after, responses, and physical actions. Whether a termination is "for cause" or not, someone's livelihood (financial situation) is being impacted, and it doesn't always bring the best out of a person. I've had name badges thrown at me, death threats sent, filing cabinets pulled over, and words said intending to hurt me as badly as I (unintentionally) was hurting the employee. Some meetings have gone smoothly or as expected, but others went off the rails. If you've seen the movie *Up in the Air* starring George Clooney, you'll know what I mean; there have been times I felt that way (other than the affair part—I'm happily married). Terminations should always be handled professionally. This means ample preparation, anticipation, and privacy. Just know, a career in HR can be viewed as boring, but there are many things that happen behind closed doors that no one else should know about. If no one finds out about the drama of a particularly tough termination, this means you did your job well. For me, this also means I've had a number of great therapists over the years. It's called balance.

Post-Termination Procedures

After the termination meeting, logistical arrangements must be addressed promptly to complete the separation process. Ensuring that the employee returns all company property, such as keys, access cards, and equipment, is essential for security. Coordinating with IT to terminate access to company systems, email accounts, and confidential information prevents unauthorized access and secures company data. These steps are integral to maintaining organizational security and protecting sensitive information following an employee's departure.

Issuing the employee's final paycheck, including any owed vacation or sick leave, as required by law, is a key component of the termination process. Providing the employee with information about benefits continuation, such as COBRA for health insurance, allows them to make informed decisions about their coverage options. Completing financial and legal matters thoroughly and promptly ensures compliance with labor laws and upholds the organization's reputation for professionalism.

Legal and Ethical Considerations

Compliance with employment laws, such as anti-discrimination regulations and wrongful termination protections, is critical for a legally sound termination process. HR must verify that all actions taken are consistent with contractual obligations and free from discriminatory practices. Maintaining thorough documentation of the reasons for termination provides a defensible record in the event of a legal claim. Adhering to legal requirements helps protect the organization from liability and supports a termination process that is both fair and compliant with relevant regulations.

Ethics play a central role in managing terminations with respect and integrity. Fairness is key, as employees deserve to be treated impartially, without discrimination or bias. Confidentiality must be maintained throughout the process, and termination details should be disclosed only to those who need to know. Providing appropriate support, such as outplacement resources or career counseling, can help the employee transition smoothly and reduce the emotional impact. An ethical approach fosters trust and upholds the organization's values, reflecting positively on both the company and its culture.

Reflection and Improvement

After completing the termination, HR and management should review the process to assess its effectiveness and identify areas for improvement. Gathering feedback from those involved can highlight potential adjustments to policies or communication practices, promoting continuous improvement. By reflecting on the termination process, the organization can refine its approach, ensuring that future terminations are handled with greater consistency, fairness, and efficiency.

Providing training for managers and HR professionals on effective performance management, disciplinary actions, and termination protocols can reduce the likelihood of future issues. Training helps managers recognize early warning signs, address performance concerns proactively, and use corrective measures to support employee development. Investing in training not only strengthens the organization's approach to employee management but also promotes a positive workplace culture where discipline is constructive rather than punitive.

Understanding Employee Terminations and Their Varieties

Employee terminations mark the conclusion of an employee's relationship with an organization. These separations can arise from various reasons and require different handling approaches based on the termination type. Here's a breakdown of the primary types of terminations:

Voluntary Terminations

Voluntary terminations occur when an employee independently decides to end their employment with the organization. Employees may resign for a variety of reasons, including personal factors, career advancement opportunities, or relocation. Some may choose to leave upon reaching retirement age, often aligning their exit with specific financial or personal milestones. Voluntary terminations generally involve a notice period, as outlined in the employment contract or company policy, which allows the organization to plan for the employee's departure and initiate a smooth transition. By understanding the motivations behind voluntary terminations, organizations can manage them effectively, preserving relationships and facilitating knowledge transfer.

Involuntary Terminations

Involuntary terminations are initiated by the employer, often due to performance issues, misconduct, or organizational restructuring. Terminations for cause may occur when an employee violates company policies, consistently underperforms, or engages in misconduct, such as theft or harassment. Terminations without cause, on the other hand, may be implemented for reasons unrelated to an employee's behavior or performance, such as restructuring or downsizing.

Involuntary terminations can be challenging and require clear communication, thorough documentation, and careful adherence to legal and organizational protocols to ensure fairness and minimize potential disputes.

Layoffs or Reduction in Force (RIF)

Layoffs are a specific form of involuntary termination in which employees are let go primarily for economic reasons, such as budget constraints, declining demand, or shifts in business strategy. Unlike terminations for cause, layoffs do not reflect on the employee's performance or behavior. Layoffs can be temporary, with the possibility of rehiring when business conditions improve, or they may be permanent if positions are eliminated. Organizations facing layoffs must carefully plan the process, including appropriate notifications, severance packages, and outplacement support, to minimize disruption and protect their reputation as a fair and responsible employer. Handling layoffs is never easy, but having a plan helps. My consulting firm has a free **Layoff Checklist** that ensures you approach layoffs with clarity, compliance, and compassion. The checklist helps you follow best practices, minimize legal risks, and communicate effectively. Go to saltandlightadvisors. com/layoffchecklist if you'd like to grab it.

Retirements

Retirement is a form of voluntary termination in which an employee leaves the workforce after reaching retirement age or achieving their financial or career goals. Retirement is often a planned transition, allowing employees to prepare financially, emotionally, and logistically for life after work. Many organizations have formal retirement processes, including notice requirements and retirement benefits, such as pensions or health benefits. Proper handling of retirements, including succession planning and knowledge transfer, is essential for minimizing disruptions and honoring the retiring employee's contribution to the organization.

Mutual Agreements

Mutual agreement terminations occur when both the employee and employer concur that it is in their best interests to part ways. This type of termination is often seen when both parties recognize a mismatch in job expectations or organizational fit. Mutual agreements may involve negotiated terms, such as severance packages or extended notice periods, ensuring a smooth transition and protecting the interests of both parties. Terminating on mutually agreeable terms allows the organization to preserve relationships and offers employees a dignified and supportive exit.

Understanding these various types of terminations equips organizations to manage each type effectively. As a result, processes are transparent, compliant, and respectful of both organizational and employee needs.

The Significance of Properly Managing Employee Terminations

Managing terminations with care is crucial for maintaining a healthy organization, complying with legal standards, and protecting employee morale. Here's why effective termination management is essential:

Organizational Health

Terminations impact organizational health by affecting productivity, reputation, and knowledge continuity. When handled respectfully and efficiently, terminations minimize disruptions to daily operations, allowing teams to remain focused and engaged. A well-managed termination process reflects positively on the organization, enhancing its reputation as a fair and responsible employer. This reputation can be crucial for attracting future talent and retaining client or partner relationships. Furthermore, a proper termination process includes knowledge transfer strategies to ensure that valuable insights and information held by departing employees are passed on, reducing the risk of knowledge gaps. Prioritizing organizational health during terminations supports continuity and strengthens the workplace environment.

Legal Compliance

Following legal requirements in termination processes is essential for avoiding costly disputes and protecting the organization from potential liabilities. Proper termination management includes adhering to employment laws, anti-discrimination regulations, and any specific contractual obligations. By maintaining detailed documentation throughout the termination process, organizations create a record that substantiates fair and objective decision-making. Documentation becomes invaluable if a termination is challenged, as it shows that policies were followed and decisions were made based on facts. Additionally, providing severance pay and benefits, when required, supports compliance with labor laws and demonstrates the organization's commitment to ethical practices, reducing the risk of legal claims.

Employee Morale

The way terminations are handled has a significant impact on the morale of remaining employees. Treating departing employees with respect and fairness reinforces the organization's commitment to ethical practices, which strengthens trust and loyalty among team members. Clear communication about terminations—including the reasons behind the decision and what it means for the team—helps alleviate concerns and preserve a positive work environment. Moreover, offering support to terminated employees, such as outplacement services or career counseling, demonstrates empathy and care. This not only benefits the departing employees but also positively influences the remaining workforce, as they see the organization as compassionate and supportive.

Key Laws and Regulations Governing Employee Terminations

Navigating the complex landscape of employment laws is essential for handling terminations legally and ethically. From at-will employment principles to anti-discrimination regulations, understanding these key areas helps organizations manage terminations responsibly while minimizing legal risks.

At-Will Employment

At-will employment is a foundational principle in many (not all) of the states in the US, allowing employers and employees to end the employment relationship at any time without cause, as long as it's not for illegal reasons. While at-will employment provides flexibility, it's subject to important exceptions. Contractual agreements or union contracts may stipulate specific conditions for termination, such as requiring just cause or a notice period. Additionally, implied contracts may arise from verbal assurances or written policies, potentially limiting at-will protections. Public policy exceptions prohibit employers from terminating employees for reasons that violate state or federal policies, such as firing an employee for whistleblowing. HR must understand these exceptions to apply terminations fairly and avoid legal challenges.

Wrongful Termination

Wrongful termination claims can arise if an employee is dismissed in violation of legal protections, contractual terms, or company policies. Such claims often involve terminations based on discrimination or retaliation. For instance, it is illegal to terminate an employee for their race, religion, sex, or other protected characteristics under anti-discrimination laws. Retaliation against employees who exercise their legal rights, such as filing a complaint or requesting family leave, is also prohibited. Contract violations, including failing to honor specific terms in employment contracts, can lead to wrongful termination claims. By thoroughly understanding these protections, HR can ensure that terminations are handled legally, reducing the risk of costly disputes.

Anti-Discrimination Laws

Federal anti-discrimination laws play a critical role in protecting employees during terminations. The Equal Employment Opportunity (EEO) principles and key laws, such as Title VII of the Civil Rights Act, the Americans with Disabilities Act (ADA), and the Age Discrimination in Employment Act (ADEA), make sure that employment decisions are free from discrimination. Title VII prohibits discrimination based on race, color, religion, sex, or national origin, while the ADA requires reasonable accommodations for employees with disabilities. The ADEA protects employees aged forty and older from age-based discrimination. Additionally, the Genetic Information Nondiscrimination Act (GINA) prevents discrimination based on genetic information. Understanding these laws enables HR to conduct fair and legally compliant terminations.

Severance Pay Regulations

Severance pay is often provided to employees upon termination, either as part of an employment contract or company policy. While no federal law mandates severance pay, companies offering it must adhere to their policies or agreements to avoid breach-of-contract claims. The Worker Adjustment and Retraining Notification (WARN) Act requires certain employers to give advance notice of mass layoffs or plant closures, sometimes including severance or benefits. Some states also have specific severance pay regulations or notice requirements. HR must be familiar with both federal and state guidelines to comply with regulations and provide appropriate financial support to employees during transitions.

Family and Medical Leave Act (FMLA)

The FMLA provides employees with job protection and continued benefits when they take leave for personal or family health issues. This law prohibits employers from terminating employees for taking FMLA leave, ensuring that employees can prioritize family and health needs without fear of losing their job. Employers must handle terminations involving employees on FMLA leave with care, as terminations perceived as retaliatory can lead to legal issues. Proper documentation and adherence to FMLA guidelines help prevent violations and support a compassionate, legally compliant work environment. As a reminder, FMLA applies to organizations with fifty or more employees within a seventy-five-mile radius (at the time of writing this book).

Occupational Safety and Health Administration (OSHA)

OSHA regulations focus on creating safe and healthy workplaces. Under OSHA, employees have the right to report safety violations without fear of retaliation. Employers cannot terminate employees for participating in OSHA investigations or raising safety concerns. HR should guarantee that any disciplinary actions or terminations are unrelated to employee safety complaints to avoid potential violations. By respecting OSHA regulations, organizations demonstrate their commitment to safety and support employees who advocate for a safe workplace.

State and Local Laws

Employment laws vary by state and may include additional protections not covered by federal law, such as mandatory notice periods, expanded anti-discrimination protections, or specific severance pay requirements. Local jurisdictions may also impose regulations affecting terminations. HR must stay informed of relevant state and local laws to achieve compliance and fairness in termination practices. Consulting legal counsel or keeping updated on regional regulations can help HR avoid inadvertent violations and conduct terminations that adhere to local requirements.

Compliance: The Importance of Adhering to Legal Requirements in Terminations

Compliance with legal standards in employee terminations is essential to protect the organization from lawsuits, penalties, and reputational harm. Let's address some reasons why maintaining compliance is critical for successful termination management.

Noncompliance with employment laws opens organizations to potential claims of wrongful termination, discrimination, or retaliation. Following legal protocols for terminations significantly reduces the risk of legal disputes. A lawsuit can be costly, both financially and reputationally, with expenses that include attorney fees, court costs, and possible settlements. By adhering to the law and having well-documented, fair processes, HR minimizes these risks and creates a legally sound foundation for handling employment disputes.

Failure to comply with employment regulations can lead to substantial fines and penalties. Regulatory bodies may impose fines for noncompliance, and employees who successfully sue for wrongful termination may be awarded damages, including back pay, legal costs, and additional compensation.

HR must prioritize compliance to avoid these financial penalties and ensure that disciplinary and termination actions are based on legally sound principles. Financially prudent compliance also strengthens the organization's ability to invest in its employees and resources.

An organization's reputation is critical to attracting and retaining talent, clients, and business partners. Compliance with employment laws demonstrates a commitment to fair and ethical practices, which fosters trust among employees, clients, and stakeholders. Legal issues arising from improper terminations can harm the organization's public image, impacting customer loyalty and business success. A strong reputation for ethical compliance builds a foundation for long-term organizational growth and credibility.

Compliance with employment laws reinforces an organization's commitment to fair and ethical treatment of employees. When an organization respects laws governing anti-discrimination, wrongful termination, and employee rights, employees are treated with respect, fostering a positive work environment. When employees see that the organization values legal and ethical standards, morale and trust improve, leading to greater engagement and loyalty. Fair treatment supports a culture where employees feel valued and secure, which boosts overall organizational health.

Legal compliance provides clear guidelines for handling employment matters, streamlining decision-making, and reducing ambiguity. Compliance fosters consistency in disciplinary and termination practices, helping managers and HR professionals approach each case with a standardized framework. This predictability creates a structured, orderly work environment where employees understand expectations and processes. That enhances operational efficiency and organizational stability.

Noncompliance can attract scrutiny from regulatory agencies, leading to audits, inspections, and heightened oversight. Regulatory investigations can be disruptive and costly, detracting from the organization's focus on core operations. Compliance reduces the likelihood of these disruptions, allowing the organization to operate smoothly and maintain positive relationships with regulatory bodies. A legally compliant organization fosters a supportive, fair, and respectful work environment, which can improve employee morale and reduce turnover. Employees are more likely to remain with an organization that upholds their legal rights and treats them fairly. Compliance-driven policies support an inclusive and positive work culture where employees feel valued, increasing overall engagement and retention. Legal compliance in employee terminations is not just about avoiding lawsuits; it is about fostering a respectful and fair workplace that supports employees and protects the organization.

Upholding Fairness and Respect in Employee Terminations

Handling employee terminations with fairness and respect is essential for maintaining ethical standards, building trust, and preserving organizational culture. Treating employees with dignity during terminations not only reflects the organization's values but also protects its reputation, morale, and integrity. The human element in termination processes cannot be overlooked; each employee, regardless of the circumstances leading to their exit, deserves to be treated with empathy and respect. This approach acknowledges their contributions and shows appreciation for the time they invested in the organization. Treating employees with dignity means valuing them as individuals, regardless of the decision to part ways, and ensuring that they leave with their self-worth intact. It can make a difficult experience more bearable, helping them move forward positively and, ultimately, protecting the organization's reputation as a fair and humane employer.

Professionalism is critical in handling terminations, as it reflects the organization's commitment to ethical practices. A professional approach involves well-prepared communication, adherence to policies, and consideration for the employee's perspective. Managers and HR professionals who handle terminations with respect and empathy set a positive example, promoting a culture where every employee feels valued. This approach also upholds the organization's reputation as a responsible and considerate employer, which resonates not only in the team but also in the broader community.

The termination process can be highly emotional and stressful, impacting the mental well-being of the affected employee. Approaching terminations with sensitivity can reduce the psychological impact, helping employees feel supported even in challenging circumstances.

Respectful terminations help prevent conflicts, grievances, and negative reactions, reducing the risk of damage to the organization's reputation. A smooth termination process allows both parties to part amicably, preserving relationships and minimizing disruptions in the workplace. How an organization handles terminations affects its reputation both internally and externally. Companies known for treating employees with respect and compassion during terminations enjoy a positive public image and are better positioned to attract and retain talent.

Word of mouth plays a significant role; terminated employees who feel they were treated fairly are more likely to speak positively about the organization, enhancing its credibility. A strong reputation for respectful and ethical terminations reflects well on the organization's values and promotes trust among current and future employees.

Respectful treatment in terminations reinforces compliance with legal standards, protecting the organization from potential lawsuits. Following company policies and procedures ensures that all employees are treated consistently and fairly. This approach helps avoid claims of discrimination or wrongful termination, reducing legal risks. A structured and fair process promotes equality and nondiscrimination, reinforcing the organization's commitment to ethical employment practices and supporting a positive workplace culture.

Clear and respectful communication is essential during terminations, helping employees understand the reasons and next steps involved. When there are transparent discussions, employees know what to expect and how to move forward. Offering outplacement services or career counseling provides additional support, making the transition easier and demonstrating the organization's commitment to helping employees succeed beyond their tenure. This support not only benefits departing employees but also reassures remaining team members of the organization's compassion and responsibility.

The way terminations are handled influences employee morale and workplace culture. Respectful treatment of employees during exits reflects the organization's values and reassures remaining employees that their contributions are valued. When employees witness fair and ethical treatment, their trust in leadership is strengthened, promoting loyalty and engagement. A positive culture is maintained even during challenging situations, as employees see that the organization upholds its values consistently, leading to a more motivated and cohesive team.

Transparency and Honesty: The Importance of Open and Honest Communication

Transparent and honest communication is fundamental to building trust and maintaining integrity in an organization, especially during challenging situations like terminations. When communication is open and truthful, employees feel valued, respected, and more secure.

Trust is the foundation of strong workplace relationships, and it's built through consistent transparency and honesty. Employees who feel informed about organizational decisions, including terminations, are more likely to trust management. This trust fosters a positive workplace culture where employees believe that leadership is committed to fairness and ethical practices. Transparent communication ensures that employees are not left guessing or worrying about hidden agendas, which strengthens trust in leadership and the organization as a whole. Transparency contributes to an open and inclusive culture where employees feel engaged and connected to the organization's mission. Employees are more likely to feel valued and secure when they're informed about decisions, especially those that affect them directly. Honest communication around changes, policies, or disciplinary actions helps maintain high morale, as employees understand the context and reasoning behind decisions. This open culture promotes trust, reduces uncertainty, and fosters a sense of belonging.

Clear, transparent communication of expectations, goals, and performance criteria reinforces accountability throughout the organization. Employees understand the standards they are expected to meet, which allows them to take ownership of their responsibilities. Honest communication about decisions and actions creates a record of accountability, ensuring that everyone is held to the same standards. When accountability is consistently applied, integrity is strengthened, leading to a more trustworthy and reliable organization. Transparent communication helps minimize misunderstandings, as it reduces the chance for assumptions or misinformation. By openly sharing relevant information, the organization fosters clarity, making it easier for employees to align their actions with company goals.

Honesty also plays a crucial role in resolving conflicts; when issues are addressed openly, misunderstandings can be clarified and resolved before they escalate. This approach creates a healthier work environment, reducing potential conflicts and promoting harmony. Transparency and honesty are fundamental components of organizational integrity. When these values are upheld, they reflect the organization's commitment to ethical standards and reinforce its reputation for fairness and respect.

Integrity strengthens the organization's reputation, making it more attractive to potential hires, clients, and business partners. Organizations known for their transparency and honesty are more likely to enjoy long-term success, as these values foster trust and credibility within and beyond the organization.

When there is transparency, decision-makers have access to all relevant information, leading to more informed and effective outcomes. Open communication about decision-making processes and criteria encourages employees to contribute to discussions, providing insights that may improve outcomes. When employees understand the rationale behind decisions, they are more likely to support and align with them, enhancing collaboration and commitment to the organization's goals. Transparent communication fosters a culture where employees feel comfortable offering feedback and suggestions for improvement. This openness to feedback promotes continuous improvement and encourages employees to contribute ideas that may enhance processes or address issues. An organization that values feedback and maintains open dialogue benefits from diverse perspectives, leading to ongoing development and progress.

Managing Voluntary and Involuntary Departures

This **step-by-step termination checklist** ensures you are prepped to handle terminations effectively.

Termination Checklist

- **Before Termination**

  - Review performance records, warnings, and improvement plans.

  - Ensure legal compliance with state and federal laws.

  - Consult with HR or legal counsel if necessary.

- **During the Termination Meeting**

  - Hold a private meeting with HR and the direct manager present.

  - Provide clear reasons for termination (performance, policy violations).

  - Offer final paycheck and details on benefits continuation (COBRA, retirement).

  - Retrieve company property (laptop, keycards, ID badge).

- **After Termination**

  - Remove system access (email, internal software, security badges).

  - Communicate the departure professionally to the remaining team.

  - Conduct an exit interview if applicable.

Top Reasons for Employee Turnover

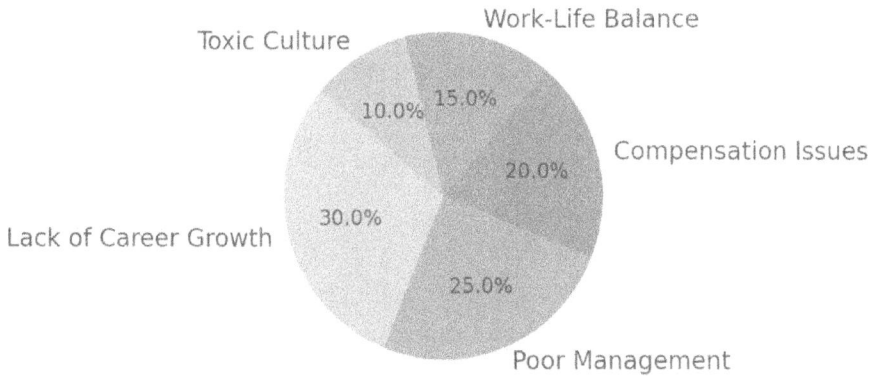

The data for the **"Top Reasons for Employee Turnover"** chart is based on commonly reported industry research, including sources like:

1. Gallup Workplace Studies: Reports that **lack of career growth and poor management** are among the top reasons employees leave.

2. SHRM (Society for Human Resource Management): Identifies **compensation, work-life balance, and toxic culture** as key turnover factors.

3. LinkedIn Global Talent Trends: Reports that employees prioritize **career growth and development opportunities** when deciding to stay or leave a company.

4. Work Institute Retention Reports: Highlights that **over 70% of turnover is preventable**, often tied to manager relationships, career stagnation, and workplace dissatisfaction.

Handling resignations and retirements effectively is key to minimizing disruptions, maintaining strong relationships, and creating continuity in the organization. Here's how to approach each type of voluntary termination:

Handling Resignations

When an employee chooses to resign, it's crucial to approach the process with professionalism and attention to detail. Start by requesting a formal resignation letter, which should specify the employee's last working day. This documentation establishes a clear timeline and provides a foundation for planning the transition. Once the resignation is received, formally acknowledge it in writing, expressing appreciation for the employee's notice and confirming their departure date.

For a smooth transition, schedule an exit interview to understand the employee's reasons for leaving, gain insights into their experience, and collect valuable feedback on workplace practices.

Collaborate with the resigning employee to create a transition plan that includes handing off responsibilities, training replacements, and documenting key contacts and processes. This knowledge transfer is vital to maintaining productivity and continuity.

Finalize the departure by updating records in payroll, benefits, and access rights. Retrieve company property, settle any outstanding matters, and consider acknowledging the employee's contributions in a positive manner, such as a farewell gathering or team message. Additionally, ensure compliance with any legal and contractual obligations, such as noncompete clauses, confidentiality agreements, and final paychecks.

Handling Retirements

Retirement is often a well-planned transition that allows both the employee and the organization to prepare for the change. Encourage employees to provide ample notice of their retirement plans, giving you time to organize a structured transition. Develop a retirement transition plan with the retiring employee, outlining timelines for knowledge transfer and the delegation of responsibilities for continuity. Succession planning is key in retirement cases. Identify a successor or team to take over the retiree's duties and provide them with the necessary training and resources. Conduct a structured knowledge transfer process that may include documentation, manuals, and training sessions. This preparation preserves institutional knowledge and minimizes disruption.

As with resignations, updating records, managing benefits, and retrieving company property are crucial steps. Ensure that retirement benefits and any financial matters are processed in alignment with company policies and legal requirements. Recognize the retiree's years of service with a thoughtful gesture, such as a retirement event or public acknowledgment of their contributions. Positive communication regarding their departure also reinforces appreciation in the organization.

Lastly, review any retirement benefits or legal obligations to confirm compliance with regulations. By approaching resignations and retirements with structured planning and clear communication, organizations can maintain continuity, protect institutional knowledge, and leave departing employees with positive last impressions.

Involuntary Terminations: Managing Firings Due to Performance Issues, Misconduct, and Organizational Restructuring

Involuntary terminations require special care to provide compliance, fairness, and respect for the affected employees. Each scenario demands a tailored approach to manage the specific reasons and impact of the termination.

Firings Due to Performance Issues

Terminating an employee for performance issues requires a thorough and well-documented process to ensure fairness and reduce legal risks. Start by consistently monitoring and documenting performance, including specific examples of underperformance or missed targets. Performance reviews and regular feedback sessions provide an opportunity to formally address these concerns and create a record of ongoing issues. Documenting each review and any employee performance improvement plans (EPIPs) builds a clear case for further action if necessary. If performance issues persist, initiate an EPIP outlining specific goals, timelines, and available resources for improvement. Schedule regular check-ins to discuss progress, offer guidance, and adjust the plan if needed. This supportive approach demonstrates the organization's commitment to employee success, even in challenging circumstances.

If the employee fails to meet the required standards despite the EPIP, it may be necessary to move forward with termination. When terminating for performance reasons, hold a formal meeting to explain the decision, referencing documented performance issues and the steps taken to address them. Comply with final pay and benefits requirements and provide relevant documentation during the termination meeting. A structured, transparent process helps the organization mitigate legal risks and uphold its commitment to fairness.

Firings Due to Misconduct

Addressing misconduct demands a fair, unbiased investigation and adherence to company policies. Begin by conducting a comprehensive investigation to gather evidence and understand the context of the alleged misconduct. Interview witnesses, collect documentation, and carefully review company policies to determine if there was a violation.

For less severe infractions, consider issuing disciplinary actions, such as verbal or written warnings, before proceeding to termination. Record each disciplinary action and communication to create a clear record of the steps taken. If termination becomes necessary, hold a formal termination meeting to discuss the misconduct and provide evidence supporting the decision. Ensure professionalism and respect during the conversation, addressing any final matters, like property returns, final pay, and potential appeal processes.

Following legal and policy guidelines is essential to avoid claims of wrongful termination or discrimination. Detailed records of the investigation, disciplinary actions, and termination decision will support the organization in the event of a dispute.

Firings Due to Organizational Restructuring

Terminations resulting from restructuring require careful planning and transparent communication to support affected employees and maintain morale. Start by evaluating the impact of restructuring on the organization's staffing needs and identifying roles that will be affected. Develop a clear restructuring plan with timelines, affected positions, and support options, such as severance packages and outplacement services.

When announcing restructuring, communicate openly with employees about the reasons for the changes and the anticipated impact. Providing a timeline and next steps helps employees prepare and reduces uncertainty. Meet with each affected employee individually to discuss their termination, providing documentation and support resources, such as career counseling or job placement assistance.

As mentioned previously in this chapter, you must comply with legal requirements related to restructuring, such as the Worker Adjustment and Retraining Notification (WARN) Act, which mandates advance notice for mass layoffs. Maintain detailed documentation of restructuring decisions, communications, and support offered to affected employees. A transparent, organized approach helps protect the organization from legal risks and preserves a respectful and supportive environment. By following structured processes for each type of involuntary termination, organizations can handle difficult transitions fairly, minimizing legal risks and maintaining a positive workplace culture.

Layoffs and Reductions in Force (RIFs): Managing the Process with Planning, Compliance, and Support

Layoffs and reductions in force (RIFs) are sensitive and challenging processes that require strategic planning, adherence to legal requirements, and a compassionate approach to support affected employees. Balancing organizational needs with employee well-being is essential for maintaining integrity and morale during these transitions.

Planning and Decision-Making

Effective layoffs or RIFs begin with a careful assessment of the organization's business needs and long-term objectives. HR and management must evaluate the underlying reasons for the reduction, whether those are financial pressures, strategic redirection, or operational inefficiencies. This step involves analyzing data on company performance, forecasting financial projections, and aligning staffing needs with the organization's future vision. When objectives are clear and specific, workforce reductions are strategic rather than reactive, which supports stability and continuity.

Once the need for layoffs or a RIF is confirmed, a detailed restructuring plan is essential to outline the process. This plan should clearly specify the scope of the layoffs, including which positions or departments will be affected, timelines, and criteria for selecting employees. Transparency in selection criteria—such as seniority, job performance, or skill relevance—reinforces fairness and compliance.

Consulting with key stakeholders, including senior management, HR, and legal advisors, guarantees that the plan aligns with organizational goals and complies with all relevant policies and laws. A well-developed plan mitigates risks, maintains organizational credibility, and provides a structured approach to an otherwise challenging process.

Legal Requirements

Adhering to employment laws is critical to avoid legal repercussions during layoffs or RIFs. Compliance with the Worker Adjustment and Retraining Notification (WARN) Act, for example, may require employers to provide advance notice to affected employees and government agencies if a mass layoff or plant closure is involved.

HR must also ensure that anti-discrimination laws are respected by conducting a thorough review to confirm that the layoff criteria do not disproportionately impact protected groups based on race, gender, age, disability, or other characteristics. Additionally, legal requirements for severance pay, final wages, and accrued benefits must be followed closely, including any contractual obligations tied to employee agreements. Clear legal compliance demonstrates the organization's commitment to fairness and minimizes the risk of disputes.

Accurate documentation is essential for defending the organization's decisions and processes in the event of a legal challenge. This involves keeping records of all decisions, including the criteria used to select employees for layoff or RIF, the communications exchanged, and evidence of compliance with legal requirements. Formal layoff or RIF notices should be drafted in alignment with legal standards, providing employees with clear, concise information about the terms of separation. Proper documentation helps safeguard the organization and provides transparency, reinforcing that decisions were made thoughtfully and in line with established criteria.

Communication

A well-planned communication strategy is critical in maintaining transparency and respect throughout the layoff or RIF process. Develop a comprehensive plan that outlines how and when the news will be delivered to affected employees, remaining staff, and external stakeholders, as well as who will deliver it. Managers should be prepared with talking points and guidance to deliver the message with empathy and clarity, allowing them to handle difficult questions with sensitivity.

By proactively addressing potential concerns and questions, a strategic communication approach helps reduce anxiety and uncertainty. The announcement to affected employees should be handled with the utmost care. Individual meetings are preferable for delivering the news in a private and respectful manner, allowing employees to process the information and ask questions. During these meetings, explain the reasons behind the decision, provide details about the separation, and outline the support resources available, such as outplacement services or career counseling. Offering clear information on the next steps and available support helps employees feel more prepared to navigate the transition.

Transparent communication with remaining employees is essential in maintaining morale and trust. Address their concerns directly, explain the business reasons behind the layoffs, and outline any changes to roles or responsibilities. Reassure employees of the organization's direction and provide support resources as needed to help them adjust to new expectations. Clear, honest communication helps maintain a sense of stability, minimizes anxiety, and reinforces the organization's commitment to its team.

Support for Affected Employees

Supporting affected employees with transition assistance reflects the organization's commitment to helping them succeed beyond their tenure. Outplacement services, including resume writing, job search assistance, and interview coaching, can make a significant difference in helping employees reenter the job market. Career counseling provides personalized support, enabling employees to explore new opportunities and feel more confident about the future. These services not only support the individuals but also strengthen the organization's reputation for treating its people with care.

Severance packages are a crucial component of financial support for laid-off employees, providing temporary income to ease their transition. Severance benefits should be communicated clearly, and continuity of benefits, if applicable, should be emphasized. Emotional support is equally important; offering counseling services or access to employee assistance programs (EAPs) can help employees cope with the stress and emotions associated with job loss. Providing both financial and emotional resources demonstrates empathy, reinforces the organization's commitment to employee well-being, and supports smoother transitions.

I have seen so many companies do virtually nothing for an eliminated employee after the actual meeting in which they learn of the reduction. It's painful. It's not much, but I built out a guide to help managers do this better, along with a guide that supports the impacted employee in the transition. Once the employee leaves, they are a bit out of sight and out of mind for HR and the remaining team. But for the person impacted, the change then becomes real. Take the extra time to care for them on their way out. You'd want someone to do it for you.

Post-Layoff and Post-RIF Considerations

After completing the layoff or RIF process, a thorough review is essential to assess effectiveness and identify areas for improvement. This evaluation can include analyzing feedback from affected employees, remaining staff, and managers to understand how the process went and where adjustments may be beneficial. Reviewing the impact on productivity, morale, and overall business outcomes provides insights into the effectiveness of the process. A comprehensive evaluation enables the organization to make informed improvements, supporting a more refined approach in future scenarios. Using feedback and insights gained from the layoff or RIF, HR and management can refine strategies to improve the process and minimize future disruptions. This might involve adjusting criteria for selection, improving communication protocols, or strengthening support resources.

Rebuilding trust is also a key focus after a layoff, as employees may feel uncertain or wary. Prioritizing communication, team-building initiatives, and professional development opportunities for remaining staff can help rebuild morale and reinforce the organization's commitment to their growth and well-being. By learning from each experience, organizations strengthen their ability to manage future challenges with integrity.

Steps for Preparation and Execution

Conducting a termination requires meticulous preparation and a structured approach to handle the process with professionalism, legality, and respect. From documentation to follow-up actions, a well-planned termination process supports both organizational needs and the employee's dignity.

Prepare and Document

Thorough documentation is essential in the termination process to substantiate the decision and protect the organization from potential legal claims. Start by collecting all performance records, disciplinary notes, and feedback that contributed to the termination decision. This includes performance reviews, attendance records, and any documented incidents or issues. Review the employee's contract, job description, and relevant HR policies so that the termination aligns with company guidelines and expectations.

Complying with legal requirements, such as notice periods, severance pay, and labor laws, is critical to upholding fair treatment and minimizing legal risks. Proper documentation demonstrates that the termination decision is based on objective criteria, supporting transparency and fairness.

The termination meeting itself requires careful planning to maintain professionalism and minimize disruptions. Schedule the meeting at a time that allows for privacy and confidentiality, ideally in a neutral setting away from other team members. Prepare an agenda outlining the key points to address, such as the reason for termination, details of the process, and any support available to the employee. Decide on the attendees, typically including the direct manager and an HR representative, to provide a balanced approach of managerial insight and HR support. This structure allows the meeting to proceed smoothly while ensuring that all necessary information is conveyed effectively and empathetically.

Plan the Conversation

Delivering clear, concise, and objective messages is crucial to the termination process. Begin with a straightforward explanation of the reason for termination, focusing on documented issues rather than personal judgments. Detail the logistics, such as the effective termination date, final pay, benefits continuation, and the return of company property. Outline any support options, like severance packages or outplacement services, showing the organization's commitment to assisting the employee during their transition.

A well-prepared script helps maintain professionalism and ensures that the employee receives all relevant information with clarity. Terminations can evoke a range of emotional responses, from shock and sadness to anger and frustration. Anticipate potential reactions and prepare to address them with professionalism and empathy. Consider possible questions or objections the employee might raise, then formulate respectful, clear responses to address their concerns. Preparing for these scenarios allows you to handle the meeting with composure and compassion, providing the employee with a sense of respect even in difficult circumstances.

Conduct the Meeting

Begin the meeting by stating the purpose clearly and directly, setting a respectful tone. Deliver the termination message in a straightforward, professional manner, avoiding ambiguous language or extraneous details that could confuse or upset the employee. Provide clear information on termination logistics, including details on final pay, benefits, and any support or severance options. Offering career transition assistance, such as outplacement services, reinforces the organization's commitment to supporting the employee's future.

Listening actively to the employee's response is essential in maintaining a respectful and supportive environment. Allow them to express their emotions and thoughts without interruption, acknowledging their feelings without becoming defensive or argumentative. Reassure the employee by recognizing their contributions and offering guidance on available support, such as counseling or job search resources. This approach not only respects the employee's dignity but also helps them process the situation constructively.

Follow Up

After the meeting, document all relevant details, including the date, attendees, and main discussion points, as well as the employee's reactions. This record provides a clear, factual account of the meeting and supports any future inquiries or legal reviews. =

Ensure that final paperwork is prepared promptly—including the termination letter, final pay calculations, and benefits information—to provide the employee with a clear understanding of their entitlements.

Terminations can impact the morale and cohesion of the remaining team, so a thoughtful communication strategy is essential. Prepare a brief, respectful statement that informs the team of the departure without revealing confidential details. Address any questions or concerns transparently, reinforcing the organization's commitment to supporting the remaining employees. This communication fosters trust, minimizes rumors, and helps employees refocus on their roles.

Complete all necessary legal and administrative tasks associated with the termination, such as updating records, revoking access to company systems, and finalizing benefits details. Complying with legal and company policies protects the organization and demonstrates respect for the terminated employee's rights. By following these administrative steps meticulously, HR maintains organizational consistency and accountability.

Review and Reflect

A thorough evaluation of the termination process is essential for continuous improvement. Review the effectiveness of the meeting, the clarity of communication, and the overall efficiency of the process. Seek feedback from those involved, including the manager and HR representative, to gain insights into what went well and what could be improved. This reflection supports the development of best practices for future terminations, ensuring that the process is fair, consistent, and respectful.

Based on feedback and lessons learned, consider making adjustments to termination policies or procedures. This might include refining documentation protocols, improving communication strategies, or enhancing support resources for affected employees. Continuous improvement not only strengthens the termination process but also aligns with the organization's commitment to fairness, transparency, and respect.

Termination Meeting: Guidelines for Conducting a Respectful and Professional Discussion

The termination meeting itself is the culmination of a well-prepared process, and it must be conducted with sensitivity, professionalism, and clarity. This ensures that the employee understands the decision, feels respected, and is supported as they transition out of the organization.

Attendees

Typically, the immediate supervisor or manager and an HR representative should be present at the termination meeting. The direct manager provides context and specific feedback about the employee's performance, while the HR representative makes sure that the termination process complies with policies and legal standards. HR can also handle administrative aspects, such as final pay and benefits, allowing the manager to focus on the conversation itself. This balanced approach supports a respectful, well-informed discussion. That said, if this is a newer leader or a team lead who has never conducted a termination meeting, it may be best to follow the approach of: "I do, you watch" as the HR professional. The next time a termination comes up for that manager, then "they do, you watch." And for the third time, you can trust that they can "do," and you are there to "do" your HR duties. This is a great model to follow to witness a manager fully step into their role. And if they are unable to take ownership of the conversation after some training and guidance, then they are likely not the best fit for a management or leadership position.

In high-risk terminations or situations where legal concerns are involved, legal counsel may be present to offer guidance and ensure compliance. Additionally, if the employee requests it, a trusted colleague or advisor can attend the meeting to provide moral support. Their presence may help the employee feel more comfortable, allowing the meeting to proceed smoothly.

Meeting Preparation

Choose a time and location that offers privacy and minimizes disruptions. Scheduling the meeting early in the workday gives the employee time to process the information and handle personal arrangements. Another option for the timing is the end of a workday, in hopes individuals have started to filter out of the office space. A neutral, private setting maintains confidentiality and helps preserve the employee's dignity, providing them with a respectful space to engage in the discussion.

Having all relevant documentation prepared in advance is essential. This includes the termination letter, information on severance pay, benefits continuation, and any support resources, such as outplacement services. When there's a prepared agenda, it's easier to guide the conversation, keep the meeting organized, and cover all necessary points. If this is a virtual termination, it is still important that the manager and the HR professional both be present. I have heard HR horror stories of an HR team member that the employee has never met offers the termination information and that employee never hears from the manager again. Unless there was an egregious reason for the termination, this is a very cold approach, and I strongly advise against it.

Conducting the Meeting

Begin the meeting with a clear, respectful introduction, stating the purpose without ambiguity. For example, "Thank you for meeting with us. Today, we need to discuss a matter regarding your employment with us." Deliver the termination message directly yet compassionately, framing it in terms of documented issues rather than personal judgments. For example, "After careful review, we have decided to end your employment effective [date] due to [specific reason]." This clarity helps the employee understand the decision while feeling respected.

Present the reasons for termination factually, referencing documented performance or conduct issues without personal criticism. Explain the effective termination date, final pay, benefits, and any severance or support options clearly. Providing detailed next steps helps the employee know what to expect, from returning company property to accessing career transition services, ensuring that they are informed and supported. Allow the employee to express their feelings, listening actively and with empathy. Maintain professionalism throughout the conversation, even if the employee responds emotionally. Acknowledge their contributions and provide reassurance, such as connecting them with outplacement services or career counseling, to help ease their transition. This compassionate approach preserves dignity and fosters goodwill. Is the employee going to be thrilled and grateful at that moment? Likely, no. But it's the right way to treat another human being. Your fifteen minutes of discomfort will end. But their season of unemployment is just beginning, no matter what the reason for separation.

After the Meeting

Document the meeting thoroughly, recording the date, attendees, and key discussion points, as well as the employee's responses. Complete any necessary paperwork, including the termination letter, final pay, and benefits details, to provide a transparent and organized closure to the process.

Prepare a respectful communication to inform remaining team members of the employee's departure, keeping details confidential. Address any questions and reassure employees of the organization's continued support. This thoughtful approach minimizes disruptions and reassures the team of the organization's commitment to their well-being.

Complete all administrative tasks, from updating internal records to revoking access to company systems, ensuring compliance and consistency. Reflect on the process with HR and management to identify areas for improvement, promoting a culture of continuous learning. By following these guidelines, organizations can conduct termination meetings professionally and compassionately, providing clarity, support, and respect for all involved. Proper preparation, communication, and follow-through help maintain dignity, compliance, and a positive organizational reputation.

Steps for a Smooth Transition and Organizational Security

Once an employee has been terminated, it's essential to follow a structured set of post-termination actions to secure company assets, finalize necessary documentation, and maintain morale in the team. Managing these steps efficiently not only protects the organization's interests but also demonstrates professionalism and respect toward the departing employee.

Collect Company Property

Gathering all company-owned assets from the terminated employee is critical to protect the organization's physical and intellectual property. Start by collecting ID badges, security cards, or other forms of physical access to the premises at the time of termination. This step secures physical entry points and maintains safety. Additionally, retrieve any company-issued devices, such as laptops, mobile phones, and tablets, which may contain sensitive data or company applications. Collect all physical documents, files, and materials that belong to the company to prevent data loss or unauthorized access.

It's important to thoroughly verify that all company property has been returned in good condition. Check each item against an inventory list or equipment log specific to the employee to ensure that nothing is missing. If all items are accounted for, have the employee sign a property return form as a record of compliance, confirming they have no remaining company assets. This step minimizes risk and provides a documented record that is essential for closing out the termination process.

Revoke Access to Systems

Immediately after termination, work with IT to deactivate the employee's access to all company systems, including email, databases, and collaboration tools. This step protects sensitive information and prevents unauthorized access to company data. For shared systems or applications that the employee had access to, it's advisable to change passwords to maintain security. Quick action in this area is critical to safeguarding company assets and data integrity. Oftentimes, I will send an email to IT moments before walking into the termination meeting, asking them to revoke access within the next fifteen minutes. That said, if there is a timing issue and the employee's access is disconnected while they are still seated at their workstation, you just created unnecessary drama in the situation. So proceed with eyes wide open.

In addition to system access, revoke the employee's physical access to the workplace. Disable electronic access cards or keys to secure areas, workstations, or buildings as needed. Conduct a thorough check to back up any work-related files or data the employee worked on, transferring them to an appropriate team member or manager to maintain continuity.

These actions prevent security risks and facilitate a seamless transition of responsibilities in the team.

Finalize Paperwork

Complete and distribute all necessary paperwork related to the termination, starting with the employee's final paycheck. The calculation must include any unused vacation or sick leave, bonuses, or other entitlements in accordance with company policies and labor laws. If applicable, prepare a severance agreement detailing terms for severance pay, benefits continuation, or other negotiated arrangements. By accurately addressing financial entitlements and agreements, the organization minimizes the risk of post-termination disputes and demonstrates fairness.

Provide the employee with information on continuing benefits, such as COBRA (or equivalent options), to help them make informed decisions about health insurance or retirement benefits. Ensuring that the employee understands their rights to unemployment benefits and how to apply for them shows consideration and helps them navigate their transition. These steps fulfill legal requirements and reinforce the organization's commitment to treating employees respectfully.

If an exit interview was conducted, gather the insights so they can be reviewed for potential improvements in workplace practices. Provide the employee with a formal termination letter summarizing the terms of their departure, including any severance and benefits details. This letter serves as an official acknowledgment and outlines what was discussed, giving both parties a documented reference for the terms of the separation.

Communicate and Provide Internal Updates

Promptly inform the HR team and payroll about the employee's departure so that final pay and benefits are processed accurately and on time. A streamlined internal notification process helps departments stay coordinated and minimizes errors. Prepare a respectful message for the remaining team members, maintaining confidentiality about the reasons for departure. Clear communication reassures employees and helps maintain a professional atmosphere. If you don't have one, this is your sign to create a termination checklist, so nothing is missed.

Accurate recordkeeping is essential. Update the employee's personnel file with termination details, including reasons for termination, severance terms, and any relevant documentation from the exit process. All internal systems and directories must be updated to reflect the employee's departure, including deactivating or transferring access rights. Properly updated records are vital for legal compliance and ongoing administrative management.

Conduct a Post-Termination Follow-Up

Conduct a final review to confirm that all property has been collected and all access revoked. Any outstanding issues, such as final pay discrepancies or unresolved benefits claims, should be resolved promptly. Thorough follow-up prevents loose ends and ensures that the termination process is complete, protecting both organizational security and employee rights. Take time to reflect on the termination process and identify any areas for improvement. Collect feedback from managers and HR representatives involved in the process, as this insight can lead to adjustments that streamline future terminations. Documenting lessons learned and updating termination policies or procedures enhances efficiency and supports the organization's commitment to continuous improvement.

Think About Additional Considerations

To protect sensitive information, conduct a security review to confirm that all systems, files, and data are secure. Verify that there are no risks associated with the former employee's access and monitor systems for any unauthorized attempts at access. Implementing robust security protocols during and after the termination mitigates risks and strengthens organizational data protection practices.

Terminations can affect team morale, so it's important to provide support for remaining employees who may feel uneasy or concerned about the future. Offer counseling services or employee assistance programs (EAPs) to help employees process the change. Reinforcing a positive work environment, addressing any concerns, and countering potential rumors show the organization's commitment to employee well-being and stability.

Documentation: Ensuring Fairness, Compliance, and Support for Employment Decisions

Maintaining thorough documentation throughout the employment life cycle—from onboarding to termination—is essential for upholding fair practices, mitigating risks, and fostering transparency. Proper documentation provides a foundation for defensible decisions, consistency, and clarity across the organization.

Importance of Documentation

Comprehensive documentation serves as vital evidence in the event of legal challenges, protecting the organization against claims of unfair practices. For example, detailed performance records and incident reports show that terminations were based on documented issues rather than arbitrary decisions. This evidence is crucial in demonstrating compliance with employment laws and helps substantiate the organization's actions as fair and legally sound. By meticulously documenting each stage, HR can build a strong foundation of proof that mitigates risks and safeguards the organization from potential disputes.

Consistent documentation practices ensure that all employees are treated equitably, fostering a culture of fairness. Standardized records, such as performance improvement plans (EPIPs) and disciplinary notes, provide a structured way to handle similar issues across departments so that policies are applied uniformly. This approach helps prevent favoritism or bias and promotes transparency in decision-making. Additionally, access to historical documentation allows managers to reference past cases, helping them make decisions in line with precedent and creating continuity in disciplinary practices.

Detailed documentation enhances clarity and communication, providing a clear record of employee interactions, incidents, and actions taken. Well-maintained records can be referenced during discussions with employees or managers, creating a shared understanding of past events and decisions. For example, having access to performance reviews, warnings, and feedback allows managers to have constructive conversations with employees and set clear expectations. These records support effective communication, reduce misunderstandings, and keep all parties on the same page.

Documentation Process

Accurate documentation starts with recording incidents and disciplinary actions as they occur. For example, incident reports should detail specific dates, descriptions of behavior, and parties involved. Written warnings, formalized with the nature of the infraction and corrective measures, provide a clear record that supports accountability. These records form the foundation for consistent disciplinary actions, helping the organization track and address issues methodically.

Detailed notes from meetings, conversations, and disciplinary discussions are essential for accurate records. For instance, HR should document key points from meetings, including any agreed-upon actions and timelines. This attention to detail allows HR to reference previous discussions, track follow-up actions, and maintain a record of the employee's progress. Documenting these interactions ensures accountability and creates a clear history of the organization's efforts to support the employee.

Maintaining the confidentiality of employee records is vital to respect privacy and comply with data protection regulations. All documentation, from performance reviews to investigation reports, should be stored securely and accessible only to authorized personnel.

Adhering to privacy laws and organizational policies regarding the handling of employee records upholds ethical standards and prevents unauthorized access, protecting both the employee's privacy and the organization's integrity.

Types of Documentation

Regular performance reviews are fundamental for evaluating an employee's work over time. These reviews may include annual or biannual evaluations, 360-degree feedback, and self-assessments. By gathering insights from various sources, performance reviews provide a comprehensive view of the employee's achievements and areas for improvement. These records create an objective foundation for any future disciplinary decisions, making them an invaluable resource.

Disciplinary records document issues related to performance or behavior, from verbal warnings to formal corrective action plans. Incident reports provide specifics on issues, while written warnings outline required improvements and potential consequences. These records demonstrate that the organization is committed to addressing issues fairly and transparently, and they offer a clear trail of documented efforts to resolve problems.

EPIPs outline clear expectations for improvement, detailing specific goals, timelines, and progress tracking. Regular progress reports document the employee's journey through the EPIP, providing an objective record of improvement or lack thereof. This documentation shows that the organization offered the employee a structured opportunity for development, supporting transparency and accountability.

Termination letters formalize the end of the employment relationship, specifying the reasons for termination, effective dates, and instructions for final pay and benefits. Detailed termination meeting notes capture what was discussed and the employee's responses. These documents are essential for finalizing the process and provide a record of the organization's efforts to handle terminations respectfully and professionally.

Exit interviews offer valuable insights into the employee's experience and reasons for leaving. The feedback gathered in exit interviews can reveal trends, highlight areas for improvement, and inform management practices. Summarizing exit interview findings provides management with actionable insights, contributing to a positive workplace culture and helping reduce turnover.

Legal records, such as employment contracts and compliance documentation, establish a framework for employment expectations and rights. Compliance documentation, like notifications of rights and benefits, ensures adherence to legal standards and provides a reference in case of disputes. These records support a transparent and legally compliant workplace environment.

Documentation of email correspondence and meeting notes related to performance or disciplinary issues results in a comprehensive record of all communication. This transparency provides context for decisions, supports accountability, and allows managers to address issues proactively and consistently.

Records of employee training sessions and certifications demonstrate the organization's commitment to professional development and compliance. Documenting these efforts also shows that the organization offered employees resources to succeed, which can be valuable if performance issues arise later.

Investigation records are essential for addressing allegations of misconduct. Detailed reports of findings, along with interview notes, create a transparent process that can be referenced if claims are disputed. These records show that the organization took fair, unbiased steps in investigating issues, reinforcing a commitment to ethical practices.

Nondisclosure agreements (NDAs) and other confidentiality agreements establish expectations for protecting sensitive information. Signed copies of these agreements are crucial for safeguarding intellectual property and organizational security. Maintaining these records is part of an overall strategy to manage risk and protect company assets.

Documentation for Employee Performance Improvement Plans (EPIPs)

EPIPs provide a structured opportunity for employees to address performance gaps. The plan should outline specific goals, expected outcomes, and timelines, ensuring that the employee understands what is required. Documenting these objectives and tracking progress through regular updates creates transparency and helps HR measure the effectiveness of the improvement plan.

EPIP documentation, including regular assessments and feedback, provides insight into the employee's commitment and ability to meet the outlined goals. Keeping these records demonstrates that the organization provided a structured improvement path, supporting fairness in any further decisions, such as termination, if necessary.

Final Steps in Documentation

Termination letters and exit documentation summarize the termination terms, reasons, and next steps. This final record closes the employment cycle and provides both parties with clear terms for separation. Documenting the termination process, including any final interviews or feedback, reinforces professionalism and legal compliance. Regularly reviewing documentation practices ensures that they stay aligned with current legal standards and organizational needs.

Providing training for HR and managers on documentation practices reinforces the importance of thorough, accurate, and confidential records. This commitment to continuous improvement fosters a fair, transparent workplace and supports ongoing compliance. As a reminder, the ideal documentation location is within the primary HR record and, with the proper security measures, is accessible to the employee's direct supervisor and to the appropriate HR staff. Managers are to forward all documentation to be saved (or upload themselves) to this location, and not save documentation in their work email, papers in unlocked drawers, or inside of a notebook on their desk.

Severance and Benefits: Supporting Employees Through Transitions

Severance packages and the continuation of benefits are essential components of a respectful and supportive termination process. They provide financial stability and necessary support during the transition period, helping employees adjust to life after employment and allowing the organization to maintain positive relationships with former employees.

Severance Packages

Severance packages are compensation and benefits offered to employees who are departing involuntarily, often due to layoffs or company restructuring. A well-structured severance package can ease the transition for the employee while helping the organization mitigate legal risks and protect its reputation.

Typical Components of Severance Packages

Severance Pay

The foundation of most severance packages is a cash payment that provides financial support as the employee searches for new employment. Severance pay is often calculated based on the employee's length of service, position, and salary. A common formula is to offer one or two weeks of salary for each year of service, although this can vary depending on company policy, industry standards, or the employee's seniority. The goal is to provide enough financial stability to assist the employee through their transition.

Continuation of Benefits

Health insurance coverage is frequently extended through COBRA, allowing the employee to continue their existing healthcare plan for a specified period, often up to eighteen months. Other benefits, such as dental, vision, and life insurance, may also be continued. By offering extended benefits, organizations help former employees maintain necessary coverage during a potentially challenging period, reducing anxiety and supporting their well-being.

Outplacement Services

Outplacement services can include career counseling, job placement assistance, resume writing, and interview coaching. These services support employees in securing new employment and provide them with tools to enhance their job search. Outplacement services reflect the organization's commitment to supporting former employees' career continuity and can be invaluable for helping them rebuild after separation.

Unused Leave or Vacation Pay

Most companies include payment for any unused vacation or personal leave that the employee accrued. This pay is typically provided in the final paycheck and helps ensure that all earned benefits are compensated fairly. Unused leave payments are essential for concluding employment fairly and show respect for the time the employee invested in their role.

Retirement Benefits

For employees with retirement plans, severance packages may include instructions on how to manage or transfer 401(k) or pension plans. This step might involve contributions to retirement accounts, explanations of rollover options, or help navigating retirement savings. Providing guidance on retirement benefits offers peace of mind and enables employees to retain access to their hard-earned funds.

Release Agreements

Legal release agreements are often part of severance packages to protect the organization from future claims related to the termination. By signing a release, the employee agrees not to pursue legal action related to their separation in exchange for the severance benefits offered. This agreement must be clearly communicated, fair, and compliant with employment law.

Other Financial Considerations

For some employees, additional financial considerations, like unpaid bonuses, commissions, or stock options, may be included in the severance package. These elements help recognize the employee's contributions and ensure that they are fairly compensated for work completed before their termination date.

Determining Appropriate Severance Pay

Determining severance pay involves evaluating multiple factors for fairness, alignment with company policies, and compliance with legal standards.

Company Policy

Review the company's severance policy to determine if there are established guidelines for severance pay. Some organizations have structured policies detailing specific formulas or caps for severance. Alignment with these policies supports transparency and consistency across the organization.

Employment Contracts

Employment contracts or collective bargaining agreements may contain terms regarding severance pay. HR should review these contracts to fulfill any contractual obligations and avoid potential disputes.

Industry Standards

Benchmarking severance packages against industry standards ensures competitiveness and fairness. Many industries have established norms for severance that can serve as a reference point, keeping the organization aligned with market expectations.

Length of Service

The employee's tenure is a significant factor in calculating severance. Longer-serving employees generally receive higher severance due to their contributions and dedication. Severance calculations may increase with tenure, creating a fair compensation structure for employees of varying service lengths.

Position and Salary

An employee's role and salary level may influence the severance amount, with higher-level or specialized roles often commanding more substantial severance due to their impact on the organization. This approach also reflects the difficulty of finding comparable roles for highly specialized or senior employees.

Legal and Regulatory Requirements

Ensure that the severance package complies with any legal requirements, including federal, state, or local laws. For example, some jurisdictions mandate minimum severance or notice periods, especially in cases of mass layoffs or plant closures. Compliance with these laws mitigates risks and demonstrates fairness.

Financial Considerations and Budget Constraints

Assess the company's budget to balance fair severance packages with the organization's financial health. HR must work with finance to make sure the severance pay is manageable for the organization, particularly in cases of large-scale layoffs.

Negotiation

In certain cases, particularly with senior employees or those with long tenure, severance terms may be negotiable. Flexibility in negotiating severance shows respect for the employee's service and supports a smoother transition, contributing to a positive post-employment relationship.

Continuation of Benefits

Post-employment continuation of benefits, especially health insurance, is a key aspect of severance packages. Offering clear options for maintaining benefits can ease the employee's transition, reducing stress and providing stability.

COBRA (Consolidated Omnibus Budget Reconciliation Act)

COBRA is a federal program in the US that allows employees to continue their group health insurance for a limited time after termination. Eligible employees may extend coverage for eighteen to thirty-six months, although they bear the full premium cost. Employers are required to notify employees of their COBRA eligibility, and employees typically have sixty days to elect this coverage. While COBRA is often more expensive than employee-paid premiums, it offers a critical bridge for employees needing continuity in healthcare coverage.

State Continuation Coverage

Some states offer their own continuation coverage, often referred to as mini-COBRA, which may have different eligibility criteria or coverage periods. This can be an option for employees at companies with fewer than twenty employees, who are not eligible for federal COBRA. HR should communicate any state-specific options to ensure that employees have all available resources for maintaining health coverage.

Spousal or Dependent Coverage

Employees may be eligible to join a spouse's employer-sponsored health insurance plan as a dependent. This option can be more cost-effective than COBRA and provides continuity for families needing coverage. HR should inform employees of this possibility, encouraging them to check with their spouse's benefits provider for details.

Individual Health Insurance Plans

The Health Insurance Marketplace allows employees to find individual or family health insurance plans. Employees may qualify for subsidies or tax credits based on income, making these plans more affordable than COBRA. Informing employees about the Marketplace and the option for subsidies gives them access to alternative, potentially more affordable, coverage options.

Medicaid

If an employee's income decreases significantly after termination, they may qualify for Medicaid, which provides low-cost or free health coverage for eligible low-income individuals. Informing employees of this option ensures that they can seek out affordable healthcare coverage during their transition.

Short-Term Health Insurance

Short-term health insurance offers temporary coverage, typically with lower premiums, although coverage is often limited. This can be a viable stopgap solution for employees between jobs, though it's not a substitute for comprehensive health insurance. HR can provide information on this option as a short-term bridge for employees seeking flexibility.

Health Savings Accounts (HSAs) and Flexible Spending Accounts (FSAs)

Employees with HSAs can continue to use funds for qualified medical expenses after termination, while FSA funds may have restricted usage based on company policies. Providing guidance on how to use these funds ensures that employees can make the most of available resources for healthcare expenses after termination.

Employee Assistance Programs (EAPs)

Many organizations offer EAPs that provide mental health support, counseling, and legal assistance. Some EAPs allow limited access after termination, providing a valuable resource for employees as they transition. Informing employees about this option shows care and commitment to their well-being.

Considerations for Employers

Communication

Clear communication about benefits options is critical during the termination process. Employees need accurate information on options like COBRA, the Health Insurance Marketplace, and spousal coverage to make informed choices about their health insurance. Proactive communication minimizes confusion and makes employees feel supported.

Documentation

Employers must provide all required notices, such as COBRA notifications, in compliance with regulations. Proper documentation minimizes liability and provides evidence that the organization met its legal obligations.

Support

Offering guidance on navigating benefits options, including COBRA and state-specific programs, supports employees in maintaining essential health coverage. This support shows empathy, maintains positive relationships, and reflects the organization's commitment to fair practices.

Handling Employee Reactions

The termination process can trigger a range of emotional responses in employees. As an HR professional, addressing these reactions with compassion and professionalism is essential for preserving dignity, minimizing tension, and supporting a respectful transition. I've put together an overview of common emotional responses and best practices for handling them effectively.

Terminations can come as a surprise to employees, leaving them in a state of shock or disbelief. This reaction is particularly common if the employee was unaware of performance concerns or impending organizational changes. Be clear and direct in your communication to prevent misunderstandings. Avoid ambiguous language and explain the specific reasons for the termination. Allow the employee time to process the news and be available to answer any initial questions they might have. Providing information about the next steps, such as severance and available support resources, helps the employee focus on moving forward.

Anger and frustration can arise, especially if the employee feels the decision is unjust or handled poorly. Employees may express their grievances, question the decision, or become defensive. Remain calm and composed, avoiding any escalation or defensive reactions. Listen empathetically to their concerns, acknowledge their feelings, and validate their frustrations by expressing understanding. Where appropriate, offer constructive feedback on performance or behavior in a respectful and factual way. Acknowledging their emotions shows respect and helps diffuse heightened emotions, ensuring a smoother conversation.

For employees with strong ties to the organization or long tenure, termination can bring sadness and a sense of loss. They may express regret over leaving or fear of the unknown. Show empathy by acknowledging the personal impact of the termination. Let them know you understand their sadness and offer support in any way you can. Providing information about counseling services or employee assistance programs (EAPs) can help them access emotional support as they navigate this transition. A compassionate approach helps preserve their dignity and contributes to a more positive closure.

The uncertainty that follows job loss can create fear and anxiety about financial stability, career prospects, and personal obligations. Employees may worry about how they will manage their next steps. Offering practical support can help ease their anxiety. Provide guidance on unemployment benefits, job search resources, and career counseling services. Encourage them to utilize available support, such as outplacement services or networking opportunities, to regain confidence in finding new opportunities. Practical assistance and encouragement can reassure them that they are not alone in this transition.

Some employees may resist the termination, holding on to hope for a reversal or expressing disbelief that it's happening. They may question the finality of the decision or seek to appeal it. Maintain a firm yet compassionate tone, reinforcing that the decision is final and explaining the process that led to it. Give them a chance to voice any remaining concerns or questions to ensure that they feel heard. Emphasize that the organization followed due process, which may include options for appeal if the company offers them. Addressing their concerns respectfully helps alleviate resistance while reinforcing transparency.

In some cases, employees may feel a sense of relief or acceptance, especially if they were dissatisfied with their role or expected the decision. This reaction can make the termination process smoother. Respect their feelings and acknowledge their readiness for change. Focus on providing the necessary resources and support to help them transition smoothly. Reiterate details about severance, benefits, and career support to set them up for a constructive exit. Acceptance of the situation can allow for a more positive parting, which benefits both the employee and the organization.

Best Practices for Handling Emotional Responses

Handling emotional responses with professionalism and empathy not only supports the individual but also reflects positively on the organization.

- **Maintain Dignity**: Always treat employees with respect and avoid language or actions that could be perceived as dismissive or condescending. Terminations should prioritize the employee's dignity, regardless of the circumstances.
- **Provide Clear Information**: Clearly communicate the details of the termination, including severance, benefits, and available resources. Clarity reduces uncertainty and empowers the employee to focus on their next steps.
- **Ensure Privacy**: Conduct termination meetings in a private setting to allow the employee to process their emotions without public exposure, maintaining confidentiality and respect.
- **Offer Support Resources**: Provide information on outplacement services, counseling, and career coaching to help

employees during their transition. Supporting their future prospects demonstrates care and fosters goodwill.

- **Document the Process**: Keep detailed records of the termination meeting and any follow-up interactions to ensure transparency and compliance with company policies. This documentation supports fairness and accountability.

Support Resources: The Importance of Providing Assistance During Termination

Offering support resources to employees during termination demonstrates the organization's commitment to their well-being and career growth. Let's discuss why these resources are essential and how they contribute to a smoother transition.

Terminations are inherently stressful, and offering counseling services provides employees with a safe space to process their feelings. Counseling can help alleviate isolation, anxiety, and depression, which may arise during this period. By providing access to mental health resources, organizations show that they value the employee's emotional well-being and support them through a challenging time. Outplacement services, including job search support, resume writing assistance, and interview coaching, empower employees to navigate the job market effectively. This support not only helps them find new opportunities but also builds their confidence as they approach new roles. Career coaching can further guide employees in planning their career paths and exploring new opportunities that align with their skills and aspirations.

An organization that provides support resources during termination reflects a culture of care and responsibility. Employees who feel supported are more likely to speak positively about their experience, preserving the organization's reputation in the industry. A commitment to helping employees transition can lead to positive word of mouth and demonstrate the company's dedication to its workforce, even in difficult situations.

Providing career counseling and outplacement services helps mitigate legal risks by showing that the organization made efforts to support the terminated employee. This proactive approach can reduce the likelihood of claims related to unfair treatment or wrongful termination. Offering support also helps reassure remaining employees, boosting morale and reducing turnover risk. With clear guidance on job search strategies, career development, and outplacement services, employees are better prepared to transition successfully into new roles.

Types of Support Resources

Providing a variety of support resources helps employees address both their practical and emotional needs as they navigate the transition.

- Outplacement Services
  - o Assistance with writing resumes and preparing for interviews
  - o Job search strategies and networking support
  - o Access to job search databases and tools
- Counseling Services
  - o Access to emotional support, therapy, and stress management
  - o Mental health resources through employee assistance programs (EAPs)
  - o Support groups for individuals in similar situations
- Career Coaching
  - o Career assessment and planning guidance
  - o Skill development support and goal-setting strategies
  - o Personalized advice on career path exploration
- Additional Resources

- Financial planning advice for managing severance and budgeting
- Legal consultation for any employment-related issues
- Access to professional networks and alumni groups for ongoing support

Internal Communication: Minimizing Disruption and Maintaining Morale

Communicating terminations internally requires a delicate balance of transparency, privacy, and support for remaining employees. Done correctly, it can help maintain morale and reassure staff while fostering a supportive, professional environment.

Plan the Communication Strategy

Consider the timing carefully to avoid unnecessary speculation or gossip. Sharing the news promptly but thoughtfully allows the team to process the change and adjust as needed. Avoid delays, which can lead to misinformation, but also be confident that you have all the details in place before announcing the departure. Craft a message that is clear, respectful, and appropriately brief. While employees may be curious, refrain from discussing the specifics behind the termination to respect privacy. The focus should be on minimizing disruption and promoting a positive, forward-looking message.

Establish Key Communication Points

Give a factual, brief explanation. For example, "We want to inform you that [Employee's Name] is no longer with the company. This decision aligns with our ongoing efforts to meet our business needs." Avoid language that may be perceived as judgmental or overly detailed. Address the potential impact on the team by highlighting plans to cover the departing employee's responsibilities. For instance, "We are taking steps to ensure that all responsibilities are covered and that projects will continue without interruption." Acknowledge the impact on the team and offer support. Encourage employees to reach out to HR or their managers if they have concerns, reinforcing the message that the organization values their well-being during this transition.

Choose the Right Medium

When the departure has a significant impact on the team, a team meeting allows managers to communicate directly, address questions, and set a positive tone. For less immediate issues or as a follow-up to a meeting, an email provides a formal record and allows employees to review the information on their own time. Ensure that the tone is supportive and professional.

Address Questions and Concerns

Encourage employees to discuss any questions or concerns privately with HR or their manager. Providing an open door for individual conversations helps alleviate potential misunderstandings. Consider providing a feedback option for employees who may prefer anonymity. Anonymous feedback can help gauge team sentiment and allow HR to address any underlying issues.

Support the Team

Recognize that terminations can affect morale. Reassure the team by emphasizing the organization's commitment to stability, employee development, and future growth. Organize team-building activities or discussions to strengthen cohesion. Acknowledging the team's contributions and focusing on unity helps rebuild trust and a sense of purpose.

Monitor and Follow Up

Schedule follow-up meetings to monitor team morale and productivity. Remaining present shows employees that their concerns are valued and allows for early intervention if issues arise. Be prepared to redistribute tasks or adjust workloads temporarily, helping the team stay focused and productive during the transition.

Maintain Confidentiality

Refrain from sharing specifics about the termination to preserve the employee's dignity. Emphasize professionalism, respecting the privacy of both the departing employee and remaining team members. Ensure that communications remain supportive and objective, setting a standard of respect in the organization.

Provide Support Resources

Remind employees of available resources, such as counseling or EAPs, which can provide valuable support. Reinforcing these resources shows a commitment to employee well-being.

External Communication: Protecting the Organization's Reputation

When communicating terminations externally, the focus should be on maintaining the organization's reputation and managing public perception. Let's dive into how to approach this communication with professionalism and care.

First, determine if external communication is necessary based on the employee's role and the potential impact on clients, partners, or the public. Not all terminations require external communication; however, a high-profile role may necessitate a carefully managed response. Consider the broader implications of the termination on the company's reputation, especially if the departure may raise questions from stakeholders.

If the termination may affect business relationships or attract media attention, a prepared statement is often beneficial. Keep the message short and focused, covering only the essential information. Avoid oversharing, as details could lead to speculation or misinterpretation. Ensure that the external message aligns with internal communications. Consistent messaging reinforces a unified approach and minimizes the risk of conflicting information.

While developing the key message points, I recommend beginning with a clear statement of purpose. For example, "We want to inform you that [Employee's Name] is no longer with [Company Name]. This decision supports our current business strategy." Emphasize the organization's ongoing dedication to quality and commitment to stakeholders to set the right tone. For instance, "Our focus on delivering exceptional service remains unchanged. We are confident in our ability to meet your needs." It's important to reassure stakeholders about continuity. For example, "We have made necessary arrangements to ensure that there will be no disruption in services and our commitment to you remains our priority."

For significant terminations that may attract media attention, a press release makes the message professional and carefully crafted. Start by coordinating with legal and PR teams to vet the message. When the departure affects clients or partners, personalized communication (email or phone call) provides a respectful, personal approach. When appropriate, brief updates on the company website or social media channels can address potential public inquiries. These channels should remain concise and professional. While people want to know the scoop, it's important to avoid revealing specifics behind the termination to protect both the organization and the employee's privacy. Respect for privacy underscores professionalism and reinforces a positive reputation. Keep the message positive and constructive, avoiding accusatory language. This tone supports the organization's image as fair and respectful.

If you don't already have one, I recommend that you assign a trained spokesperson, such as a PR manager or senior executive, to handle media inquiries. This provides consistency and helps maintain control over the message. It's better to choose this individual in advance and ensure that they have a clear policy to follow in this area. After a termination or during the planning process, prepare statements in advance to manage any anticipated questions and provide consistent responses. Having statements ready can prevent misstatements during spontaneous inquiries.

Have someone on your marketing or communications team monitor feedback on social media, news outlets, and other channels. This tracking helps gauge public sentiment, allowing for timely adjustments if needed. If negative feedback or misinformation arises, address it promptly with factual clarifications. Being transparent without revealing private details helps control the narrative, which is important during potentially uncertain times.

While external communications are important, make sure someone on your team completes internal communications *before* making external announcements to prevent premature leaks. Informing employees before informing the public demonstrates respect and maintains internal trust. A best practice is to train staff on how to respond to external inquiries, ensuring that they understand company policies regarding termination-related communications. Generally, this is identifying that trained spokesperson and requiring all communications or inquiries be sent to that individual for response.

Lastly, to help make the future better based on lessons learned, evaluate the effectiveness of the external communication strategy after it has been executed. It's helpful to review feedback to identify areas for improvement. Using insights gained to refine future communication strategies, improving both internal and external messaging will help your organization improve and grow stronger, even if the plan is not to conduct a termination of the same nature in the future.

While employee terminations can be one of the most challenging aspects of managing a workforce, they are also an essential part of maintaining a healthy, productive organization. By approaching terminations with fairness, empathy, and adherence to legal and ethical standards, HR professionals and managers can minimize disruption and uphold the dignity of everyone involved. Remember, how you handle a termination reflects the integrity of your organization and can significantly impact morale, culture, and even your employer brand. Treat every termination as an opportunity to reinforce accountability, compassion, and respect, ensuring that your organization remains a place where people and performance thrive together.

CHAPTER 5

HR Compliance and HR Law

Compliance is one of the trickiest parts of HR for small businesses. Laws around wages, employee rights, hiring, and termination can feel overwhelming, but staying compliant is crucial to avoiding lawsuits, fines, or reputational damage. This chapter breaks down the key HR laws every business owner should know, from fair hiring practices to wage and hour regulations, so you can confidently manage HR without legal headaches.

HR law encompasses a wide range of regulations and legal standards that govern the employer-employee relationship, which is critical for maintaining a compliant and productive workplace. This legal framework covers various aspects, including hiring practices, workplace safety, employee benefits, discrimination, and termination procedures. A deep understanding of HR law is essential for businesses that want to ensure compliance, minimize legal risks, and foster a fair and safe work environment.

It should go without saying, but HR law, just like compliance and regulations in most industries, is changing at a rapid pace to keep up with the demands of the workplace. I am not an attorney, and I highly recommend that you connect with one so that you can be sure that you are following the letter of the law in your region, state, and country. Also, these laws change regularly, so while this chapter will give you a solid idea of what you need to consider, be sure to stay up to date with any adjustments in regulation. I have referenced several of the laws in previous chapters where they were directly applicable but want this chapter to be somewhat of a stand-alone resource, so let's dive in.

One of the key areas of HR law is employment contracts and agreements, which define the terms of employment, such as job responsibilities, compensation, and duration. These contracts establish clear expectations and protect both the employer and employee. Another crucial component is anti-discrimination laws, which include regulations like Title VII of the Civil Rights Act, the Americans with Disabilities Act (ADA), and the Age Discrimination in Employment Act (ADEA). These laws prohibit discrimination in the workplace based on race, color, religion, sex, national origin, age, or disability, promoting fair treatment for all employees.

Labor laws, such as those set by the Fair Labor Standards Act (FLSA) and the National Labor Relations Act (NLRA), govern minimum wage, overtime pay, child labor, and collective bargaining rights. Understanding these laws helps organizations comply with wage and hour regulations. Additionally, health and safety regulations enforced by the Occupational Safety and Health Administration (OSHA) guarantee safe working conditions, protecting employees from hazards and ensuring a healthy work environment. Employee benefits and compensation are also governed by legal requirements, with the Employee Retirement Income Security Act (ERISA) setting standards for pension and health plans. The Family and Medical Leave Act (FMLA) provides eligible employees with the right to take unpaid, job-protected leave for specific family and medical reasons, further safeguarding employee rights. Another significant aspect is workplace privacy, which involves regulations related to monitoring employee communications and handling personal data, such as the General Data Protection Regulation (GDPR) for organizations operating in the European Union.

Termination and severance are crucial areas in HR law that set legal standards for fair and lawful employment termination, addressing issues such as wrongful termination claims and severance package requirements. It is vital that employers understand these laws while navigating the complexities of employee separations. The significance of HR law in managing employer-employee relationships cannot be overstated.

First and foremost, compliance with these legal standards ensures that companies reduce the risk of lawsuits, fines, and reputational damage. By promoting fair treatment and equal opportunity for all employees, HR law fosters a positive and inclusive workplace culture. It also protects the rights and well-being of employees, guaranteeing that they work in a safe and respectful environment. Moreover, HR law provides mechanisms for resolving workplace disputes, preventing escalation to legal actions, and offers a legal framework that guides employers in making informed decisions regarding hiring, management, and termination practices.

Ultimately, complying with HR law can boost morale and productivity, as a fair and legally compliant work environment enhances employee trust and engagement. HR law plays a critical role in safeguarding the rights of both employees and employers, keeping workplaces fair, safe, and productive. This comprehensive framework encompasses various regulations and legal standards that uphold employee rights while providing employers with the necessary guidelines for managing their workforce effectively.

Fundamental Legal Principles

One of the foundational concepts in HR law is employment-at-will, a legal doctrine that governs the employer-employee relationship in the United States (in some but not all states). This principle stipulates that, in the absence of a specific contract that states otherwise, an employer has the right to terminate an employee—at any time, for any reason, or for no reason at all, and without prior warning—as long as the reason for termination is not illegal, such as discrimination based on protected characteristics. Conversely, employees also have the freedom to leave their jobs at any time without obligation to provide notice or justification.

This flexibility can have significant implications for both parties involved. For employers, the implications of employment-at-will include enhanced flexibility in workforce management. They can hire and fire employees based on evolving business needs without being constrained by long-term contracts. This ability to quickly adjust the workforce allows organizations to remain agile in a competitive landscape. Additionally, employers can address performance issues more swiftly, enabling them to dismiss underperforming employees without lengthy disciplinary procedures.

However, this flexibility comes with risks. Employers must navigate the potential for wrongful termination claims, ensuring that any termination does not violate anti-discrimination laws, public policy, or any implied contracts. To safeguard against such challenges, it is essential for employers to maintain thorough documentation of employment actions. Moreover, the at-will nature of employment can impact employee morale and retention. The absence of job security may lead to concerns among employees about their stability in the workplace, resulting in lower morale and increased turnover. Consequently, employers may need to invest in creating a positive work environment and fostering transparent communication to alleviate fears of arbitrary dismissal.

On the employee side, the implications of employment-at-will can be both liberating and anxiety-inducing. The ability to leave a job without being tied to long-term contracts provides employees with significant job flexibility, allowing them to pursue better opportunities or personal interests. This freedom can also serve as a negotiation tool, giving employees leverage in discussions regarding their employment terms. However, this flexibility comes at a cost; employees may grapple with a sense of job insecurity. Knowing that they can be terminated at any time without cause can create feelings of instability and lead to financial uncertainty and stress.

Legal protections exist to mitigate some of these concerns. Anti-discrimination laws safeguard employees from terminations based on race, color, religion, sex, national origin, age, disability, and other protected characteristics. Furthermore, the public policy exception to employment-at-will provides an additional layer of protection, preventing terminations for reasons that violate public policy, such as refusing to engage in illegal activities, reporting violations of the law, or exercising legal rights.

While employment-at-will is the standard framework, there are important exceptions that may affect its application. One is the implied contract exception, where verbal or written assurances of job security can create an implied contract, limiting an employer's ability to terminate at will. Another is the covenant of good faith and fair dealing, recognized in some states, which suggests that employment decisions should be made fairly and in good faith, even in an at-will context. Finally, the public policy exception protects employees from termination for exercising legal rights, such as filing for workers' compensation, reporting illegal activities, or serving on a jury.

Employment-at-will provides significant flexibility for both employers and employees, allowing either party to end the employment relationship without the need for a contractually defined reason or notice period. However, it also introduces challenges, such as potential job insecurity for employees and the risk of wrongful termination claims for employers. To navigate these challenges, employers must comply with legal protections and foster a supportive work environment, while employees should be aware of their rights and the conditions of their employment.

Employment Contracts: Essential Components of the Employer-Employee Relationship

Employment contracts are formal agreements that delineate the terms and conditions governing the relationship between employers and employees. These contracts take various forms, including offer letters, noncompete agreements, and confidentiality agreements. Each serves a distinct purpose in protecting the interests of both parties and creating clarity in the employment relationship. Understanding these documents is crucial for creating a robust and transparent work environment.

Offer Letters

An offer letter is often the first formal document exchanged between an employer and a prospective employee, serving as confirmation of the job offer and outlining the fundamental terms of employment. Given that studies show that approximately one in six job offers is declined, organizations should examine their offer letters closely to ensure that they are compelling and comprehensive.[2] If offers are being declined, there are several strategies that can help mitigate this

---

2   Glassdoor Economic Research posted on February 27, 2020

issue. One important tactic is to clearly advertise the salary or at least provide a salary band in job postings. If candidates are surprised by the compensation at the offer stage, this could lead them to decline, reflecting poorly on the employer's transparency. Employers should remember that, while they are committing to pay the new hire, they are also marketing the role to the candidate. Therefore, it is essential to highlight the unique opportunities and benefits that come with the position to generate excitement.

Additionally, the format of the offer should not be overlooked. Utilizing informal emails may signal a lack of professionalism. Instead, offer letters should be presented in a polished format—such as a Word document saved as a PDF—to underscore the seriousness of the opportunity.

Employers might also consider enhancing their interview processes by incorporating more steps, such as questionnaires or video submissions. Research indicates that candidates are statistically more likely to accept an offer if they perceive the interview process as challenging and engaging.

The benefits of a well-crafted offer letter are manifold. It provides clarity and transparency by clearly communicating the details of the job offer, thereby preventing misunderstandings. Furthermore, an offer letter serves as a legal record that can be referenced in case of disputes regarding employment terms.

Noncompete Agreements

Noncompete agreements (NCAs) are another critical element of employment contracts. They restrict employees from joining competitors or starting a competing business for a specified time after leaving the company. These agreements aim to protect an employer's trade secrets, confidential information, and customer relationships, which are vital for maintaining a competitive edge in the market.

Key elements of an NCA include the scope and duration of the restrictions, as well as the consideration exchanged for the agreement to be enforceable. For instance, an employee may receive additional training or a promotion in exchange for signing the agreement. The benefits of NCAs are significant; they safeguard a company's intellectual property and prevent former employees from leveraging insider knowledge to benefit rival organizations. As with all HR law, it's always evolving, so it's best to partner with a seasoned HR professional or pay for membership in an organization that can keep you up to date with potentially changing legislation in this space.

Confidentiality Agreements

Confidentiality agreements, commonly referred to as nondisclosure agreements (NDAs), require employees to keep certain business information confidential during and after their employment. These agreements are essential for protecting sensitive information, such as trade secrets, business strategies, and client data.

Key components of confidentiality agreements include a clear definition of what constitutes confidential information and a specified duration for which the employee is obligated to maintain confidentiality after leaving the company.

The benefits of these agreements are substantial. They provide a legal basis for action if confidential information is improperly disclosed and encourage a culture of trust in the organization, allowing for open communication without the fear of sensitive information being leaked.

Key Employment Laws and Regulations

If you're thinking TL; DNR at this point (too long, did not read) like I do sometimes, here's a quick list of legal considerations for businesses, but I highly recommend you refill that coffee and come back for the context and additional details after you cruise through my short list.

Basic Legal Considerations for Businesses

- **Fair Labor Standards Act (FLSA):**

    o   Classify employees correctly (exempt vs. non-exempt).

    o   Ensure compliance with overtime and minimum wage laws.

- **Americans with Disabilities Act (ADA):**

    o   Provide reasonable accommodations when required.

    o   Maintain a discrimination-free hiring process.

- **Equal Employment Opportunity (EEO) Laws:**

    o   Prohibit discrimination based on race, gender, age, disability.

    o   Maintain fair hiring and disciplinary practices.

- **Occupational Safety and Health Administration (OSHA):**

    o   Implement workplace safety standards.

o   Conduct required safety training for hazardous job environments.

Misclassifying employees can lead to legal issues and financial penalties. My consulting firm has an **Exempt vs. Non-Exempt Guide** which makes it easier to determine the right classification and stay compliant. The guide helps you understand key differences in the two statuses, avoid costly compliance mistakes and stay aligned with labor laws. Go to saltandlightadvisors.com/exemptvsnonexempt to grab it.

Anti-discrimination laws play a crucial role in promoting equality and protecting employees from unfair treatment in the workplace. These laws create a fair environment for all workers and address various forms of discrimination. Among the most significant anti-discrimination laws in the United States are Title VII of the Civil Rights Act, the Age Discrimination in Employment Act (ADEA), and the Americans with Disabilities Act (ADA). Each of these laws has specific provisions and protections that are essential for fostering an inclusive work environment.

Title VII of the Civil Rights Act of 1964

Title VII aims to eliminate workplace discrimination based on race, color, religion, sex, or national origin. This landmark legislation established a framework for fair employment practices.

Under Title VII, several key provisions are outlined to protect employees. First, it identifies protected classes, which include race, color, religion, sex (encompassing gender identity and sexual orientation), and national origin. The law prohibits discrimination in various employment practices, such as hiring, firing, promotion, compensation, and other terms and conditions of employment.

Additionally, Title VII explicitly outlaws workplace harassment based on these protected classes so that employees are not subjected to a hostile work environment. It also prohibits retaliation against individuals who file a discrimination complaint or participate in an investigation, providing critical protections for those who seek to assert their rights.

Enforcement of Title VII is carried out by the Equal Employment Opportunity Commission (EEOC). Victims of discrimination can file a charge with the EEOC, and if the issue is not resolved, they may pursue a lawsuit. The impact of Title VII is significant, as it promotes diversity and inclusion in the workforce while holding employers accountable for discriminatory practices.

Age Discrimination in Employment Act (ADEA) of 1967

The ADEA protects employees and job applicants aged forty and older from discrimination based on age. Its primary purpose is to ensure that older workers are treated fairly in all aspects of employment, including hiring, firing, promotions, compensation, and benefits. The ADEA prohibits employers from denying benefits to older employees based solely on their age, although cost considerations may serve as a defense in certain situations.

Like Title VII, the ADEA also prohibits harassment based on age that creates a hostile work environment and prohibits retaliation against individuals who complain about age discrimination or participate in investigations. The ADEA is also enforced under the jurisdiction of the EEOC, requiring individuals to file a charge with the agency before pursuing legal action. The ADEA's impact is profound, as it protects the rights of older workers and encourages fair treatment and equal opportunities regardless of age.

Americans with Disabilities Act (ADA) of 1990

The ADA prohibits discrimination against individuals with disabilities, ensuring that they have equal opportunities in the workplace. This law defines a protected class as individuals with disabilities who can perform the essential functions of their job, with or without reasonable accommodations. The ADA requires employers to provide reasonable accommodations to qualified individuals unless doing so would impose an undue hardship on the business.

Like the other laws, the ADA prohibits discrimination in hiring, firing, promotions, compensation, and other employment terms, and it outlaws harassment based on disability that creates a hostile work environment. Retaliation against individuals who assert their rights under the ADA or participate in investigations is also prohibited.

Enforcement of the ADA is managed by the EEOC, and individuals must file a charge with the agency before pursuing a lawsuit. The impact of the ADA is significant, as it promotes accessibility and inclusion in the workplace so that individuals with disabilities can succeed.

Minimum Wage Provisions

The **Fair Labor Standards Act (FLSA)** is a cornerstone of US labor law that establishes essential standards for wages, overtime pay, and child labor. Enacted in 1938, the FLSA protects workers from unfair pay practices and substandard labor conditions, ensuring that every worker receives fair compensation for their efforts.

The primary purpose of the FLSA's minimum wage provisions is to guarantee that workers receive a baseline level of pay for their labor. The act establishes a federal minimum wage, which has stood at $7.25

per hour since 2009 and holding there still in 2025. However, states and municipalities have the authority to set higher minimum wages, reflecting the varying cost of living across different regions. For tipped employees, the law allows employers to pay a lower direct wage of $2.13 per hour, provided that the employee's total earnings—including tips—meet or exceed the federal minimum wage. Additionally, the FLSA permits employers to pay employees under the age of twenty a minimum wage of $4.25 per hour during their first ninety consecutive calendar days of employment. These provisions collectively ensure a basic standard of living for workers and provide a foundation for wage regulations across various states and localities.

Overtime Pay Provisions

Overtime pay provisions in the FLSA serve to compensate employees for hours worked beyond the standard workweek, promoting fair compensation for extended labor. The standard workweek is defined as forty hours, and nonexempt employees must receive overtime pay at a rate of at least one and a half times their regular pay for hours worked over this threshold. Certain employees, however, are exempt from these overtime provisions, including executive, administrative, and professional employees, as well as outside sales personnel and certain computer professionals, provided they meet specific criteria regarding job duties and salary levels.

These overtime provisions provide additional compensation for workers who exceed standard working hours and encourage employers to manage labor more efficiently to avoid excessive overtime costs.

Child Labor Provisions

The child labor provisions of the FLSA protect minors' educational opportunities and prevent their employment in roles that may be harmful to their health and well-being. The act sets the minimum age for employment at fourteen years for non-agricultural jobs and imposes restrictions on the number of hours minors can work.

For example, minors aged fourteen to fifteen are restricted to a maximum of three hours of work during school days and a total of eighteen hours during a school week. On non-school days, they can work a maximum of eight hours, not exceeding forty hours in a non-school week. Individuals aged sixteen to seventeen have no hourly restrictions, but they are prohibited from working in hazardous occupations.

The act also explicitly prohibits minors under the age of eighteen from working in jobs deemed hazardous by the secretary of labor, such as operating heavy machinery or being exposed to harmful substances. These regulations ensure that young workers can pursue their education while being protected from exploitation and dangerous working conditions.

In summary, the Fair Labor Standards Act (FLSA) plays a crucial role in safeguarding workers' rights in the United States by establishing minimum wage standards, regulating overtime pay, and setting restrictions on child labor. A solid understanding of and compliance with the FLSA is essential for employers in creating fair and equitable workplaces while protecting the well-being of their employees. This foundational labor law continues to evolve, addressing contemporary labor issues and reflecting changes in the workforce and economy.

Occupational Safety and Health Act (OSHA)

The **Occupational Safety and Health Act (OSHA)** of 1970 represents a significant advancement in the effort to improve workplace safety and health across the United States. Enacted with the aim of preventing workplace injuries and illnesses, OSHA was designed to create safe and healthful working conditions for all employees. This landmark legislation established the Occupational Safety and Health Administration, an agency in the US Department of Labor, and made it responsible for setting and enforcing safety and health standards.

OSHA's primary goal is to ensure that employers provide a working environment free from recognized hazards to safety and health. This includes protection against exposure to toxic chemicals, excessive noise levels, mechanical dangers, extreme temperatures, and unsanitary conditions. By setting forth a framework for workplace safety, OSHA aims to mitigate risks that could harm workers. It also promotes an overall culture of safety in the workplace.

One of the key provisions of OSHA is the General Duty Clause, which mandates that employers must maintain a workplace free from recognized hazards that could cause death or serious physical harm. This clause acts as a catch-all provision for hazards not explicitly covered by existing OSHA standards. In addition to the General Duty Clause, OSHA establishes specific standards and regulations tailored to various industries, such as construction, maritime, agriculture, and general industry. These standards address a wide range of workplace hazards, including exposure to hazardous chemicals, electrical safety, fall protection, and safe machinery operation.

OSHA's enforcement mechanisms are crucial for compliance with safety and health standards. Compliance safety and health officers, or OSHA inspectors, have the authority to inspect workplaces to verify adherence to these standards. Inspections may be prompted by worker complaints, accidents, referrals, or as part of routine monitoring programs.

Furthermore, employers are required to maintain records of work-related injuries and illnesses, with a mandate to report within eight hours any incidents resulting in a fatality or the hospitalization of three or more employees.

Employer responsibilities under OSHA are comprehensive and include compliance with all safety standards, ensuring that employees have access to safe tools and equipment, and establishing safety and health programs that encompass training and education.

Employers must also inform employees about potential hazards through various means, such as training sessions, labeling, alarms, and safety data sheets. On the other hand, employees have the right to a safe workplace and can raise safety concerns without fear of retaliation. They also have the right to receive appropriate training, work with safe machinery, and be provided with necessary safety equipment.

OSHA standards encompass a wide array of regulations tailored to different sectors.

- General Industry Standards (29 CFR Part 1910) cover numerous safety topics, including machinery, fire safety, hazardous materials, and personal protective equipment (PPE).
- The Construction Standards (29 CFR Part 1926) focus on safety measures specific to the construction industry, including fall protection and scaffolding regulations.
- Additionally, maritime safety standards address regulations for shipyards and marine terminals, while agriculture standards focus on safety concerns unique to agricultural operations.

OSHA also supports several related programs and initiatives that enhance workplace safety.

- The Safety and Health Achievement Recognition Program (SHARP) acknowledges small businesses that demonstrate exemplary injury and illness prevention programs.
- The Voluntary Protection Programs (VPP) encourage industries and federal agencies to adopt proactive approaches to prevent workplace injuries and illnesses through hazard control and employee involvement.
- The OSHA Training Institute (OTI) offers educational resources and training in occupational safety and health for compliance officers, state consultants, and private sector personnel.

The **Family and Medical Leave Act (FMLA)**, enacted in 1993, is a significant piece of federal legislation in the United States that grants eligible employees the right to take unpaid, job-protected leave for specific family and medical reasons. The primary aim of the FMLA is to help employees balance their work and family responsibilities by allowing them to take time off without risking their employment status. By providing this framework, the FMLA helps to alleviate the stress associated with juggling personal and professional obligations.

To qualify for FMLA leave, both employers and employees must meet certain requirements. The FMLA applies to employers with fifty or more employees within a seventy-five-mile radius, ensuring that this protection extends to a significant portion of the workforce. For employees, eligibility requires a minimum of twelve months of service with the employer and at least 1,250 hours of work in the twelve months preceding the leave.

Eligible employees can take up to twelve weeks of unpaid leave during a twelve-month period for various reasons, including the birth or adoption of a child, caring for a spouse, child, or parent with a serious health condition, addressing the employee's own serious health condition, or managing exigent circumstances related to a family member's military service.

The FMLA also includes provisions specifically for military families. Qualifying Exigency Leave allows eligible employees to take up to twelve weeks of leave for urgent needs arising from a family member's deployment. Furthermore, Military Caregiver Leave provides up to twenty-six weeks of leave in a single twelve-month period to care for a covered service member who has sustained a serious injury or illness.

Importantly, the FMLA includes strong job protection guarantees, requiring that employees be restored to their original or an equivalent position upon returning from leave. Employers are also mandated to maintain health insurance coverage for employees during their FMLA leave under the same terms and conditions as if the leave had not been taken.

In addition to the FMLA, several other regulations and laws impact employee leave rights.

- The Americans with Disabilities Act (ADA) prohibits discrimination against individuals with disabilities and may require employers to provide additional leave as a reasonable accommodation.
- The Pregnancy Discrimination Act (PDA), an amendment to Title VII of the Civil Rights Act, mandates that pregnancy-related conditions must be treated the same as other medical conditions regarding benefits and leave.
- Furthermore, state and local leave laws can offer more generous benefits than those provided by the FMLA, including paid sick leave and parental leave.

- Other relevant legislation includes the Uniformed Services Employment and Reemployment Rights Act (USERRA), which protects the employment rights of individuals who serve in the military, safeguarding their reemployment rights and continuation of health benefits upon returning from military duty.
- Additionally, workers' compensation laws provide benefits to employees who become injured or ill due to work-related activities, covering medical care and job protection during recovery.

Compliance with the FMLA and related leave regulations is critical for employers. Staying informed about federal, state, and local leave laws is essential to ensure compliance and avoid legal repercussions. Clear documentation and open communication regarding employee leave rights are vital. Employers should develop transparent leave policies and procedures that comply with applicable laws and provide HR personnel and managers with proper training on FMLA and other leave regulations. Consistent application of leave policies is necessary to prevent discrimination claims, and maintaining confidentiality regarding leave requests and medical information is paramount to protecting employee privacy.

The **Health Insurance Portability and Accountability Act (HIPAA)**, enacted in 1996, plays a critical role in safeguarding sensitive patient health information from unauthorized disclosure. Its primary purpose is to protect individuals' medical records and other personal health information, ensuring that this data is not disclosed without the patient's consent or knowledge.

The law established the Privacy Rule, which sets standards for the protection of medical records and applies to health plans, healthcare clearinghouses, and healthcare providers engaged in certain electronic healthcare transactions. Under this rule, appropriate safeguards must be implemented to protect personal health information, and there are strict limits on the use and disclosure of such information without patient authorization.

HIPAA includes several other key provisions. The Security Rule outlines a series of administrative, physical, and technical safeguards necessary to maintain the confidentiality, integrity, and availability of electronic protected health information (e-PHI).

Moreover, the Breach Notification Rule mandates that covered entities notify affected individuals, the secretary of health and human services, and, in some cases, the media in the event of a breach involving unsecured protected health information.

Finally, the Enforcement Rule provides the standards for enforcing all Administrative Simplification Rules established by HIPAA. Overall, HIPAA is essential for ensuring that patient health information remains protected while facilitating the necessary flow of information required for high-quality healthcare delivery.

On a global scale, the General Data Protection Regulation (GDPR), implemented in May 2018, represents a comprehensive approach to data protection and privacy for individuals in the European Union (EU) and the European Economic Area (EEA). The GDPR is built upon a set of key data protection principles, including lawfulness, fairness, transparency, purpose limitation, data minimization, accuracy, storage limitation, and integrity and confidentiality. One of its significant features is the expansion of the rights of data subjects, which encompasses the right to be informed, the right of access, the right to rectification, the right to erasure (often referred to as the right to be forgotten), the right to restrict processing, the right to data portability, and the right to object, along with rights related to automated decision-making and profiling.

Organizations that fall under the GDPR are also required to appoint a data protection officer (DPO) to oversee compliance with the regulation. Furthermore, the GDPR mandates that data breaches must be reported to the relevant supervisory authority within seventy-two hours of becoming aware of the breach, highlighting the importance of rapid response in safeguarding personal data. Noncompliance with the GDPR can result in substantial fines, which may reach up to 4 percent of annual global turnover or €20 million, whichever is greater. This regulation has established a high standard for data protection and privacy, influencing data protection laws around the world and significantly enhancing the protection of individuals' personal data.

Beyond HIPAA and GDPR, several other privacy-related laws contribute to the protection of individuals' personal data. The California Consumer Privacy Act (CCPA) grants California residents enhanced rights concerning the collection and use of their personal data, including rights to access, delete, and opt out of the sale of personal information.

Similarly, the Children's Online Privacy Protection Act (COPPA) imposes requirements on operators of websites directed toward children under the age of thirteen, necessitating verifiable parental consent before collecting personal information from children.

The Gramm-Leach-Bliley Act (GLBA) requires financial institutions to disclose their information-sharing practices and safeguard sensitive data, while the Family Educational Rights and Privacy Act (FERPA) protects the privacy of student education records and grants parents certain rights regarding these records.

Canada's Personal Information Protection and Electronic Documents Act (EPIPEDA) governs the collection, use, and disclosure of personal information by private-sector organizations, and the Payment Card Industry Data Security Standard (PCI DSS) establishes security standards for companies handling credit card information.

Collectively, privacy-related laws—such as HIPAA, GDPR, and others—protect individuals' personal data and ensure that organizations handle this information responsibly. Compliance with these laws not only secures sensitive data but also fosters trust and accountability among stakeholders. In a world increasingly reliant on digital communication and data sharing, adherence to these regulations is essential for safeguarding personal information and maintaining the integrity of organizations.

National Labor Relations Act (NLRA)

The National Labor Relations Act (NLRA), enacted in 1935, serves as a cornerstone of US labor law, establishing the rights of employees to engage in collective bargaining and participate in union activities. The NLRA's primary objective is to safeguard workers' rights to organize, form, join, or assist labor organizations and engage in collective bargaining, fostering a balanced relationship between employees and employers.

Key provisions of the NLRA outline essential employee rights, including the right to organize and form labor unions, the right to bargain collectively over wages, hours, and other working conditions, and the right to engage in concerted activities aimed at improving workplace conditions. This means employees can legally strike or protest, provided these actions are conducted lawfully.

Moreover, the NLRA imposes specific obligations on employers and unions, prohibiting unfair labor practices, such as employer interference with employees' rights to organize and union coercion of employees to join a particular union. The NLRA mandates that both parties must bargain in good faith regarding employment conditions; failure to do so can constitute an unfair labor practice.

The enforcement of the NLRA is overseen by the National Labor Relations Board (NLRB), an independent federal agency tasked with investigating complaints related to unfair labor practices and conducting union elections. The NLRB plays a vital role in determining whether employees wish to be represented by a union and mediating disputes that arise between employers and employees or unions.

Labor-Management Relations Act (Taft-Hartley Act)

Enacted in 1947, the Labor-Management Relations Act, commonly known as the Taft-Hartley Act, amended the NLRA to better balance the power dynamics between unions and employers. This federal law imposes restrictions on union activities while also protecting the rights of employees and employers. Among its key provisions, the Taft-Hartley Act prohibits unions from engaging in secondary boycotts, where they might pressure neutral parties to cease doing business with an employer involved in a labor dispute. It also outlawed closed-shop agreements, which required workers to be union members prior to employment. However, the law does permit union shops, which mandate that workers must join the union after being hired.

Additionally, the act ensures employee protections, granting workers the right to petition for the decertification of a union if they choose to no longer be represented by it, and safeguards their freedom of speech to express anti-union views without fear of retaliation.

Labor-Management Reporting and Disclosure Act (LMRDA)

The Labor-Management Reporting and Disclosure Act, also known as the Landrum-Griffin Act, was enacted in 1959 to protect the rights of union members and promote transparency in labor organizations. This legislation establishes a bill of rights for union members, granting them essential rights, such as the ability to vote in union elections, participate in union meetings, and be safeguarded from arbitrary suspension or expulsion.

In addition to these rights, the LMRDA mandates that unions file detailed financial reports with the Department of Labor and conduct regular elections for union officers, promoting accountability and transparency in union operations.

State Laws and Right-to-Work Laws

Beyond federal regulations, many states have enacted their own labor laws governing labor relations and collective bargaining, including right-to-work laws. These laws prohibit agreements between employers and unions that make union membership or the payment of union dues a condition of employment. The intent of right-to-work laws is to provide employees with the autonomy to choose whether or not to join a union without facing discrimination or risking their employment.

Immigration Reform and Control Act (IRCA) of 1986

The Immigration Reform and Control Act (IRCA) of 1986 stands as a pivotal piece of legislation in the United States, directly addressing immigration and its implications for employment. This act regulates the hiring of immigrants, promotes lawful employment practices, and provides pathways for undocumented workers.

One of the key provisions of IRCA is the requirement for employers to verify the identity and employment authorization of all employees hired after November 6, 1986, using the I-9 form. Under this mandate, employees must present documentation that proves both their identity and eligibility to work in the US. Employers are responsible for retaining these I-9 forms for a specified duration and must make them available for inspection by authorized government officials when requested.

In addition to employment verification, IRCA prohibits discrimination based on national origin or citizenship status, ensuring that employers cannot hire or continue to employ individuals who they know are unauthorized to work in the United States. The act includes sanctions and penalties for employers that fail to comply with its verification requirements or knowingly hire unauthorized workers, with penalties increasing for repeated violations.

Furthermore, IRCA established legalization programs that offered pathways to legal status for certain undocumented immigrants who had continuously resided in the US since before January 1, 1982. Among these programs were the Special Agricultural Worker (SAW) and the Replenishment Agricultural Worker (RAW) initiatives, designed to address labor shortages in the agricultural sector.

Related Immigration Laws Affecting Employment

IRCA's framework is complemented by several related immigration laws that impact employment practices in the US. One of the most significant is the Immigration and Nationality Act (INA), which governs US immigration law and outlines provisions for employment-based immigration. The INA establishes various visa categories for both temporary (nonimmigrant) and permanent (immigrant) workers. Common employment-based visas under this act include the H-1B visa for specialty occupations, the L-1 visa for intracompany transferees, and the EB-1 through EB-5 visas for employment-based immigrants.

Another crucial component of the immigration landscape is E-Verify, an online system that allows employers to confirm an employee's eligibility to work in the United States. While participation in E-Verify is voluntary for most employers, certain federal contractors and employers in specific states are mandated to use this system to verify work eligibility.

Additionally, the Deferred Action for Childhood Arrivals (DACA) policy permits certain individuals who arrived in the US as children to request deferred action from deportation and obtain work authorization, allowing them to receive renewable two-year work permits.

Temporary Protected Status (TPS) is another relevant legal provision, granted to eligible nationals from specific countries experiencing armed conflict, environmental disasters, or other extraordinary conditions. TPS beneficiaries are allowed to work and reside in the US for a limited time.

Moreover, the H-2A and H-2B visa programs facilitate the employment of foreign nationals in temporary agricultural and nonagricultural jobs, further emphasizing the critical role of foreign labor in various sectors of the US economy.

Impact on Employers and Employees

The implications of IRCA and related immigration laws are significant for both employers and employees.

For employers, compliance with these laws is paramount to avoid legal penalties, which can be severe. Companies must implement robust verification processes and train their HR personnel on compliance requirements to ensure adherence. Failure to follow these regulations can lead to costly fines, legal repercussions, and damage to the company's reputation.

On the employee side, individuals must provide appropriate documentation to prove their eligibility to work. Noncompliance or the provision of false information can result in job loss and serious legal consequences.

IRCA and related immigration laws profoundly influence the employment landscape in the United States, aiming to control illegal immigration, protect workers' rights, and foster a fair and legal workforce. It is imperative for both employers and employees to understand and comply with these laws to maintain a lawful and equitable working environment.

Employment-Related Torts

Employment-related torts are civil wrongs that can occur in the workplace, leading to potential harm for either employees or employers. These torts are significant because they can result in legal action, where a party found liable may have to pay damages. Some of the key employment-related torts include defamation, invasion of privacy, and intentional infliction of emotional distress, each of which has distinct definitions, elements, examples, and implications for both parties involved.

Defamation

Defamation involves making false statements about an individual that harm their reputation. In the workplace, this can occur between employers, employees, or third parties.

There are two primary types of defamation: libel and slander. Libel refers to written defamation, such as false statements made in emails or performance reviews, while slander pertains to spoken defamation, such as verbal statements made during meetings.

For a defamation claim to be successful, certain elements must be established: The statement must be false, it must be communicated to a third party, it must cause harm to the person's reputation, and the defendant must be at fault in making the statement, either through negligence or malice. For example, if an employer falsely accuses an employee of theft in a staff meeting or a manager writes an untrue negative reference about a former employee, these actions can be considered defamation. The legal consequences for defamation are significant, as the defamed party can sue for damages. Additionally, defamation can create a toxic work environment, leading to decreased morale and productivity among employees.

Invasion of Privacy

Invasion of privacy refers to intruding upon an employee's private affairs, publicizing private information, or misusing an employee's identity without their consent. This tort encompasses several types of violations.

Intrusion upon seclusion involves unwarranted invasions of an employee's personal space or affairs, such as unauthorized surveillance or searching personal belongings.

Public disclosure of private facts occurs when private information that is not of public concern, like medical records or personal finances, is shared.

False light refers to publicizing misleading information about an employee, while appropriation of name or likeness involves using an employee's identity for commercial gain without their permission.

For instance, an employer monitoring an employee's personal emails without consent or a supervisor sharing an employee's medical condition with coworkers can constitute an invasion of privacy.

The legal ramifications for such actions can lead to lawsuits for invasion of privacy, and breaches of privacy can significantly erode trust between employees and management, damaging the workplace culture.

Intentional Infliction of Emotional Distress

Intentional infliction of emotional distress occurs when an employer or coworker engages in extreme and outrageous conduct that intentionally or recklessly causes severe emotional distress to an employee. To establish a claim, certain elements must be proven: conduct must be extreme and outrageous, there must be intent or recklessness in the actions taken, the conduct must directly cause the emotional distress, and the distress must be substantial and enduring.

Examples of such behavior include a manager repeatedly humiliating an employee in front of colleagues or an employer making false threats of termination to intimidate an employee. The legal consequences for this type of tort can involve compensatory and punitive damages, and such conduct can contribute to a hostile work environment, severely impacting overall employee morale and productivity.

Understanding employment-related torts, including defamation, invasion of privacy, and intentional infliction of emotional distress, is crucial for maintaining a fair and lawful workplace. Employers must be mindful of their actions and communications to avoid legal liability and foster a respectful and supportive work environment. Simultaneously, employees should be aware of their rights and the legal remedies available to them if they encounter harmful conduct in the workplace. By proactively addressing these torts, organizations can mitigate risks and promote a culture of trust and integrity, ultimately benefiting everyone involved in the workplace.

Compliance and Risk Management

Effective compliance and risk management are crucial for organizations aiming to navigate the complexities of employment law while minimizing legal risks.

A comprehensive understanding of legal requirements is the foundation of any successful compliance strategy. This begins with thorough research to identify the applicable federal, state, and local laws that impact the organization. Key areas to consider include employment laws, safety regulations, anti-discrimination laws, wage and hour laws, and data protection regulations.

Organizations should prioritize staying updated on any changes in legal frameworks by consulting with legal professionals, subscribing to legal updates, or joining relevant industry associations. Engaging with employment lawyers or legal consultants can further ensure that the organization's policies are tailored to meet legal requirements and the organization's specific needs.

The development of clear and comprehensive policies is a vital next step. This requires assessing the organization's unique needs, culture, and business objectives and considering the size of the organization, its industry, and its geographical location. Once these aspects are understood, HR leaders should draft detailed policies that cover essential areas, including recruitment, onboarding, employee conduct, performance management, compensation, benefits, leave policies, workplace safety, and termination.

It is imperative to use clear and unambiguous language so that all employees can easily understand the policies. Moreover, policies must incorporate legal requirements relevant to the organization, such as the Family and Medical Leave Act (FMLA), the Fair Labor Standards Act (FLSA), the Occupational Safety and Health Act (OSHA), and various anti-discrimination laws while also protecting employee rights, ensuring safety, and maintaining confidentiality.

Following the drafting process, a thorough review and approval stage is essential. Policies should be shared with key stakeholders, including management, department heads, and HR staff, to gather feedback and make necessary revisions. Legal experts should then review the final draft for compliance with all applicable laws and regulations. The policies must be presented to senior management or the board of directors for approval, guaranteeing alignment with the organization's strategic goals and values.

Implementation is the next critical phase, where policies are clearly communicated to employees. Organizations can disseminate policies through employee handbooks, internal websites, or orientation sessions. It is vital that all employees receive, read, and acknowledge the policies. Training sessions should be provided to educate both employees and managers about the new policies, their responsibilities, and compliance expectations. Addressing questions or concerns during training will facilitate better understanding and adherence.

Furthermore, it is important to integrate these policies into daily operations, aligning HR processes—such as recruitment, performance reviews, and disciplinary actions—with the new policies while updating relevant forms, systems, and procedures.

Monitoring and enforcement are ongoing responsibilities for HR leaders. Regular reviews of policy compliance should be conducted, promptly addressing any issues or violations. Implementing mechanisms for confidential reporting of policy violations is also essential. Periodic audits should be performed to ensure that policies remain compliant with evolving laws and regulations while evaluating their effectiveness and making necessary adjustments.

Finally, continuous improvement is vital for maintaining effective HR policies. Regular updates should reflect changes in laws, organizational shifts, and feedback from employees. Communicating these updates and providing training on new or revised policies is critical in keeping all employees informed.

Soliciting feedback from employees and managers can provide insights into the effectiveness of policies and identify areas for improvement. Using this feedback to make data-driven adjustments enhances policy effectiveness and supports a compliant workplace culture.

Developing and implementing HR policies that comply with legal requirements involves thorough research, careful drafting, and ongoing management. By remaining informed about legal obligations, involving stakeholders throughout the process, and maintaining clear communication, organizations can create effective HR policies that protect both employees and the organization. Regular reviews and updates ensure that policies continue to meet legal standards and align with organizational needs, ultimately fostering a positive and compliant workplace environment.

Training HR professionals and managers on legal compliance and ethical practices is vital for fostering a fair, safe, and productive workplace. This training serves multiple purposes, all of which contribute significantly to the organization's overall health.

First and foremost, legal compliance is critical in avoiding legal risks. Comprehensive training equips HR professionals and managers with the necessary understanding of laws and regulations that govern employment practices, including anti-discrimination laws, workplace safety standards, and other relevant statutes. By reducing the likelihood of legal disputes, penalties, and costly litigation, organizations can mitigate the risks associated with noncompliance. Additionally, investing in training can minimize compliance costs; well-trained staff are less prone to making errors that could lead to legal challenges or financial repercussions.

Promoting ethical behavior is another essential aspect of this training. By fostering a culture of integrity and trust, organizations can create an environment where employees value honesty, fairness, and respect in their interactions. Training on ethical practices not only helps employees understand the importance of ethical behavior but also sets clear expectations regarding acceptable conduct. This proactive approach is effective in preventing unethical practices, such as discrimination, harassment, and conflicts of interest.

Informed decision-making is enhanced through proper training as well. HR professionals and managers who are well-versed in legal requirements and ethical standards are better equipped to make decisions that result in fair treatment of employees. This training is particularly important when handling sensitive issues, such as employee complaints, conflicts, and terminations, allowing staff to approach these situations in a manner that is both legally compliant and ethically sound.

A company's organizational success also heavily relies on the effectiveness of its HR training programs. Well-trained HR professionals and managers can foster positive employee relations, leading to higher satisfaction and retention rates. Furthermore, organizations that prioritize legal compliance and ethical behavior tend to enhance their reputation as fair and responsible employers. This reputation not only attracts top talent but also fosters a positive public image.

Adapting to changes in the business environment is another critical benefit of ongoing training. Regular updates keep HR professionals and managers informed about evolving employment laws and regulations, allowing the organization to respond quickly and effectively. Moreover, as new ethical challenges emerge, continuous training equips staff to navigate these complexities while upholding high standards of conduct.

Lastly, training empowers leadership in the organization. It strengthens the leadership skills of HR professionals and managers by providing them with the tools necessary to lead by example. When leaders value and encourage ethical behavior, they cultivate an environment where such conduct is the norm. Additionally, understanding their roles and responsibilities concerning legal and ethical issues enables HR professionals and managers to hold themselves and others accountable, ensuring adherence to policies and standards.

The hiring process is a critical function in human resources, and it involves several legal considerations regarding compliance with employment laws and minimizes the risk of legal disputes. Each stage, from job advertisements to background checks, carries legal implications that organizations must navigate carefully.

Job advertisements play a pivotal role in attracting the right talent while adhering to nondiscrimination laws. Compliance with federal, state, and local anti-discrimination statutes, including Title VII of the Civil Rights Act, the Age Discrimination in Employment Act (ADEA), and the Americans with Disabilities Act (ADA), is essential. Job advertisements must be crafted to avoid language that discriminates against or excludes candidates based on race, color, religion, sex, national origin, age, disability, or genetic information. Using inclusive language can help attract a diverse pool of candidates, steering clear of terms that might be interpreted as discriminatory, such as *young* or *recent graduate.*

Moreover, the accuracy and clarity of job descriptions are paramount; they must accurately reflect the position's duties and requirements to avoid potential claims of misrepresentation or breach of contract.

When it comes to **job applications**, it is vital to ensure that application forms comply with equal opportunity laws. Organizations should avoid collecting information that could lead to discrimination—such as marital status, religious beliefs, or disabilities—unless such details are relevant to the position. Privacy considerations are also critical; protecting candidates' personal information is essential, especially in light of data protection regulations, such as the General Data Protection Regulation (GDPR). Organizations must store personal data securely and use it solely for its intended purpose.

Interviews present another layer of legal considerations. To uphold nondiscrimination principles, interview questions should focus on the job's requirements and refrain from addressing protected characteristics, such as age, race, religion, or disability. Implementing structured interviews can help create consistency and fairness throughout the hiring process. Additionally, maintaining records of interview questions and candidate responses is important for supporting hiring decisions and demonstrating compliance with equal employment opportunity laws.

Furthermore, providing reasonable accommodations during the interview process for candidates with disabilities, as mandated by the ADA, is essential for fostering inclusivity. This may involve offering accessible interview locations, assistive technology, or modifications to the interview format.

Background checks are a final critical element of the hiring process that must be approached with legal compliance in mind. Organizations using third-party services for background checks must comply with the Fair Credit Reporting Act (FCRA), which regulates the conduct and reporting of these checks. This includes obtaining written consent from candidates, providing them with a copy of the report, and allowing them the opportunity to dispute any inaccuracies. It is equally important to be aware of and adhere to state-specific laws regarding background checks, as these may impose additional requirements or restrictions.

Ensuring the relevance of background checks to the job position is another legal consideration; for instance, checking a candidate's criminal history should relate directly to the nature of the job and not serve as a blanket exclusionary criterion. To maintain fairness and avoid claims of discrimination, background checks must be applied consistently across all candidates for the same position.

Equal Employment Opportunity (EEO) compliance is essential in recruitment practices, serving as a cornerstone for fairness, inclusivity, and legal adherence in the workplace. The importance of EEO compliance extends across various dimensions, beginning with the organization's **legal obligations**. EEO laws, such as Title VII of the Civil Rights Act, the Age Discrimination in Employment Act (ADEA), and the Americans with Disabilities Act (ADA), explicitly prohibit discrimination based on race, color, religion, sex, national origin, age, disability, or genetic information. By adhering to these laws, organizations can significantly reduce the risk of discrimination claims and legal disputes, thereby protecting themselves from costly lawsuits and penalties. Furthermore, compliance ensures that recruitment practices align with federal, state, and local laws, promoting fair treatment throughout job advertisements, applications, interviews, and hiring decisions.

Beyond legal adherence, EEO compliance plays a vital role in **promoting diversity and inclusion** in the workplace. Organizations that embrace EEO principles encourage the recruitment of a diverse pool of candidates, which enriches the workforce with a variety of perspectives and ideas. This diversity enhances creativity, problem-solving abilities, and innovation in the organization. Additionally, by fostering an inclusive culture, organizations demonstrate their commitment to equal opportunity, thereby creating a positive work environment where all employees feel valued and respected.

Moreover, compliance with EEO regulations enhances an **organization's reputation**. Organizations that prioritize fair hiring practices build a positive image as employers of choice. This reputation not only attracts top talent but also boosts employee morale and strengthens the organization's standing in the community. A commitment to fair and inclusive recruitment practices broadens the candidate pool, as potential employees are more likely to apply to and stay with organizations that demonstrate a dedication to equality and fairness.

EEO compliance also contributes to **reducing turnover and improving retention** rates. By creating a supportive work environment where employees feel they are treated fairly and equitably, organizations can enhance job satisfaction and encourage long-term commitment among their workforces. Furthermore, implementing EEO policies allows for early identification and resolution of potential issues during the recruitment process, thus reducing the likelihood of disputes and fostering a more harmonious workplace.

Finally, EEO compliance protects **fairness in hiring** by standardizing recruitment practices. Organizations must utilize objective job descriptions, consistent interview questions, and fair assessment methods, ensuring that candidates are evaluated based on their qualifications and suitability for the role rather than personal characteristics. Adhering to

EEO principles guarantees that all candidates receive equal consideration for positions based on their skills, experience, and fit for the role, free from biases or discriminatory factors.

Ensuring Compliance with Wage and Hour Laws

When I was early in my HR career, we received notice of a required external audit regarding exempt and non-exempt employee classifications, specifically in our IT department. To make a very long story short, we had our IT department team members misclassified as exempt when they should have been non-exempt. The employees were asked to go back through three years' worth of their tenure and estimate each week how many overtime hours, if any, they were working. We were then required to apply back pay to each applicable employee (which was all of them in certain titles) as well as pay an overall penalty for the mistake. Many employers want to push the easy button and state that most all employees are either exempt or non-exempt (whatever is easiest for them), but I urge you to learn the laws and classify correctly from the start.

Compliance with wage and hour laws is critical for employers aiming to avoid legal issues and maintain fair employment practices. Key areas of focus include salary basis requirements, overtime regulations, and equal pay provisions. Understanding these components is essential in fostering a respectful and legally compliant workplace.

The Fair Labor Standards Act (FLSA) establishes salary basis requirements for employees classified as exempt. These employees must be paid a fixed salary each pay period, regardless of the number of hours worked. As of 2023, the FLSA sets a minimum salary threshold for exempt employees at $684 per week, or $35,568 annually. Employees earning less than this amount typically do not qualify for exempt status. It is essential to distinguish between nonexempt and exempt employees. Nonexempt employees are entitled to overtime pay and must be compensated on an hourly basis or a salary basis that includes overtime. In contrast, exempt employees—often found in executive, administrative, or professional roles—are not entitled to overtime pay, but they must meet specific job duties and salary criteria to qualify for this classification.

Overtime regulations further clarify employee compensation. Nonexempt employees must receive overtime pay for hours worked beyond forty in a workweek, calculated at a rate of 1.5 times their regular hourly wage. The FLSA defines a workweek as a fixed and regularly recurring period of 168 hours, which can start on any day and at any hour but must remain consistent for each employee.

Employers should also consider special state laws that may allow for compensatory time (comp time) in lieu of overtime pay, though this practice is not permitted under federal law for private-sector employees. Awareness of state and local regulations is vital, as they may impose stricter requirements or additional rules regarding overtime pay, including daily overtime mandates.

Equal pay provisions are another critical area under wage and hour laws. The Equal Pay Act of 1963 mandates that employers provide equal pay for equal work, irrespective of gender. This means that jobs requiring equal skill, effort, and responsibility performed under similar working conditions must be compensated equally. To comply, organizations should conduct regular compensation audits to identify and address any pay discrepancies. Promoting transparency in compensation practices is essential, as clear communication with employees about pay structures and criteria for pay decisions fosters trust and accountability. Employers should also implement strategies to identify and rectify pay gaps, which may involve revising job descriptions, adjusting salary ranges, and providing training on equitable pay practices.

Maintaining accurate records is crucial for compliance with wage and hour laws. Employers must keep detailed records of hours worked, wages paid, and overtime calculations for both exempt and nonexempt employees. Utilizing reliable timekeeping systems is essential for accurately tracking employee hours while complying with federal and state recordkeeping requirements.

Additionally, job descriptions should accurately reflect the duties and responsibilities associated with each role to support the correct classification of employees as exempt or nonexempt. Documenting pay policies, including salary basis, overtime procedures, and equal pay practices, is also necessary for keeping employees informed and facilitating adherence to these policies.

Staying informed about regulatory updates is vital for ensuring compliance with wage and hour laws. Employers should regularly review changes in federal, state, and local regulations and consult with legal experts or employment law attorneys to navigate complex compliance issues effectively. Training HR staff and managers on wage and hour laws, including proper employee classification and overtime calculations, is essential for fostering a compliant workplace.

Conducting internal audits and reviews can help assess compliance with wage and hour laws, allowing employers to address any discrepancies or issues promptly, thereby mitigating potential liabilities.

Paid Sick Leave and Leave Laws

In addition to the FMLA, various states and local jurisdictions have enacted laws mandating paid sick leave or other types of leave for employees. These laws can differ significantly from federal requirements, necessitating that employers stay informed about the specific regulations that apply to their operations. Employers must ensure compliance with these local and state laws, as they can impact employees' rights to paid leave, thus affecting overall workplace morale and employee satisfaction. By offering paid sick leave, employers not only fulfill legal obligations but also foster a culture of care and support in their organizations.

Disability Insurance

State requirements regarding disability insurance are another critical aspect of employee benefits. Some states mandate that employers provide short-term disability insurance to their employees, offering financial protection for workers unable to perform their job due to a nonwork-related illness or injury. This insurance typically covers a portion of an employee's wages during their time away from work, alleviating some of the financial burdens associated with health issues. By giving employees access to disability insurance, employers demonstrate commitment to their workforce's well-being and financial security.

Workers' Compensation

Workers' compensation is a vital safety net for employees who experience injuries or illnesses related to their job. This insurance provides benefits, including medical care and wage replacement, to employees who are injured on the job. Depending on state laws, employers are required to carry workers' compensation insurance or may choose to be self-insured. By adhering to these requirements, employers not only fulfill their legal obligations but also promote a safer workplace environment, reinforcing the importance of employee health and safety.

Compliance and Documentation

Effective management of employee benefits requires rigorous compliance and documentation. Employers must maintain detailed records for all employee benefit plans, including plan descriptions, amendments, and compliance reports. This documentation is essential not only for regulatory compliance but also for ensuring that employees understand their benefits. Additionally, employers are obligated to file annual reports with the Department of Labor (DOL) and the Internal Revenue Service (IRS), which includes submitting Form 5500 for Employee Retirement Income Security Act (ERISA) plans and complying with Affordable Care Act (ACA) reporting requirements.

Communication with employees is equally crucial. Employers should provide clear and accurate information about available benefits, including eligibility criteria, coverage details, and claims filing procedures. By maintaining transparency and open lines of communication, employers can foster trust and satisfaction among their workforces.

Understanding HR compliance doesn't mean you have to become a legal expert; it's about knowing the basics and having the right policies in place. By following fair hiring practices, wage laws, and documentation requirements, businesses can operate legally and ethically.

IN CLOSING

After more than twenty years in HR, I've come to appreciate that success in managing people boils down to doing the basics well. For businesses without the resources to hire a seasoned HR professional, this book arms you with the tools, strategies, and mindset needed to create a solid HR foundation. While hiring, onboarding, disciplinary actions, terminations, and compliance with HR law may seem daunting, you don't need a massive budget to manage these areas effectively. What you need is clarity, consistency, and a commitment to doing things right. If your eyes have glazed over at this point, let me remind you of the basics of the last five chapters so you're ready to put some plans in place to make improvements in your business today.

1. Hiring and Recruitment

When it comes to hiring, you don't need a fancy recruiter or expensive tools to find great people. Focus on:

- **Leveraging Free and Low-Cost Platforms**: Platforms like LinkedIn, Indeed, and even your own social media channels are cost-effective ways to reach candidates.
- **Standardizing Interviews**: Create a structured process with consistent questions to ensure fairness and compliance.

The goal is not just to fill a role but to find someone who aligns with your culture and can grow with your business.

2. Onboarding

The first thirty to ninety days are critical in shaping an employee's success. A strong onboarding program doesn't have to be costly; it just needs to be intentional. These two priorities are a great start:

- **Make It Personal**: Regular check-ins during the onboarding period show employees you value them.
- **Invest in Documentation**: A simple employee handbook can save you hours of answering repeated questions and ensures that everyone understands the rules.

Remember, a well-onboarded employee is more productive, engaged, and likely to stay with your company.

3. Disciplinary Actions

No one likes having tough conversations, but they are necessary for maintaining accountability. Here's how to navigate discipline effectively:

- **Be Clear and Direct**: Employees can't improve if they don't understand what's wrong. Clearly outline expectations and consequences.
- **Focus on Solutions**: Approach discipline as an opportunity to correct behavior rather than just a punishment.

Consistency is the key to fairness. Employees are more likely to respect the process if they see it applied uniformly.

4. Terminations

Terminations are often the most challenging part of managing people, but they can be handled with dignity and professionalism if you do the following:

- **Follow the Process**: Ensure that you've documented performance issues or policy violations leading to the termination.
- **Show Compassion**: How you let someone go says a lot about your company's values. Treat the individual with respect, even if the decision is difficult.
- **Minimize Risk**: Understand basic legal requirements for terminations, such as providing final paychecks promptly and avoiding language that could be interpreted as discriminatory.

When they're handled well, terminations can protect your culture and reputation while preserving the departing employee's dignity.

5. HR Law

You don't need a law degree to manage HR compliance, but you do need awareness of the following:

- **Focus on the Basics**: Know your responsibilities around wages, safety, anti-discrimination, and employment classifications.
- **Use Free Resources**: Government websites (like the Department of Labor and EEOC) offer a wealth of information.
- **Ask for Help When Needed**: When in doubt, consult a local HR professional or attorney for clarity.

Compliance isn't just about avoiding lawsuits. It's about creating a fair, respectful workplace.

Key Takeaways for Small Businesses

Be Proactive, Not Reactive: Don't wait for problems to arise. Set clear expectations and systems from the start.

Invest in Relationships: Treat your employees like the valuable assets they are, and they'll reward you with loyalty and productivity.

Document Everything: Whether it's a great hire or a difficult termination, having proper documentation protects both you and your employees.

Leverage Technology: Affordable tools like HR software, online training platforms, and cloud-based document storage can save you time and money.

Stay Curious: The HR landscape evolves constantly. Make it a habit to learn about new laws, trends, and best practices to keep your business compliant and competitive.

HR doesn't have to be expensive, but it does have to be intentional. With a commitment to fairness, consistency, and respect, even a small business with limited resources can build an HR foundation that supports growth, mitigates risk, and fosters a thriving workplace. You don't need a twenty-year HR veteran on staff full-time to succeed—you just need the right tools, strategies, and a willingness to lead with integrity.

I hope this book can serve as a guide or a road map. My last intention is for it to be overwhelming. While there are a ton of things we can do to positively (or negatively) impact our people, I'll tell you what I tell my podcast listeners every single week—just start somewhere. Pick one chapter, one section, or one paragraph that you think you could implement, and do it. Maybe schedule thirty minutes a week to hop into this book and tackle one thing per month. Or schedule that meeting with your leadership team to map out your current process and then chat about things you can do to improve it. What's working? What isn't? And if you don't know what isn't, knock out an employee engagement survey. You can do this for free, and it will set the stage for your next year. Your people will see if you're trying.

We all started a business, chose to lead, or chose the field of HR because we wanted to make an impact. One of the best ways you can make an impact today is by taking the time and energy to truly care about your people. The success of your business isn't just about the bottom line. It's about the people who drive it. Invest in them wisely, and the results will follow. I'm rooting for you.

ACKNOWLEDGMENTS

Writing this book has been a journey, and I owe so much of it to the people and teams who have shaped me into the HR professional and business owner I am today.

To William Burke, my first HR boss and mentor, thank you for challenging me at every turn, pushing me to think critically, and setting the foundation for my career (even when I thought for sure you weren't going to make me a job offer).

To my first HR department, thank you for being my very first HR playground. It was there I discovered the art and science of this profession and learned to navigate the intricacies of people and processes (even processes on how to distribute apples and bananas).

To the HR team that let me build the Learning & Development function and an eLearning team from the ground up, you taught me the value of environments where everyone's contributions are recognized—and the wisdom to leave when that's no longer the case.

To my third HR team, thank you for showing me the strengths and challenges of the public sector. While it wasn't the best fit for me, I found myself surrounded by incredibly intelligent, compassionate, and fun individuals. Special thanks to Allen Johanning and Erik Smetana—you were truly some of the best colleagues I've ever had.

To the team that gave me the opportunity to step through the challenging C-suite door and tackle M&A work, thank you for helping me cut my teeth on some of the toughest, most rewarding aspects of this profession, teaching me about variable compensation, sales, and how to truly negotiate and advocate for myself.

To my final employed Operations & HR teams, thank you for saying yes to becoming my very first client. That leap of faith propelled me into business ownership and start-up life, and I'll always be grateful for your trust in me.

To my current team - thank you for your unwavering support, for never being too shocked when I start another book, launch a new service line, or set a seemingly audacious goal. With you, I've finally found my people, and I know we're capable of achieving every goal we set.

To Carly, my editor, and my entire publishing team, your expertise and hard work have brought this book to life. Thank you for your guidance, patience, and dedication throughout this process.

To the readers who have chosen to invest their time and hard-earned money in this book, thank you. This is the first of three HR books I plan to write, and it's my hope that each one provides you with practical tools, valuable insights, and a renewed perspective on the power of great HR.

And last, to every person I have recruited, hired, disciplined, had a one-on-one meeting with, mentored, challenged, led, questioned, laid off, terminated, coached, taught, debated, and lived through a meeting that should have been an email with, this book is a culmination of the lessons, challenges, and growth so many of you have contributed to. Thank you for being part of my story.

AUTHOR BIO

Kerri M. Roberts has devoted her career to strategic human resources. She earned her bachelor's degree in business administration from Columbia College and MBA from William Woods University. Her expertise includes training in the Malcolm Baldrige National Quality Award criteria [previously a Senior Examiner for the Missouri Quality Award].

Kerri is the founder of Salt & Light Advisors, a People Operations and HR Firm based in Missouri. She also hosts the podcast Don't Waste the Chaos and writes for a variety of online publications on HR and leadership.

Kerri has been named to Women of Excellence, Women in Power, Women Who Move the City, 20 Under 40, Hot 100, Elite Women, and Graduate and Professional Alumni of the Year by different publications and organizations and was nominated for the Young Professional Award by Athena International.

She spends her favorite days on the Mark Twain Lake, baking new sourdough recipes, or exploring the woods on her 140-acre farm with two yellow labradors.